*Industrialization
and
development*

Industrialization and development

A comparative analysis

Ray Kiely

Lecturer in Development Studies,
University of East London

Routledge
Taylor & Francis Group

LONDON AND NEW YORK

First published in 1998 by Routledge
2 Park Square, Milton Park, Abingdon, Oxon, OX14 4RN
270 Madison Ave, New York NY 10016

Transferred to Digital Printing 2007

The name of Routledge is a registered
trade mark used by Routledge with the consent of the owner.

British Library Cataloguing-in-Publication Data
A CIP catalogue record for this book is available from the British Library.

Library of Congress Cataloging-in-Publication Data are available

ISBNs: 1-85728-544-1 HB
       1-85728-545-X PB

Typeset in Bembo.

Publisher's Note
The publisher has gone to great lengths to ensure the quality of this reprint
but points out that some imperfections in the original may be apparent

Contents

Acknowledgements

Many thanks to those who made the passage of the book from original draft to publication a surprisingly painless process. In particular, I would like to thank Caroline Wintersgill, Margaret Christie, David Stewart and Mina Gera-Price.

Part I
Industrialization and development: definitions and debates

Chapter One
Introduction:
defining industrialization and development

This book addresses three principal questions: first, what is the relationship between industrialization and development?; second, who or what are the agents that promote industrialization?; and third, what is the relationship between late industrialization and the global economy? These questions are examined through a case study approach, which seeks to draw out the common features, and the contrasts between, various industrialization processes. The work can therefore be regarded as an attempt to construct a "post-impasse" historical sociology of development, as recommended by (among others) Nicos Mouzelis (1988).[1] A previous knowledge of the debates around the impasse in development sociology is not, however, a requirement for understanding the arguments in this book.

Industrialization can be defined in three ways (Hewitt et al. 1992a: 3–6): first, as "the production of all material goods not grown directly on the land", or second, as the economic sector comprising mining, manufacturing and energy. Most interesting for our purposes is the third definition, which sees industry as "a particular way of organizing production and assumes there is a constant process of technical and social change which continually increases society's capacity to produce a wide range of goods" (Hewitt et al. 1992a: 6). In this definition, industrialization is regarded as a total process, impacting on society through an unprecedented increase in goods and services.

For this reason, it is often assumed that there is a close link between industrialization and development. Development theory in the 1950s and 1960s often implicitly defined development as an increase in Gross National Product, and assumed that the increase in wealth associated with industrialization would trickle down to the bulk of the population. Writers such as Seers (cf. Chapter Two) have questioned this view, without necessarily rejecting the idea that industrialization is necessary for development. Definitions of development now often include attention to basic needs such as decent health-care, education, income for all, and environmental sustainability. For instance, the Human Development Index (HDI) measures development according to life expectancy, educational attainment and real GDP per capita (UNDP 1995: 12).

3

More recently, a Gender-related Development Index (GDI) has been used to incorporate gender inequality into the measurement of HDI (UNDP 1995: 73). Clearly then such measures question the view that industrialization and development are one and the same thing, although (as we shall see) they do not necessarily undermine the view that there is a close correlation between the two.[2]

Technical, economistic accounts of industrialization are also criticized in my discussion of agency. A long tradition of scholarship has regarded industrialization as a technical issue, impacting on different societies in ways that promote convergence (Kerr et al. 1962). This is because it is technology which largely determines the shape of society – other factors are secondary to the primary role of technological development. Others, however, argue that technology embodies particular social relations and so the decision to introduce new technology is a political one, and the effect of such technology is far from neutral (Leys 1984). This has implications for how we think about the relationship between industrialization and development, but it also forces us to think carefully about the issue of historical process. Technology does not exist in a vacuum, and so a close examination of the "pioneers" of technological development, and the social and political context in which such development arises, is crucial. Thus, major consideration is given to the role of entrepreneurs and markets (or capitalists and capitalist social relations), and the role of the state in industrialization processes.

Finally, the relationship between industrialization and the global economy is examined. Technicist approaches tend to regard the prospects for late industrialization as relatively unproblematic – if the correct policies are adopted, and market forces are given free rein, then appropriate industrial development will follow.[3] Although there are opportunities offered by the world economy for potential late industrializers, constraints also exist. A recognition of these constraints and opportunities is crucial for an understanding of industrialization strategies in the periphery since the Second World War.

These three interlinked questions are examined in the chapters that follow. Chapter Two examines one particular case for industrialization, the "Kitching thesis". Although I argue that this case is in many ways convincing, it also has its weaknesses and omissions. In criticizing the thesis, an argument is made for the case study approach adopted in the rest of the book, based on the similarities and contrasts of "actually existing industrializations" (Sutcliffe 1992: 333). Chapters Three and Four examine historical "models" of industrialization, both capitalist (Britain and Japan) and socialist (the Soviet Union and China). Chapters Five to Nine examine cases of late industrialization. The global constraints and opportunities faced by late industrializers are scrutinized in Chapter Five, while Chapters Six and Seven explore local responses to the global economy. Case studies include Brazil, India, South Korea, Taiwan, Hong Kong, Singapore, and the Chinese Special Economic Zones. Some reference is also made to the second-tier newly industrializing countries (NICs) in South-East Asia. Chapter Eight brings together the arguments by reassessing the three core questions in the light of these case studies. Chapter Nine examines new constraints and opportunities faced by potential late industrializers in the "global, post-Fordist" era, and Chapter Ten summarizes the arguments of the whole book.

Notes

1. Unlike many of the "post-impasse" writers however, I attempt in this book to show the continuing validity of the core of a Marxist methodology, without falling into the trap of a Marxist dogma (cf. Kiely 1995c).
2. These issues are taken up in more detail, particularly in Chapters Two and Eight. The brief discussion here of meanings of development has not examined the important work of writers who have deconstructed the idea of development (Crush 1995; Cowen & Shenton 1996). These writers argue that the idea of development is based on a particular way of viewing the world which implies the need for some to speak on behalf of others – a form of trusteeship. This argument is largely convincing as development, a highly political process, has often been reduced to a purely technical issue (cf. Kiely 1997a). Nevertheless, as these writers point out (Cowen & Shenton 1996: 452–72), a crude anti-development position (cf. Sachs 1992a) is based on a similar form of trusteeship and so hardly constitutes a satisfactory alternative. This work does not focus on these issues in any detail, but there is some discussion of anti-development and populist positions in Chapter Two. Moreover, by focusing on agency and emphasizing a *contingent* (but not accidental) relationship between industrialization and development, I hope to have avoided some of the problems associated with technicist approaches to development. The shortcomings of all quantitative measures of development are discussed throughout the text, particularly in Chapter Eight.
3. According to this school of neo-liberal thought, development may not always be led by industrialization. Countries may have comparative advantages in predominantly agrarian products or in service industries such as tourism. The point is that this can only be established through the adoption of unrestricted competition, so that countries will find out what it is that they can produce effectively.

Chapter Two

Debating industrialization

This chapter is concerned with debates around the relationship between industrialization and development. The case that industrialization is necessary for development is explored, mainly through a critical assessment of the work of one writer, Gavin Kitching. These arguments are then scrutinized by introducing some populist and anti-development objections to the claims of the pro-industry position. In assessing these debates some further consideration of the meaning of development is necessary.

I am not exclusively concerned with arguments of the "Kitching thesis". Nevertheless, his work is paid considerable attention in this chapter for two reasons: first, it is the best defence of the old growth orthodoxy; second, some of Kitching's contentions, and indeed his omissions, are very useful as an introduction to the debates about industrialization that are taken up in the rest of the book.

These debates are outlined in two main sections. First, the case of the pro-industrializers, and Kitching in particular, is outlined. Second, the views of the critics are considered. Finally, I provide a preliminary summary of the debates, and an argument is made for a case study approach of "actually existing industrialization" (Sutcliffe 1992).

Arguments for industrialization

Gavin Kitching's book *Development and underdevelopment in historical perspective* (1982) must be situated in the context of specific disputes about development, and his concern to defend the view that "if you want to develop you must industrialize" (Kitching 1982: 6). Such a view was commonplace amongst theorists and practioners of "development" in the 1950s and much of the 1960s. Perhaps the most famous advocate, Walt Rostow (1985: 21), argued that the transition from a traditional to modern society "can be described legitimately as a rise in the rate of investment to a level which regularly, substantially and perceptibly outstrips population growth".

However, from the late 1960s onwards such certainties were increasingly challenged on the grounds that industrialization and economic growth were not the same as development, and that output had expanded without meeting the basic needs (health, education and so on) of the population. Some writers went further and argued that the whole notion of development was Eurocentric, and designed to promote the interests of specific social groups in the West (together with their allies in the Third World). For example, George (1976: 17) argued that

> The West has tried to apply its own conceptions of "development" to the Third World, working through local elites and pretending that the benefits showered on these elites would trickle down to the less fortunate, especially through the wholesale application of Western-inspired and Western-supplied technology. These methods have not produced a single independent and viable economy in the entire Third World – and in fact were not meant to. "Development" has been the password for imposing a new kind of dependency, for enriching the already rich world and for shaping other societies to meet its commercial and political needs.

Such views, which have become even more forceful in recent years, were rejected by Kitching. While it would be unfair to simply lump Kitching together with the modernization theorists of the 1950s and 1960s, it is the case that he shares the view that progress and development are desirable goals, and that the most effective way to achieve these is through the promotion of industrial growth.

Nevertheless, before examining the details of Kitching's case, it should be noted that the precise relationship between Kitching (who identifies with the political left) and modernization theory (which is broadly on the right or centre-right of the political spectrum) is ambiguous. This should become clearer throughout the chapter, but two points need to be introduced immediately. First, Kitching's case for industrialization is not *explicitly* political – it is one that could be, and indeed is shared by many conservatives, liberals and socialists. This is not to deny the importance of politics in assessing Kitching's claims – indeed, this book is concerned to show that industrialization is very much a political issue – but it is the case that an argument can be made for industrialization that cuts across political ideologies. Second, Kitching's case is basically a technical one which largely omits social factors from consideration. It would be totally erroneous to suggest that Kitching is unaware of the importance of social factors in influencing economic growth (Kitching 1982: chs 2–5), but it is the case that, as with modernization theorists before him, his technical case is somewhat weakened by such neglect. In particular, whilst Kitching examines the social consequences of industrialization, he does not adequately examine the social causes of industrial development, and the question of who are the agents of such strategies. This point will become clearer in due course.

The starting point of Kitching's argument is to take an imaginary society of small-scale farmers living in a closed economy – that is, a society where no imports or exports are made. At least initially, farmers will produce for their own consumption, but they will soon begin to trade among themselves to achieve some variety in their consumption patterns. As this process increases farmers will begin to specialize in producing certain crops, and as they become more skilled at doing so, they increase their productivity. Each specialist farmer is thus able to produce more food, and so exchange surplus food with fellow farmers. The result is that both individual and total incomes increase. However, at this point the process reaches definite limits, "for the need of human beings for food is finite, and after a while the need of the peasants (as consumers) for food will not grow as fast as their output and income is growing" (Kitching 1982: 8). So, Kitching's argument is that as income rises beyond a certain point, the demand for food rises less quickly than each rise in income. There is what economists call a "low income elasticity of demand" for agricultural products.

At this point, then, farmers will want to exchange their surplus food products, not for other farmers' surplus food, but for clothes, shelter and so on. However, such a situation presupposes the existence of industrial production. Therefore, further development (defined either as economic growth or meeting basic needs) requires some form of industrial production.

But as Kitching (1982: 9–10) himself points out, in the real world economies are not closed and are part of a global system in which nation-states trade with each other. Is it not possible, then, for some agrarian countries to trade their surplus food with the products of industrial countries? In such a scenario some countries do not need to industrialize, and can expand output and incomes through increasing their productivity in agriculture. This is the basis of the theory of comparative advantage, which holds that countries should specialize in producing those goods in which they are cheap, efficient and competitive. However, as Kitching (1982: 9) tells us, the low income elasticity of demand for agricultural products operates beyond imaginery closed economies, and exists at a global level. The potential effect, as the old orthodoxy reminds us (Prebisch 1959), is that demand for food products rises less quickly than demand for industrial products, and so the terms of trade can potentially decline for agrarian producers as against industrial producers. The result of such a decline is that agrarian producers pay relatively more for their industrial imports against the amounts they receive for their exports. This is not the place to examine the empirical claim that such a decline has indeed taken place, but there appears to be some evidence that this has been the case (Spraos 1983). Agrarian economies would therefore have to "run faster" in order to maintain even a slow increase in living standards. In the real world, where massive surpluses of cheap food exist, it is simply not viable for nations to try to develop solely on the basis of agricultural production.

There may also be political imperatives in the drive to industrialize – to decrease dependence on foreign suppliers for a particular technology, and to build up an independent military capacity (Kitching 1982: 10). It seems then that there is an "economo-political" logic, which suggests that "the rulers of agricultural economies will try hard to industrialize them once other industrialized nation-states have come into existence" (Kitching 1982: 10).

Kitching then moves on to argue a case for large-scale industrialization based on economies of scale. These economies derived from investment in large-scale, capital-intensive technologies which have the effect of decreasing the unit cost of production as the volume of output increases. Thus a country with output per annum of 1,000 units may have production costs of 100 per unit. However, with technological innovation output per annum may increase to 2,000 units, but unit costs will decrease to say, 75. The primary reason why unit costs are likely to decrease is that labour productivity is intensified as technological innovation increases. Such internal economies of scale are reinforced by external economies such as access to decent infrastructural facilities, to suppliers and to established markets, which are usually located in towns – hence the historical tendency of industries to "cluster" in certain localities.

So, to summarize, Kitching's case for industrialization is based on three principal arguments:

(i) Agricultural production comes up against definite limits because of the low income elasticity of demand for food products;
(ii) Economies of scale exist in mass production;
(iii) External economies arise from the spatial concentration of industry in urban areas (Kitching 1982: 17–18; cf. R. Chandra 1992: ch. 1).

There is one more case for industrialization which really brings us to the heart of the matter. The basic argument is that there is a significant correlation between industrialization and development. Kitching (1982: 15–17) argues that classical political economy from Adam Smith to Karl Marx shared an implicit view of development as the increase in production of goods.[1] This is contrasted with the views of nineteenth-century populists who particularly objected to the concentration of economic power and wealth that arose from industrialization, and were more concerned with issues of distribution. If one accepts that development is primarily about increasing productivity, output and incomes, then there is a close connection – indeed, a causal one – between industrialization and development (see Allen 1992: 382; Sen 1992: 10). However, others have argued that the meaning of development is wider than simply economic growth, and have criticized the case for industrialization on this basis.

Industrialization and its critics

Kitching's defence of the old, growth-led orthodoxy is a powerful one, but these issues need further attention. This section presents a critique of the growth-led orthodoxy. My presentation of the arguments is divided into three parts: first, a rejection of the notions of development, progress and growth;

second, an examination of populist alternatives to industrialization based on mass production; and third, a critical account of some of the claims of pro-industrialization writers, which focuses on agency and industrial strategy.

The rejection of development

The first set of criticisms concerns not only the question of industrialization, but that of development. Some writers (Sachs 1992a,b; Escobar 1995) argue that the very idea of development is a form of cultural imperialism, "nothing more than projecting the American model of society onto the rest of the world" (Sachs 1992b: 5). Although this model may take a number of forms – mixed-economy, market-led, or basic-needs approaches – the basic rationale remains the same, namely the imposition of a set of values onto cultures that are mis-represented as backward (Esteva 1992).

This critique, which closely parallels some of the concerns of postmodern social theory (cf. McLennan 1992), has far-reaching implications, not just for the growth-orthodoxy outlined above, but for *all* forms of development. Such a critique is also far more wide-ranging than a simple rejection of industrializa-tion, but this school of thought is obviously highly critical of scholars who claim that it is necessary to industrialize. Indeed, a central argument of "anti-development" theory is that industrial technology has not liberated the people of the West, so it is hardly likely to liberate people in the rest of the world (Ullrich 1992).

The strength of this school of thought is that it asks important questions about industrialization and development, which tend to be neglected by growth-based theorists. To take one example, the argument that industrializa-tion increases development can at least in part be seen as a tautology: for if development is defined as an increase in Gross National Product, then it is hardly surprising that the more industrialized nations are also the most developed. This is because GNP figures are more likely to take account of industrial rather than agrarian production, because the former is far more likely to pass through official channels than the latter, where goods may not be exchanged but directly consumed, or may be exchanged through unofficial markets. Moreover, GNP figures do not account for wider measures of social development such as income distribution, literacy rates, life expectancy or environmental destruction (indeed, the last of these may actually increase GNP figures). These points do not completely undermine the case of the growth-based theorists, but they do show that there is a need for some refinement of the arguments (Allen 1992; Sachs 1992b: 19; Escobar 1995: ch. 3).

Furthermore, anti-development writers stress that the optimism of modernizers is misplaced, and that the world of industry has brought new social problems, social inequalities and environmental destruction. Contem-porary concerns over global warming and the partial destruction of the ozone layer are pressing reminders of the fact that the industrial world has intensified pollution, while there is some question over the degree to which resources can be renewed if *all* nations choose (or are able to choose) the route of rapid industrialization. This is not the place for a full discussion of these global debates,[2] but as anti-development theory implies, the relationship between *local* industrializations and the environment needs to be addressed.

However, whilst anti-development theory asks a number of important questions, there are strong grounds for suggesting that it stretches its case too far. One can certainly accept the viewpoint that industrialization is a *contradictory* process, without completely rejecting the notion of development, or the strategy of industrialization. Cases for industrialization and development do not have to rest on the "Western-centric" view that this is simply a way for "them" to become more like "us". Many of the needs that exist in the West are socially and historically constructed and do not necessarily apply to other societies. However, the difficulties in outlining a case for universal needs and justice should not entail a rejection of such principles in the name of a cultural relativism.[3] For without some commitment to universal needs, it seems very difficult to be critical at all. On what basis can we argue for or against industrialization without some measure (with all the difficulties this involves) of its effects on "living standards", and some notion of "progress"?

Such a commitment to universal principles may for instance include Seers' (1979: 10) six criteria for development:

(i)   the capacity to buy/command access to necessities such as food and health-care;
(ii) access to employment of some kind;
(iii) relatively equal income distribution;
(iv) adequate educational levels;
(v)   participation in politics;
(vi) belonging to a nation of true independence.

In usefully deconstructing models of economic growth, anti-development theory provides one with the basis for an alternative approach more in keeping with the "limited universalism" proposed by Seers. Certainly, the implication is that this school is more sympathetic to the social development indicators outlined above, rather than the technocratic measure of Gross National Product. However, the argument that there is *no* connection between economic growth and basic needs is difficult to substantiate. To take one example: the figures in Sachs (1992b: 19) illustrate that those countries with the lowest infant mortality rates (Japan, Canada, United Kingdom and so on) are precisely the more industrialized ones. It is true that industrialization in itself does not automatically lead to lower mortality rates, and I would accept that other factors (such as poverty, organizational forms of health service and so on) are important – Cuba and the Indian state of Kerala, for instance, have far better rates with their collective systems of health-care than many more industrialized countries. Similarly, the health-care records of industrialized societies may vary – the predominantly private system in the United States performs far worse than the more collective system in Sweden. Nevertheless, there is still a significant correlation between industrialization and low infant mortality, which suggests that the former can at least facilitate the latter. A comparison of life expectancy now with that of two hundred years ago suggests a similar conclusion.

Furthermore, the argument that development through industrial growth is *just* a form of cultural imperialism is difficult to prove, as it rests on the *a priori* assumption that decisions by Third World leaders *must* reflect their "contamination" by Western ideas. For instance, Sachs (1992b: 5) writes that " [t]he leaders of the newly founded nations – from Nehru to Nkrumah, Nasser to Sukarno [sic] – accepted the image that the North had of the South, and internalized it as their self-image". One need not deny the impact of Western ideas on many leaders in the post-war new states, but to argue that this was the *sole* cause of them adopting industrialization strategies is nonsense, and indeed patronizing – it *assumes* that people in the Third World are incapable of making their own decisions (Kiely 1995b). Industrial strategies may have been influenced by the West, but they were also taken on the pragmatic grounds that this was the way to improve living standards, build nations and alleviate unequal terms of trade. The case for industrialization made by new leaders was thus not unlike those arguments made by Kitching outlined above.[4] Indeed, in some respects the decision in parts of the periphery to industrialize constituted a *challenge* to the West, a point that at least one anti-development writer appears to recognize (Escobar 1995: 29).

Such arguments may have been misguided, and they may have been based on particular one-sided interpretations of factors like living standards, but this alone does not explain the initial motive for industrialization. Furthermore, without some universal account of what constitutes an increase (or decrease) in the standard of living, we have no way of assessing the success or failure of particular industrialization strategies.

Finally, anti-development theory's case against industrialization is very close to a mirror-image of the technocratic optimism of the most excessive growth-based theorist.[5] For while the latter posits an industrial utopia where conflict is eradicated (or substantially reduced), the former is in danger of romanticizing a pre-industrial past (or present, in parts of the Third World) where proper communities existed and were not torn asunder by the impersonal relations and expansionary drive of industrial capitalism or socialism (cf. Latouche 1993). Such patronizing and frankly naive views[6] put the anti-development school firmly in the camp of the crudest populists (cf. Kitching 1982: ch. 2; also Hyden 1980: 2), whom I examine below.

On the whole then, anti-development theory does not provide a particularly penetrating alternative to growth-led strategies. Nevertheless, it asks some important questions about the effects of industrial development strategies (although they are hardly the first to do this), and some of the proposed alternatives.

Populism and development

Kitching identifies a broad tradition of political thought that is suspicious of the growth-led policies of "production-based" economics (1982: 15–17). These thinkers, whose work spans a time period of around 150 years, are described as populist and neo-populist. Both doctrines are said to "oppose industrialization and large-scale production in the name of small-scale individual enterprise" (Kitching 1982: 21).

The populist critique of industrialization is rooted in the social consequences of industrialization in early-nineteenth-century Europe, and Britain in particular (Kitching 1982: ch. 2). Writers such as Owen and Proudhon criticized the inequalities both within and outside of the factory, and the dehumanization of modern urban life. This was contrasted with the life of the peasant and artisan in the pre-industrial age, where work was far more independent of hierarchical management and unskilled divisions of labour, and communities were based on more personal and human social relationships. Thinkers such as Proudhon and the "Ricardian Socialists" wanted to preserve small-scale peasant production based on a relatively equal distribution of private property, in which each farm would trade with each other in a system of laissez-faire-type perfect competition (Kitching 1982: 26–35).

Such concerns were taken up in late-nineteenth-century-Russia in the context of the fate of the agrarian commune, which was said to be the basis for both a more organic community *and* a more humane modernizing process which avoided the excesses of British industrialization. Writers such as Chernyshevsky and Danielson espoused the virtues of Russian communal life in the countryside, against the modernizing influences of large-scale industry – and, incidentally, against the claims of Russian Marxists such as Plekhanov and Lenin who saw the destruction of the former by the latter as an inevitable process.[7] These views were then expanded by neo-populists such as Chayanov in the context of the Soviet industrialization debate in the 1920s, and the question of the relationship between industry and agriculture.

Populism in this sense thus refers to the fundamental belief that "small is beautiful" (Schumacher 1973). This philosophy is part of a tradition of thought which focuses on the viability and desirability of small-scale production, and which concentrates on the problem of distribution more than the problems of raising productivity and increasing output.

One such contemporary neo-populist strategy is that associated with the International Labour Organization (ILO) in the 1970s (Kitching 1982: 70–84; cf. Chenery et al. 1974). The ILO argued the case for labour-intensive industrialization and development of the informal sector, as this would provide employment and create a market for the goods that such industry produced. It was not against large-scale industry *per se*, but rejected the widespread commitment to such industries, particularly when they were often high-cost and inefficient and did not increase output (Kitching 1982: 75). When capital-intensive industries were efficient, and did not enjoy the protection of states promoting import substitution industrialization (ISI), then there was little objection to them.[8] The strategy was combined with a commitment to land reform in agriculture, which would facilitate the development of peasant farming, reinforced by the extension of new, labour-enhancing (rather than labour-displacing) technologies. These included the improvement of simple irrigation systems, new seed varieties, and better fertilizer applications, as opposed to large tractors, and mechanized harvesting (Kitching 1982: 73).

The ILO therefore put forward the case for small-scale industry and agriculture, combined with a focus on greater equality of distribution. Such a concern with distribution is justified not simply as an end in itself, but also as "a necessary means of achieving development – expanding demand for the products of labour-intensive industry" (Crow and Thomas 1983: 18).

Growth theorists are sceptical of such concerns. In his discussion of development in China, Kitching argues (1982: ch. 5) that successful development occurred because the static efficiency implicit in the ILO's strategy was rejected in favour of a more dynamic approach. This alternative championed the dynamic gains that could be made from securing economies of scale, even though this meant making short-term sacrifices. For Kitching (1982: 139), it was the capital-intensive producer goods industries in China such as cement, fertilizer, iron and steel and machinery which facilitated both industrialization and the expansion of Chinese agriculture. His argument therefore suggests that for sustained development to occur, there must be an increase in technical skills and linkages, and these are secured by the development of producer goods and economies of scale.

A key part of Kitching's argument, then, is that economies of scale are highly efficient compared to small-scale production. It should be noted, however, that while Kitching is an advocate of the "large is efficient" school of thought, he does at times qualify his position (see below), and he is explicitly against a universal Stalinist model of industrialization for contemporary developing countries. For smaller and resource-poor developing countries he advocates an industrialization policy of initially expanding primary products, moving to the manufacture of simple inputs and basic consumption goods for primary producers (including peasants), and from there to the manufacture of labour-intensive consumer and producer goods for domestic consumption and export (Kitching 1989: 192). Although such a strategy says little about scale, there is an undoubted correspondence between elements of this strategy and some neo-populist policies, which are generally *not* against industrialization (Bideleux 1985: 53–70).

Nevertheless, Kitching's primary concern is with the development of dynamic efficiency and how this can be achieved through economies of scale. There is an undoubted history of economies of scale developing with industrialization, but this is not the whole story. The development of economies of scale, particularly those internal to the firm, is only a tendency which is subject to some counter-tendencies. This point applies to industry, but especially to agriculture. Second, while it may be the case that the development of scale economies is a dominant tendency, it is also true that growth-based economics lacks an adequate account of why such economies occur.

On the first point, some writers (Piore and Sabel 1984) have argued that we have entered a new period of capitalist development, where the importance of internal economies of scale are less crucial than they were in the "Fordist" era of mass production. The new period of "post-Fordism" is based on smaller-scale but efficient production, utilizing the latest microelectronic technology, and serving small and volatile niche markets. Much is made of the emergence of new industrial districts such as the so-called "Third Italy", which has enjoyed substantial economic growth on the basis of the small-scale production of textiles and some machinery (Sabel 1982; Scott 1988: 43–59).

Writers strongly disagree about the significance of such flexibility for industrial workers – to oversimplify, the flexible specialization school (Piore and Sabel 1984) can be described as optimistic, while the regulation school (Lipietz 1987) is pessimistic.[9] More relevant to our concerns is the argument that mass production, and with it mass markets, has declined in importance. The clear implication is that potential late industrializers may be able to adopt flexible methods of industrial production, and thereby compete effectively with the early industrializers in the "advanced" industrial societies. Sabel (1986: 46–8) has argued that late industrializers actually have certain advantages – first, "poor organization" within existing large factories may effectively lead to the existence of a cluster of independent – and flexible – producers, specializing in small-scale production and therefore more able to respond to the flexibility of niche markets; second, there is the massive informal sector, which may also be similarly placed to benefit from the new opportunities afforded by post-Fordism.

Some of the claims for a new period of flexible capitalism are exaggerated (Amin and Robbins 1990), and the existence of small-scale production is hardly a new phenomenon (Pollert 1991). Nevertheless, for all the weaknesses of the specific arguments of these theories,[10] they do point to the continued existence and viability of small-scale industrial production in some sectors of the economy. This point does not question Kitching's argument that industrialization is necessary for development, but it does show that his focus on mass production is exaggerated (cf. Humphrey 1995b: 5–6).

This problem is even more apparent in the case of agriculture. In both the "First" and "Third" worlds, the development of capitalism in agriculture has not always led to the collapse of peasant-based agriculture. Capitalists may be reluctant to invest directly in the uncertain conditions of natural farming, and there is a greater difficulty in supervising wage labour in the field than in the factory. Also, in agriculture production-time is greater than labour-time because of the growth cycle of plants and livestock, and so capital is tied-up and unable to realize profits until crops are harvested (Bernstein 1994: 51–2). Moreover, there may be instances where peasant production is able to compete more than effectively with large-scale farming. This is because of the nature of peasant farming as opposed to capitalist farming, as the neo-populist Chayanov argued in the 1920s. For the capitalist farmer, labour is hired and fired with the sole intention of producing enough commodities to enable the farmer to make a profit. On the other hand, the peasant's primary purpose for working the land is to provide for his or her family, i.e. for subsistence. According to Chayanov, the size of a peasant's holding and intensity of cultivation is therefore determined by the size and composition of his/her family. Although this particular contention is questionable,[11] the important point to note here is the clear implication that peasants can compete with capitalists because they are prepared to work long hours for little return, and do not (unlike capitalists) cost out their labour when they sell their produce (Johnson 1988). In technical terms, Chayanov's basic argument is that while the output per labourer may be lower for the peasant (who lacks complex machinery, etc.), the marginal cost may still be lower as the peasant does not face wage bills and his/her only concern is reaching a basic subsistence level (cf. Kitching 1982: ch. 3). While this may not be the case for all agricultural sectors, it is certainly true for some, especially cases where production may be difficult to mechanize and so labour productivity may not be significantly higher in the capitalist sector. Kitching (1982: 138) himself appears to concede this point when he states that

> In agriculture no general arguments from economies of scale or anything else can serve to establish the superiority of large-scale over small-scale production; both in theory and in reality the matter is decided by complex combinations of factors which may vary from situation to situation. They include the nature of the crop itself, the land and terrain, the skills of peasants and the structure and organization of markets.

It seems then, that Kitching's case for economies of scale, in both industry and agriculture, is exaggerated. On the other hand, it could be argued that these exceptions are counter-tendencies, and no more than that, while the *dominant* tendency over the last two hundred years has been the establishment of economies of scale. I believe that this contention is in fact true, but we need to establish *why* this is the case. It is at this point that we arrive at the heart of the matter, because we begin to understand the key omission in the work of Kitching.

The emergence of economies of scale is not the intrinsic product of particular technologies, but is rooted in a particular set of social relations. Economies of scale emerged as a strategic consideration made by individual firms in the context of the competitive accumulation of capital. Such economies enabled firms to control labour more effectively, and thereby increase labour productivity, and to internalize the supply of inputs and thus escape the uncertainties of the market place. Thus, "[e]conomies of scale ... emerged as a key dynamic in the competitive process *after*, and not before significant increases in capital concentration and centralization" (O'Donnell & Nolan 1989: 9). Thus the development of plant size, work organization and so on, is not (solely) a product of a particular technology, but is rooted within a particular social and political framework.

Sutcliffe (1971: 15) has similarly argued that "it makes no sense in a capitalist economy to ask if a more labour intensive technique is available than that actually in use, if the existing technique is the most profitable and if the state is not prepared to subsidize a different technique". This statement is used by Sutcliffe to criticize some of the naive views of the neo-populists outlined above, particularly that appropriate technology should be adopted because it is more humane than capital-intensive technology.[12] However, the quotation also shows that the decision to secure economies of scale is not a neutral one, but one that exists in a particular social context; that it is a choice made by capitalists (or socialist bureaucracies) not to expand development, but to increase profitability (Kaplinsky 1990: ch. 3). I now turn to a consideration of this social context.

The determinants of industrialization

Industrialization is best considered as a social process. By this I mean not simply arguing that the (technical) process of industrialization leads to a number of social problems, such as urban squalor and environmental degradation. It is the very *process* of industrialization that is ultimately socially determined.

Technological development is an intrinsic part of any industrial revolution, but the decision to innovate through the introduction of new technology is made within a specific social and political context. While Kitching is clearly aware of this fact,[13] his failure to fully incorporate a convincing account of the social basis of industrialization is an important omission, which clearly shows the weakness of the old growth-based orthodoxy. In fairness to Kitching, the intention of his work is to expose the weaknesses of development strategies that idealistically "wish away" the problem of production (1989: 185–95). In this respect, his work is successful, and his central contention that industrialization is necessary for development (in both an economistic *and* a social sense) is convincing. However, to simply argue that industrialization is necessary for development does not take us very far, as it provides us with no analysis of the *form* that "actually existing industrializations" (Sutcliffe 1992: 333) take, a point that Kitching himself accepts (1989: 192). For as Sutcliffe (1992: 333) argues,

It is surely a fact that the standard, universally accepted *theoretical* defence of industrialization has never been the main motive for any actually existing industrialization. Real-world industrializations have not been motivated directly by the desire to satisfy human needs in general.

Moore (1966: 506) has similarly argued that "[a]t bottom all forms of industrialization so far have been revolutions from above, the work of a ruthless minority".

In other words, while it may be true that industrialization can and indeed has in some respects improved living standards (for some), it is not the case that this was the main motivation for particular people to inaugurate *actual* processes of

17

industrial development. This is why it is crucial to examine the motives of those social and political agents who have promoted industrialization, whose primary interest may have been to make a profit or increase military strength, rather than to improve the health or education of the population.

These questions are further complicated by the cases of "late" industrialization in the so-called Third World which may be radically different from the experiences of the early industrializers, and where there may be even wider discrepancies between the theoretical case for industrialization, and the actual concrete experiences of industrial development. Kitching's case for industrialization largely ignores the practical problems, and particularly the constraints and opportunities, faced by late industrializers in the global economy.[14]

Such comments are very much at odds with the work of early growth-based theory. Modernization theorists argued that in the industrial age, all nation-states would become increasingly alike as industrialism imposed its own logic on the social and political structures of all societies. The advance of science and technology would induce rapid changes in the labour market as a more complex division of labour emerged. Industrial technology required large-scale social organization to support mass production – thus industrial societies would be concentrated in cities, and administered by large-scale, bureaucratic organizations. Industrial societies would become alike because "[t]he science and technology on which ... [they are] based speak in a universal language" (Kerr et al. 1962: 54).

The problem with this approach is that it works with an implicit model of an ideal industrial society. In the real world, while there may be important similarities between industrial (or capitalist) societies, there are important differences too. Kerr et al. (1962: 29) argue that industrialization

tends under any political and economic system to raise materially the level of wages, to reduce the hours of work, and to raise living standards as meas-ured by such conventional means as life expectancy, health and education.

However, this leads us back to problems already discussed: namely that such a perspective rests on a very one-sided and optimistic account of the effects of industrialization; it tells us nothing about who carries out concrete industrial strategies; it fails to address the question of which kinds of government policies or indeed political regimes are most conducive to industrialization; nor does it tell us why there have been such discrepancies in living standards between actual cases of industrializing societies.

Kitching also rejects the technological determinism of modernization theory, and accepts that processes of technological diffusion are not neutral and benefit certain social classes more than others. His focus is therefore on *capitalist* rather than industrial society. Nevertheless, Kitching *has* argued (1983: 54) that regrettable though it may be, the best way to achieve (economic and social) development is through the development of the productive forces under the auspices of a capitalist class. Thus,

materially poor societies cannot produce the democratic public life which is an essential prerequisite of the creation of socialist democracies, because gross material poverty and isolation as well as the illiteracy and narrowed intellectual vision which accompanies these material conditions make the majority of their citizens inactive or ineffective as continuous monitors and controllers of the use of public power.

"Third World" societies *must* therefore pass through a stage of development based on capitalist industrialization (cf. Warren 1980). Arghiri Emmanuel (1982: 105) has similarly argued that

> if capitalism is hell there exists a still more frightful hell: that of less developed capitalism ... if development does not *ipso facto* lead to the satisfaction of "social needs", it nonetheless constitutes, via the political struggles made possible by a certain pluralism inherent in the higher phase of the industrial revolution, a much more favourable framework for a satisfaction of those needs than those of past class regimes.

Clearly then, for some Marxists *capitalist* industrialization is a necessary bridge towards a better future, based on the fulfilment of wider development objectives and the achievement of a socialist society. Such views have become stronger with the collapse of state socialist development strategies in the 1980s. These views are also prepared to accept that "development is an awful process ... [which] varies only, and importantly in its awfulness" (Kitching 1989: 195). Compared to some of the "quick-fix" solutions of many underdevelopment theorists, Marxists and Third-Worldists, such views are a breath of fresh air (Smith 1981; Kiely 1995b).

However, the approach is also flawed. It conflates a model of capitalism with the varieties of capitalisms that exist in the real world (Kiely 1995a: 85). In this respect it mirrors the errors of convergence theory which takes an ahistorical model of industrial society as the norm and measures all others as deviations from that ideal. Thus, we arrive back at Sutcliffe's point that there is a need to analyze not just theoretical cases for industrialization, but the experience of actually existing (capitalist or socialist) industrializations. In doing so, we are in a position to expand on the point made in passing by Kitching, but which he fails to give sufficient attention, namely that industrializations vary in their degrees of awfulness. The question of why some industrializations are more humane – or less awful – than others is thus a *social* question, which cannot be answered by resort to an ahistorical model of capitalist or industrial society.

Finally, one should briefly point out the political dangers of a simplistic one-sided pro-industrialization strategy (be it capitalist or socialist). First, such a strategy tells us little about *how* to undertake rapid industrialization, a not inconsiderable problem for "late" industrializers. Second, it says nothing about the relationship between rapid industrialization and damage to the environment. Third, the view that the short-term sacrifices of one generation are necessary for long-term and inevitable industrial development is particularly dangerous. As Allen (1992: 388) argues, "Such a grimly determinist view could lead to a position that there is little point in doing anything to help the poor or change society".

A preliminary summary

Growth-based theorists in the 1950s and 1960s made a powerful case for all nation-states to industrialize. These views were challenged from the late 1960s as industrial development failed to alleviate poverty in much of the world. This paved the way for a number of alternative development strategies, which focused on fulfilling basic needs and social development, rather than simply increasing industrial output. Kitching showed that such strategies were far from original and were similar to populist and neo-populist strategies in nineteenth-century Europe and twentieth-century Russia. His theoretical case for industrialization – based on the limitations of agriculture and the efficiency of economies of scale – remains the most powerful argument in favour of the proposition that "in order to develop, you must industrialize".

However, there are a number of omissions in the work of the growth-based theorists, which relate to the realities of *actual* processes of industrialization and the question of the social and political agents that lead it. Therefore, in order to assess the relationship between industrialization and development, one needs to assess the experiences of actually existing industrializations. This task is taken up in the rest of the book, which takes a case study (rather than hypothetical) approach. The case studies are used to show the complexities of industrial development, the social and political basis of industrial strategies, and the relationship between industrialization and the global system.

Notes

1. This view of Marx is rejected as one-sided in Kiely 1995a.
2. Cf. Redclift 1987; Pearce 1989; Banuri and Appfel Marglin 1993.
3. Cf. Corbridge 1994; Kiely 1995b; more generally on universalism versus particularism, see Habermas 1987; Alexander 1995; Geras 1995.
4. The argument here should not be misunderstood. These points tell us little about who led the industrialization process, and their interests in doing so. As will become clear, a theoretical case for industrialization is no guarantee of an implementation of pro-industry policies. This will depend on the political and social power of a particular group of people who favour industrial development. My point here is to stress the fact that these people cannot be reduced to being passive puppets of an omnipresent Western discourse, and that "hypothetical" cases for industrialization may be one means by which popular support for such a strategy can be won.
5. Cf. Long and Villareal 1993: 163, fn. 9.
6. One of the best contemporary examples of such romantic approaches is that of ecofeminism – for examples, see Mies and Shiva 1993; Banuri and Appfel Marglin 1993. These approaches put forward the proposition that the environmental struggles of women in local communities form the basis for non-patriarchal societies that are at one with "Mother Earth" (Mies and Shiva 1993: 13). Such views, in keeping with the "relativist turn" in social theory, simply discount the realities of conflict and hierarchy (not least those based on gender) in "other" localities, romanticize and homogenize women, and reject rationality as a Western concept. Jackson's (1995) critique of ecofeminism does a very effective job in demolishing such notions.

7. Though with some important qualifications in the case of Lenin.
8. ISI is discussed in more detail in Chapter Six.
9. See Chapter Nine.
10. See Chapter Nine for further discussion.
11. The principal weakness of Chayanov's work is that he fails to demonstrate that peasants are only interested in maintaining a constant level of living standards and are disinterested in accumulation. He therefore underestimates the potential for class differentiation between peasant households. On the other hand, Chayanov's critics, such as Lenin, underestimate the degree to which peasant differentiation can be limited by state regulation. The issue of peasant differentiation is further addressed through an examination of the industrialization debate in the Soviet Union in Chapter Four.
12. He has since radically altered his views (cf. Sutcliffe 1992).
13. See, for example, Kitching 1982: 19–22; 1980.
14. It is true, however, that Kitching's work does include an important discussion of development theory – see Kitching 1982: ch. 6. This particular chapter is principally concerned with showing that the prospects for development in the periphery are not all bad, and that many varieties of dependency theory are unduly pessimistic, empirically wrong and theoretically inconsistent. I share these conclusions – see Kiely 1995c: ch. 3 and Chapter Five of this book. Nevertheless, it remains the case that Kitching's argument in support of industrialization is based on "national economies", and lacks a consideration of how such economies relate to the world economy. In this respect, his approach may tell us more (although still not enough) about an earlier, "Fordist" era of national economic growth, but less about industrialization in a so-called post-Fordist, global era.

Part II
Historical "models"

Chapter Three
Capitalist models of industrialization

This chapter is concerned with comparatively early capitalist industrializations. Britain is examined in some detail, with particular attention paid to the questions of agency, development and the world market. The difference between Britain and later capitalist industrializations is very briefly examined, with a particular focus on the role of the state. I then illustrate these differences through an examination of Japanese industrialization.

The British industrial revolution

The industrial revolution in eighteenth- and nineteenth-century Britain is the first case of large-scale industrialization. For some writers (e.g. Rostow 1985) it is regarded as a model for other countries to follow. My brief account of the industrial revolution below is intended to do two closely related things: first, to question the assumption that Britain represents a "model" for late industrializers; and second, to question the idea that the industrial revolution in Britain was *primarily* a revolution in economic growth caused by expanding output, which in turn was *simply* a consequence of neutral technological innovation. These questions are addressed in three parts: (a) an assessment of technological and social factors; (b) an assessment of the relationship between British industrialization and the international division of labour; (c) an assessment of the relationship between industrialization and "living standards".

Technological and social factors in the British industrial revolution
For a number of writers, the causes of the British industrial revolution are quite simple. This revolution was primarily caused by a particular set of human values combining with certain technologies, and thus producing the world's most far-reaching industrialization process. The implication is that the British industrialization experience can be replicated elsewhere and so constitutes a model for the Third World today. Eisenstadt (1966: 1) has outlined this position:

> Historically, modernization is the process of change toward those types of social, economic and political systems that have developed in Western Europe and North America from the seventeenth century.

The particular values which promoted industrialization were self-interest and an entrepreneurial spirit. Such acquisitive values led to the creation of wealth which benefited the individual, but also benefited "society" in general. British industrialization was therefore caused by "the desire to do something better, faster, more efficiently, with less effort" (McClelland 1961: 4). This crude interpretation of Adam Smith's *The Wealth of Nations* thus became the basis for modernization theory in the 1950s and 1960s. As regards technological development, it was argued that the Third World could draw on the technology produced by the "First World" and therefore – so long as it adopted the "universal" values of individualism and acquisitiveness – could actually reap the advantages of "late development" (McClelland 1961).

Modernization theory (in both its neo-liberal and mixed-economy forms) has been the subject of many devastating critiques, which need not detain us here.[1] It should be borne in mind, however, that it believes that modernization is essentially achieved through industrialization, and that the latter process is largely a technologically driven one. Industrialization is regarded as having its own dynamic independent of social and political factors, and this "logic of industrialism" (Kerr et al. 1962) will lead to a convergence between industrial societies irrespective of political ideology and social structure.

Other writers have challenged the argument that British industrialization was *simply* a product of technological innovation by entrepreneurs. Hobsbawm (1962: 45–6) has shown that in matters of science, technology and education, both the French and the Germans were ahead of Britain. For instance, the French produced more original inventions, such as the Jacquard loom in 1804, and had a more effective shipbuilding industry. The key difference for Hobsbawm was that technological innovation and self-interest existed in a *particular social context* in Britain, which facilitated a more rapid and (for a time) far-reaching process of industrialization.

The most important social factor that facilitated industrialization was the *unique* British[2] solution of the agrarian problem. In Britain there existed a "triad" of landowners, who leased land to capitalist farmers, who in turn employed wage labour. A relatively free and mobile labour force employed by a comparatively dynamic, accumulating class of capitalist farmers facilitated rapid economic growth, which in turn laid the basis for the industrial revolution, and further growth in the late eighteenth century (Snooks 1994).

The emergence of this unique social structure was encouraged by the defeat of royal absolutism and the emergence of a strong, centralized state. Contrary to popular myth, Britain had a strong state in the sense of a public administration that effectively extracted financial resources from society. In terms of revenue extraction, "the British state was probably the most highly developed in Europe in the eighteenth century" (Weiss & Hobson 1995: 43–4). In 1694 the Bank of England was formed, which paved the way for the emergence of a close relationship between the Treasury and the City in the eighteenth century. In addition there were the Enclosure Acts (1760–1830), which forced peasants off the land and into a new relationship of wage labour with capitalist farmers (Moore 1966: ch. 1; Hilton 1976; Marx 1976: ch. 27). In the rest of Europe, on the other hand, the peasantry had successfully maintained (or been forced to maintain) direct access to land. The British social structure thus facilitated relatively early industrialization in at least three ways:

> to increase production and productivity, so as to feed a rapidly rising non-agricultural population; to provide a large and rising surplus of potential recruits for the towns and industries; and to provide a mechanism for the accumulation of capital to be used in the more modern sectors of the economy. (Hobsbawm 1962: 47)

This social structure was very different from, say, the case of France, where a potential labour force for industry was hindered (not entirely, but certainly in comparison to Britain) by the success of the peasants in remaining on the land, which in turn limited the development of a mass market and so encouraged the production of luxury goods or investment in foreign industry (Hobsbawm 1962: 218). It was in Britain, then, that capitalist relations of production first developed, which laid the basis for the accumulation of capital and industrial development. Brenner (1986: 33) identifies the particular social relations that emerged in Britain:

> Under what conditions, then, will the economic actors adopt patterns of economic action conducive, in the aggregate, to modern economic growth? ... [T]hey can be *expected* to do so, only where all the direct producers are separated from their means of subsistence, *above all the land*, and where no exploiters are able to maintain themselves through surplus extraction by extra-economic coercion. It is only where the organizers of production and the direct producers (sometimes the same person) have been separated from direct access to the means of subsistence, that they *must* buy on the market the tools and means of subsistence they need to reproduce themselves. It is only where the producers must buy on the market their means of reproduction, that they must be able to sell *competitively* on the market, i.e. at the socially necessary rate. It is only in the presence of the necessity of competitive production – and the correlative absence of the possibility of cutting costs, or otherwise raising income, by forcefully squeezing the direct producers – that we can expect the systematic and continual pressure to increase the efficiency of production which is the *sine qua non* of modern economic growth.[3]

If we regard industrialization as a social process, then this has implications for how we think about *all* processes of development. It *is* the case that entrepreneurship and technological innovation were crucial factors in shaping industrial development, but it is equally true that these factors *in themselves* are not sufficient as explanations for Britain's success. More important is the social context in which these factors exist. This in turn means that Britain cannot be a model of industrialization for any "late developer" because the British experience rested on the emergence of social relations *which were unique to that particular country's history.* This does not mean that comparisons cannot be made between different industrialization processes, or that *specific* lessons cannot be learnt, but simple, technicist accounts should be rejected.

British industrialization and the international division of labour

The notion that Britain represents a model deserves rejection for a second reason, which relates to the relationship between the industrial revolution and the world economy. The effects of the industrial revolution were not of course confined solely to Britain. Most importantly, the fact that one country had industrialized at a faster pace than others meant that the "rules of the game" for later industrializers had completely changed. When Britain industrialized, it faced limited competition from others. There was competition for colonies, and the access to protected markets that such acquisition guaranteed, but no country effectively competed with Britain in terms of comparatively high productivity. Therefore, any later industrializing country was likely to protect itself from the competition of an already powerful British economy.

Moreover, British industrialization promoted a new international division of labour in which different regions produced different goods. The leading sector in Britain's industrialization was the cotton industry, which had a major impact on the rest of the world. The raw material for cotton was acquired from slave plantations in both the West Indies and the southern USA, while the finished cotton goods found a ready market both at home and abroad. This included Europe and the United States, but also markets in the "periphery" of the world system, namely West Africa and India (Hobsbawm 1968: 57–8). The case of India is striking because this was one part of the world that could successfully compete with Britain in terms of exporting finished cotton goods. However, Britain was able to use its semi-colonial status over India to protect British industry through the manipulation of import duties, and to impoverish Indian urban society through the appropriation of colonial revenue, which had the effect of destroying demand for domestic products (Alavi 1989: 11). The result was that over the period from 1813 to 1830, India shifted from being a textile exporter to a source of raw cotton exports for Europe, and a market (albeit one limited by Britain's colonial policies) for finished textile products imported from Britain (Mukherjee 1974).

British industrialization therefore had an impact on much of the world, so that parts of it became suppliers of raw materials which helped to fuel Britain's so-called "take-off". Furthermore, these suppliers often used "archaic" forms of labour control such as slavery and other forms of forced labour, often with British encouragement. Marx (Marx & Engels 1965: 40) argued that "[d]irect slavery is as much the pivot of our industrialism today as machinery, credit etc. Without slavery no cotton; without cotton no modern industry." British industrialization changed the rules of the game and in doing so subordinated some parts of the world.

The social consequences of British industrialization: the "living standards" debate
One of the major debates concerning the industrial revolution in Britain
concerns the impact that industrialization had on living standards. Optimists
such as Ashton (1948) believe that the results were largely favourable, while
pessimists such as Hobsbawm (1969: ch. 4) argue the opposite. There are
problems with both sides of the argument, not least because of the difficulty
involved in defining and measuring living standards. A close parallel can thus be
drawn between the living-standards debate in eighteenth- and nineteenth-
century Britain, and the problematic relationship between industrialization and
development discussed in the previous chapters.

Thus, measuring improvements in living standards in terms of increases in
per capita GNP is highly problematic. Per capita *consumption* is a more reliable
method, and the evidence appears to show that from 1760 to 1820 this was
largely unchanged for most sections of the (male) population, but then
improved (Snooks 1994: 13). In terms of life expectancy, there was a slight
improvement before 1820, but little change from 1820 to 1860 (ibid.).

Perhaps more important than simple statistical analysis is the fact that the
industrial revolution represented "not merely a process of addition and
subtraction, but *a fundamental social change*" (Hobsbawm 1968: 80). The agrarian
landlords benefited from increased rents which were facilitated by increased
demand for farm produce, and increased prices for land in both town and
country. The emerging class of industrial capitalists benefited from high rates of
profit. For the working class, however, the situation was different. Deprived of
direct access to the means of production, workers became dependent on a wage
for access to basic entitlements (Sen 1981). Although this provided some
workers with opportunities, it also presented significant risks. Workers were
dependent on the successful selling of their labour power to employers. In
periods of economic slump, when labour requirements were low, many
workers were deprived of any means of support, beyond the harsh inadequacies
of "poor relief". In the slump of the early 1840s, around 10 per cent of the
population were paupers (Hobsbawm 1969: 72), and deprived of any proper
means of support.

Even when workers did enjoy considerable job security, they were subject to
new means of discipline (Thompson 1991: 394–5). Wage increases alone did
not necessarily entail an improvement in the quality of life. Thompson (1963:
231) has recognized

> those trades, such as coal mining, in which real wages advanced between
> 1790 and 1840, but at the cost of longer hours and greater intensity of
> labour, so that the breadwinner was "worn out" before the age of forty.
> In statistical terms, this reveals an upward curve. To the families
> concerned it might feel like immiseration.

Optimistic versus pessimistic views of the industrial revolution also pervade
debates around the issue of gender, and the position of women before and after
industrialization. The pessimistic view, most famously presented by Alice Clark

(1919), argued that before industrial capitalism employers hired the whole family. With the coming of factory production the "independent" wage workers gradually displaced women, who were excluded from skilled work and became economically dependent on the male breadwinner. The optimistic position, espoused by Ivy Pinchbeck (1930), argued that the growth of factory production led to higher wages, and the *family wage* recognized the fact that women performed work within the household. Moreover, industry offered women more jobs, which in turn increased women's bargaining position within the family.

Both sides in this debate tend to over-generalize their arguments. A closer examination of the evidence suggests that the experiences of women were quite diverse, even within the working class. Industrialization led to the separation of production from consumption, and the replacement of the household as the basic unit of production by the factory system (Maynard 1985: 77). The nineteenth century also saw the emergence of domestic ideology (Davidoff & Hall 1987), in which motherhood came to be regarded as the natural role for women.

The experience of working-class women was very different from this picture, and they were constantly criticized for being poor housewives and bad mothers. In the early years of the industrial revolution, women were employed in large numbers in the cotton industry, both as homeworkers and in factories. With technological innovation, spinning – a traditionally female task – was gradually moved out of the home into the factory, where the work was monopolized by skilled men. Weaving – regarded as men's work before industrial capitalism – was in turn affected by the mechanization of spinning, which increased the demand for handloom weavers. As they were increasingly displaced from their traditional role of spinning, women and children came to fill the gap in weaving. However, in the long run weaving went into decline with the introduction of power looms in the 1830s and 1840s (Hall 1982: 23–5).

It is therefore difficult to generalize about the impact of industrialization on women. The case of the pessimists is partly undermined by a tendency to romanticize the position of women before the industrial revolution, where there was a pronounced sexual division of labour. As Pinchbeck (1930) points out, in the family economy women were in a subordinate position. Suicide and mortality rates were particularly high and in the towns there were high rates of prostitution among women who escaped from oppressive husbands. On the other hand, it is too simplistic to suggest that the modernizing thrust of industrialization swept away archaic and unequal gender relations and liberated women. In the public sphere, women were largely excluded from the most innovative and highest paid sectors, and their role in paid employment (as domestic servants for instance) was largely seen as an extension of their "natural" role as mothers and housewives (Richards 1974). As a result, women were paid less than men, their paid employment tended to be regarded as unskilled, and they faced the double burden of work in the "public" and "domestic" spheres (Phillips & Taylor 1980). The so-called family wage still left women economically dependent on men, and was often unequally distributed within families, with sometimes devastating results for women's health (Nicholas & Oxley 1994).

Overall then, the industrial society had a contradictory impact on working-class women, providing opportunities (mobility, waged employment) on the one hand, and constraints (economic dependence, domestic ideology) on the other. It was only from the late nineteenth century that substantial gains were made with the coming of compulsory education (which alleviated some domestic burdens and widened the base of female employment) and legislation which allowed women to own property within a family.

Later capitalist industrializations

The rhetoric of laissez-faire that accompanied British industrialization was problematic for two reasons. First, it did not fit the reality of the British case, where the state played a vital role in the transition to capitalist industrialization. Second, laissez-faire was of little use to potential competitors, because free trade benefited the already powerful, as established industries could out-perform weak rivals. The work of Frederick List (cf. Cowen & Shenton 1996: 158–65) is significant here. He argued that the collective interest took precedence over the interests of isolated individuals, and that the development of manufacturing was important because it was economically progressive and rested on the use of social, rather than isolated, labour. Manufacturing must therefore be developed as part of the process of nation-building, and this should occur through the use of protectionist measures (tariffs, import controls) against foreign competition.

These points were not lost on later industrializers. Private enterprise was still deemed to play a key, leading role in industrialization, but it was to be accompanied by an actively interventionist state. Thus in Germany from the 1870s, most major products were regulated by price cartels and import controls. Marketing syndicates were also established, whereby the entire output of member firms was in the hands of a single agency, which effectively eliminated competition. In France too, the market was restricted by the role of the state which promoted the growth of giant industrial complexes which were shielded from foreign competition (Kemp 1978: 120–21).

In the United States, the ideology of laissez-faire was more openly embraced. The Constitution adopted the principle of free enterprise (with important qualifications), while "open" frontiers encouraged the development of family farms producing wheat for the market[4] (Byres 1991: 29). As Kemp (1990: 18) states, "[t]he state in America was expected to play only a limited role and not to enter the social or economic arena except under very special circumstances". However, the reality of US industrialization does not confirm the limited government thesis. As early as 1791, the first Secretary of the Treasury,

Alexander Hamilton, made a case for government assistance to manufacturing. He argued that it was impossible for the United States "to exchange with Europe on equal terms" (cited in Cowen & Shenton 1996: 155), and so argued for state controls on imported finished goods and state promotion of what is now known as research and development in new technology (ibid.: 157). Such protectionism and support for industry has been an enduring feature of US industrial development.[5]

However, perhaps the most successful case of capitalist state–industry relations is Japan.

Japanese industrialization

Many Western stereotypes about Japan implicitly reject the need for a historical analysis. The success of the country is "explained" by recourse to "culture". While such views usually betray a lack of knowledge about Japan, more informed analyses have attempted to explain the rise of Japan through its Confucianist heritage. Confucianism can be regarded as a social philosophy, which focuses on the need for hierarchy, authority and tradition. The Confucianist tradition thus propagates the need for a loyal and compliant workforce, which is often taken to be the essence of the Japanese miracle (Hofheinz & Calder 1982). This claim lacks any historical grounding because "[i]n East Asia, Confucianism developed in the fifth century B.C.; thus it took two and a half millennia before it supposedly fostered any local capitalism" (Johnson 1995: 40). Moreover, such a cultural reductionism falsely homogenizes Japanese culture. As Morris-Suzuki (1994: 3) points out,

"culture" tends to be presented as something created in remote antiquity, and somehow handed down intact to the present day. The sense of history as an ongoing process of human conflicts and human choices is often lost, and therefore theories which seek to explain and elucidate serve, in the end, only to intensify the aura of mystery surrounding Japanese society.

To understand Japanese industrialization, then, a historical approach is required. I undertake this task in four parts: (i) 1868 onwards, the Meiji restoration and its impact; (ii) the early twentieth century, to 1945; (iii) 1945 to the present; (iv) industrialization and development in Japan.

From the Meiji restoration to the First World War, 1868–1914

In 1867–8, bands of lower-ranking samurai successfully took power and undertook the task of building a new state. The Tokugawa regime, seemingly powerless to protect the region from Western imperial dominance, was replaced by the restored Meiji dynasty (Anderson 1974: 459–61). The new regime undertook the task of modernizing Japan through agrarian reform and industrial development.

In the Tokugawa period, land ownership was restricted to the *shogunate*, which comprised around 300 lords, plus a small number of wealthy farmers. The Meiji state granted land ownership to ordinary farmers in return for payment in the form of land taxes. Restrictions on the buying and selling of land were also removed (Byres 1991: 49). Thus, there emerged both a rural landlord class and a set of small, relatively poor, tenant cultivators (Fukui 1992: 201–2). Land tax was payable to the state and up to 1914 constituted the most important source of government revenue (Byres 1991: 49). In 1890, land tax constituted as much as 85.6 per cent of total government tax revenue, and even by 1910 the figure was still as high as 42.9 per cent (Karshenas 1995: 142).

The state also led the industrialization process. It established new enterprises which were often run at a loss, directly invested in some sectors, and took the lead in importing and adapting technology to local conditions (Bronfenbrenner 1982: 99; Inkster 1991). The state contributed over 40 per cent of total investment in the period from 1868 to 1910 (Weiss & Hobson 1995: 85). An effective alliance was formed between the state and the nascent industrial capitalist class. The latter co-operated with the state

> not because they were necessarily more community-centred and less profit-oriented than, say, their American counterparts. It was partly because cooperation with government gave business access to important resources; and partly because such cooperation was publicly sanctioned, being closely linked to the cause of strengthening the nation. (Weiss & Hobson 1995: 180)

Industries developed in coal and silver mining, cotton spinning, silk reeling, shipyards and cement factories (Fukui 1992: 201). The nationalist state established a corporate framework in which there were strong controls over trade unions, but some progressive legislation was introduced. Thus, independent unions were suppressed in the period of uprisings in 1910–11, while a Factory Law in 1911 banned the employment of children under twelve years of age, and limited the working day to 12-hour shifts (Fukui 1992: 201).

Although most labour power was still used by agriculture, Japan had made significant strides in industrial development by the beginning of the twentieth century. Kemp (1983: 19–20) is therefore right to claim that

> unlike any other Asian country, Japan entered the twentieth century under the guidance of a modernizing elite committed to building a strong national economy both to preserve the independence of the state and also to extend its power and influence on the Asiatic mainland and the Pacific area.

1900–45

Japan responded to the second industrial revolution (1880s to 1920s) in Europe and the United States by increasing its research and development facilities, establishing links with foreign firms and importing foreign technology. Industrial development received a boost during the First World War, as domestic production was increased to replace lost imports, and new export markets were won as the major protagonists in the war were otherwise occupied. Moreover, the 1914–18 period was a particularly favourable time for industrial experiments, as the world market was unusually "forgiving" (Morris-Suzuki 1994: 116).

After the First World War, the economy went into recession as competitors began to recover and overseas demand shrank. In the early 1930s the economy again suffered as a result of the world depression. However, recovery was swift as military spending soared. In 1937 Japan invaded China and closer relations were established with Germany and Italy, culminating in the Tripartite Pact of 1940 and war with the Allies from 1941 to 1945.

In this period of militarization, the government's industrial policy was strengthened. In 1927 the Bureau of Resources was established, which empowered government officials to assess data on the output and finances of all enterprises. In 1931, the Major Industries Control Law encouraged large firms in key industries to form cartels to regulate production, and required these same firms to report their activities to the government. Between 1934 and 1941, a series of measures were passed which allowed the government to control private entry into various industries, such as automobiles, steel and machine tools (Morris-Suzuki 1994: 137–9, 146). The effect of these measures was to concentrate big business in the hands of a few large corporations, known as the zaibatsu, "which enjoyed a privileged relationship with the government and worked closely with it and the armed forces to increase production for war purposes" (Kemp 1983: 28).

At the other end of the scale, many small businesses continued to operate, often serving as suppliers to the large companies. A government survey in 1934 showed that 76 per cent of companies with more than 100 workers, and as many as 42 per cent of companies with 30–100 workers relied on outside suppliers (Morris-Suzuki 1994: 132). This dense network of suppliers and subcontractors laid the basis for alternative forms of industrial organization, such as the Just-in-Time (JIT) system. Under JIT, which was established by Toyota in 1938, supplies were not stored in warehouses but were produced and delivered just in time for the day's production, thus cutting down on storage and waste, and enhancing flexibility (cf. Chapter Nine).

By the eve of war, industrial production had grown at an impressive rate. Agricultural labour constituted around 75 per cent of the workforce in 1867–8; by 1939, the figure was around 40 per cent. Manufacturing output rose from 6 per cent of GDP at the end of the nineteenth century to 30 per cent by 1939 (Fukui 1992: 206–7). Despite this growth, defeat in the war exposed Japanese weakness in the face of far more powerful economies.

Recovery and the miracle, 1945 to the present

Defeat in the war plunged Japan into a state of chaos. US bombs destroyed around one-quarter of the country's factories and infrastructure. At the end of the war, the Allied Occupation forces set about dismantling the military machine, and some attempts (later abandoned) were made to dismantle the zaibatsu. However, conditions for recovery were also laid down very quickly. Higher wages for workers forced companies to invest in new technology, and laid the basis for a mass market for consumer goods. Plans for harsh reparations were gradually abandoned as the US came to regard Japan as a potential ally in the Cold War. Only one-quarter of the material originally planned for reparations was appropriated, and the rest was authorized for sale to Japanese companies (Morris-Suzuki 1994: 174). Thus, Japanese industry was effectively paying war reparations to itself. Japan was also a major recipient of aid from the United States.

In 1946, the US insisted on a further land reform, which abolished the "militaristic" landlord class by transferring ownership to the peasants (Byres 1991: 47–50). Four million farmers became owner-cultivators, and the end of high rents payable to landlords meant that their purchasing power was increased. Furthermore, in reducing ties to the land, the reform effectively released labour for employment by industrial capital. Between 1950 and 1970, the primary sector shed about 10 million people, while manufacturing employment rose from 6 million to nearly 14 million (Kemp 1983: 32).

The state continued to play an active role in facilitating industrialization. In 1949, the Foreign Exchange Control Law was passed, requiring all importers to apply to the Ministry of International Trade and Industry (MITI) for foreign exchange to complete their transaction. This allowed MITI to favour certain kinds of imports over others, giving it considerable leverage over industrial planning. The shipbuilding, steel, chemicals and machinery industries were all successfully targeted by MITI in the 1950s, with the state providing subsidies and protection from foreign competition. Although government spending on research and development was lower in Japan than in other (First World) nations, this reflected Japan's much lower military spending, and ignored the country's success in diffusing the benefits of R&D to smaller companies – largely through the active role of local government (Morris-Suzuki 1994: 183).

Japan also imported technology on very favourable terms, with few conditions attached, as it was not regarded as a major competitor in the world market. This import of technology was combined with successful local adaptation and innovation, so that imports complemented (rather than competed with) domestic innovation. In fact in only one industry in the early 1960s (oil refining) did spending on imported technology exceed investment in local research and development. Although this figure partly reflects the favourable terms on which Japan imported technology, it also shows the interdependence between foreign and local innovation (Morris-Suzuki 1994: 171).

By the 1950s, then, the conditions for a rapid boom were in place. Japan's economy grew by an annual average of 7 per cent from 1954 to 1958, 10.8 per cent from 1959 to 1963, 10.9 per cent from 1964 to 1968, and 9.6 per cent from 1969 to 1973 (Tsuru 1993: 67). Although growth rates slowed down after the oil shocks of 1973–4, Japan continued to outpace its rivals, successfully penetrating the markets of the advanced capitalist world (cf. Chapter Nine).

Industrialization and development in Japan

Industrialization since the Second World War has gone hand in hand with an increase in living standards. Health, literacy, and life expectancy have all improved dramatically. Furthermore, income inequalities are not as great as in other First World nations such as the United States (Bradshaw & Wallace 1996: 101–2). On the other hand, Japanese industrialization has "imposed massive burdens on the human workforce and the natural environment, and . . . provoked repeated protests, large and small, from those who bore a disproportionate share of the burden" (Morris-Suzuki 1994: 203). The dark side of the miracle includes high levels of air pollution, long working hours, and substantial inequalities between male and female workers (*New Internationalist* 1992b: 19).

Conclusion

Capitalist industrialization rested on the leading role of private entrepreneurs appropriating the surplus produced by workers, and therefore laying the basis for the development of industrial techniques. In Britain this occurred through a process of "primitive accumulation", through which the peasantry were divorced from direct access to the means of production. The seemingly "spontaneous", even accidental, nature of this process faciliated an ideology of laissez-faire, which championed the entrepreneurial individual unfettered by state collectivism – even though the centralization of a state apparatus was crucial to British success. However, in industrializing first, Britain had changed the rules of the game in the world economy. Later industrializers were prepared for a more active role for the state, even although private enterprise was still deemed the leading sector.

None of the capitalist industrialization processes were carried out in order to "promote development". The intentions were to increase profits in a competitive environment, and to protect national security from more powerful economic and military competitors. These two motives are not mutually exclusive. The relationship between industrialization and development was therefore far from straightforward, but included both costs and benefits, the legacies of which persist to this day.

Notes

1. See among many others Larrain 1989: ch. 3; Kiely 1995c: chs 2 and 6.
2. One should be careful about generalizing from concrete processes of history. The "British" solution of the agrarian problem in fact varied from region to region, and it is a simplification to say that the peasantry no longer existed on the British mainland by the

nineteenth century. There were significant exceptions, most obviously in Scotland, but also in rural England (cf. Reed 1986). Nevertheless, these exceptions qualify, but do not alter, the fact that agrarian capitalism existed to a far greater extent in Britain than elsewhere. Cf. Aston and Philpin (1985) and more generally, Byres (1991).

3. This point needs to be qualified in the case of later capitalist industrializations, which have often taken place in the context of the relative absence of wage labour in agriculture, as the examples in this book show.

4. Both central government and local states still played a crucial role in the recruitment of labour, law and order and so on, even though such forced mechanisms coincided with laissez-faire ideology. For example, on slavery, see Frederickson 1981: ch. 6. In the 1930s, of course, laissez-faire pretences were abandoned. Among other activities, family farming was protected by the role of the state from the Roosevelt period onwards (Byres 1991: 33).

5. What *is* true about US state intervention is its relative incoherence compared to other advanced capitalist countries. The pattern of state formation after the Civil War was a product of compromise between the interests of Northern industrialists and Southern commercial interests (Bensel 1990: 97). One of the legacies of weak state–industry relations in the United States has been that government spending in support of industry has been "shaped largely by special interest pressure and not by a coherent strategy for industrial development" (Weiss & Hobson 1995: 225). The state therefore played a key role in protecting US economic interests, including industry, from foreign competition, without in the long term providing a long-term strategy to deal with competitors. Since the 1970s, the effects of this legacy have been visible, with economic and social decline.

Chapter Four
Socialism and industrialization

This chapter examines an alternative historical "model" to that of capitalism – socialist industrialization. After a brief examination of the idea of socialism, I detail the history of the industrialization experiences in the Soviet Union and China. I then use this historical approach to examine the social context in which industrialization occurred, paying particular attention to living standards, class and gender.

Socialist industrialization

The nature of socialism and communism are matters of fierce debate. Following White (1982: 1–2; cf. Bahro 1978), a distinction can be made between "full" socialism, marked by an absence of classes and the state, and the existence of a radical democracy, on the one hand, and the reality of "actually existing socialisms". Neither of the cases examined in this chapter, nor indeed any other "socialist" country, could have been described as "fully" socialist. My reference to China and the Soviet Union as socialist (or state socialist) is intended as a shorthand, and in no way entails approval for the Communist Party leaders in either of the countries.

Having said that, both Soviet and Chinese industrializations were very different from the experiences of capitalist industrializations.[1] White (1982: 1) correctly argues that state socialist countries broke with the power of capital over politics, production and distribution, and embarked on a development path which did not principally rely on the power of private ownership and entrepreneurship. Instead, development was based on nationalized industries, socialized agriculture, abolition or limitation of markets, state control of foreign trade, state control of labour supply which guaranteed virtual full employment, state control of prices, and a central planning system which determined output, distribution and co-ordination between individual enterprises. This strategy was led in both cases by a single, Marxist-Leninist party, claiming to rule in the name of the working class and the peasantry (White 1982: 1; Kilmister 1992: 238–9).

Soviet industrialization

Although Russia was the first country to experience socialist revolution, the context for building a socialist society was far from favourable. Marx and Engels (1964: 206) had argued that a socialist society could only arise where there had been a sustained development of the productive forces, "otherwise all the old filthy business would necessarily be produced". Classes were inevitable in societies where the surplus product was relatively small, and so socialism could only rest on advanced industrial development and abundance.[2] In Russia there had been significant industrial development from the 1880s onwards, but in 1913 large-scale industrial output was only 6.9 per cent of American gross output (Nuti 1979: 236). Moreover, the industrial working class was small (2.5 million in 1913), and the peasantry made up 80 per cent of the population (Nuti 1979: 236).

While Marx in his later years envisaged a transition to communism in Russia based on the peasant commune (Shanin 1984), most of his Russian followers took the "orthodox" view that Russia must first develop along the lines of industrial capitalism before it could move to socialism (Plekhanov 1976). Lenin (1977a: 75, 99) also held a (qualified) stagist view before 1917, arguing that *capitalist* development could be promoted by a "democratic dictatorship of the proletariat and peasantry". Trotsky on the other hand argued that uneven development in Russia made it necessary that the working class, supported by sections of the peasantry, lead the revolution and that it would therefore have to take a socialist character. Industrial development had been largely undertaken by the state, and financed by foreign loans. To retain solvency, the peasant sector was heavily taxed, which blocked the development of a large internal market for industrial goods, which was necessary to promote further development. Nonetheless, significant pockets of large-scale industry had developed, and with it a small but highly concentrated working class. It was therefore this class, rather than a classical bourgeoisie, which would lead Russia to revolution. The revolution would therefore take on an immediately socialist character as the working class would not be content to allow the bourgeoisie to rule as a class (Trotsky 1976; cf. Anderson 1974: pt II ch. 6). By 1917, Lenin effectively shared Trotsky's view. In addition he argued that Russia, whose economy was influenced by foreign finance capital, was a "weak link" in the imperialist chain, and so could undertake a socialist revolution which would spread rapidly to the imperialist countries (Lenin 1977b).

It was on these grounds that the Bolsheviks led the socialist revolution in November 1917. However, on seizing power they faced numerous problems. There was the question of building socialism in an economically backward country. While the Bolsheviks had the support of industrial workers, these were a minority, and the question of the peasant majority had to be addressed. There were also the problems of internal opposition and foreign isolation and hostility. These issues dominated debates in the Bolshevik (Communist) party in the

39

following years. This can be seen through an examination of (i) the civil war of 1918–21; (ii) the industrialization debate; and (iii) Stalinist industrialization.

Civil war and War Communism, 1918–21

On taking power a decree was issued which nationalized the land, but effectively gave peasants the right to use it. This involved a substantial redistribution of land, although in practice villages carried out the reform and some richer peasants took more land for themselves. On the whole, though, there was an increase in the number of peasants holding land, and so the poor and landless peasants gained from the reform (Nove 1969: 48). In addition the Bolsheviks nationalized the banking system, repudiated foreign debts, and encouraged the movement for workers' control in factories (Nove 1969: 49–50).

By 1918, however, the Bolsheviks faced opposition from the "Whites" who wanted to restore Tsarism, and from foreign powers hostile to Communism and Russia's withdrawal from the First World War. A policy of War Communism was introduced, which involved rapid nationalization of industry, hierarchical management and the militarization of labour, obligatory delivery and requisition of agrarian surplus, the abolition of private trade, rationing, and a system of bartering within the state sector (Carr 1952: ch. 17).

By 1921, the Bolsheviks had won the civil war but at great cost. Many of the measures of War Communism were extremely unpopular, the economy was devastated by war, and millions had died in famine. Furthermore, the expected revolutions in Western Europe had not happened,[3] and so the country now faced the task of rebuilding the economy and socialism. It was in this context that the New Economic Policy was introduced.

NEP and the Soviet industrialization debate

The New Economic Policy, introduced in 1921, replaced grain requisition with a tax in kind set at a lower level (Nove 1969: 84). Thus, after paying a tax in kind (and from 1923 money tax), peasants could market the rest of their output. Private trade was legalized and some private enterprise was also allowed in small industry and services. The state continued to control large and medium-sized industry, finance and foreign trade (Nove 1969: 85).

The NEP era saw a great debate within the Communist Party over the future direction of development in the Soviet Union. Divisions arose over both the economic and political future of the country. The economic debate, which centred on the degree to which the Soviet state should support NEP, was strongly influenced by the political debate, which concerned the growing bureaucratization of the party-state apparatus. Lenin, who died in 1924, was particularly concerned with the separation of the Party from the working class and feared that a dictatorship of the proletariat had become a dictatorship over the proletariat (Lewin 1974). Questions concerning the future of NEP were therefore also questions concerning the future leadership of the Communist Party and the Soviet state.

The main critic of NEP was Evgeny Preobrazhensky. He argued for an industrialization strategy based on "primitive socialist accumulation" (Preobrazhensky 1965). By this he meant that the peasantry should be exploited through the state fixing the price of industrial goods at an artificially high level, and similarly depressing the price of agricultural goods. Through this unequal exchange, a surplus would be extracted from agriculture to finance industry. Other leaders such as Bukharin rejected these proposals on the grounds that they were politically unacceptable and would leave peasants with little incentive to produce goods in the first place (see below).

Trotsky was united with Preobrazhensky in the Left Opposition. However, such unity was over the growing power of a bureaucratic elite with Stalin at the helm, rather than economic strategy. In fact, Trotsky was embarrassed by Preobrazhensky's proposals for developing the Soviet economy (Day 1977).[4] Trotsky's main concern was how the Soviet Union could actively draw on the opportunities offered by the world economy, while at the same time using the state monopoly of foreign trade to eliminate the constraints. He argued that Soviet pricing must be guided (but not determined) by the world market through comparative coefficients, which would measure the effectiveness of Soviet goods in terms of price and quality (Trotsky 1975: 347–54). A poor coefficient would signal the need for controlled imports and simultaneous investment, and so "serve as guides to the optimal pattern of specialization to be pursued within the world division of labor" (Day 1977: 82). Trotsky (1975: 358–62) used such measures to argue that it was necessary to import highly capital-intensive machinery, and specialize at home in simpler types of equipment. These imports would have to be financed by the export of farm goods and so it was imperative to encourage the development of agriculture:

> We require a development of the productive forces in the village. The *kulak*, the rich peasant, who sells grain by way of the state, enables the state to acquire foreign currency with which it can import machines for our factories. This is a positive factor. It promotes movement towards socialism. (cited in Day 1973: 114)

Another position was that taken by Bukharin and the Right Opposition, who gave qualified support to NEP. He believed that it was necessary to win the support of the peasantry, the majority of the population. He also believed that it made good economic sense to support accumulation in agriculture because "[a]ccumulation in socialist industry cannot occur for long without accumulation in the peasant economy" (cited in Cohen 1973: 174). This was because the peasantry constituted the source of demand for industrial products, and in turn technological advance in agriculture depended on the availability of industrial products such as fertilizers and machinery. He therefore envisaged a "virtuous circle" in which state industry would receive grain, industrial crops, food for workers and export revenue, and industry would provide inputs into agriculture, thereby stimulating agicultural productivity. In 1925 Bukharin called for peasants to "get rich, accumulate, develop your farms" (cited in N. Chandra 1992: 103).

This perspective was later caricatured by Stalin as encouraging the restoration of capitalism in the countryside. However, Bukharin was never an advocate of unregulated market forces, and always believed that industrialization was necessary. His differences with colleagues was over how to proceed. He argued that industry could be financed from the profits of industry itself, from a progressive income tax on the richer peasants (the kulaks), and through voluntary savings deposited in Soviet banks. In this way, peasant differentiation could be limited. For Bukharin, higher industrial prices alone would be counter-productive because they would undermine peasant demand (cf. Cohen 1973: 178). Furthermore, from 1927 he called for "curtailing the role of capitalist elements", arguing that it was "possible to delimit the kulaks' exploitative tendencies" through an increase in agrarian co-operatives and more restrictions on the kulaks (cited in N. Chandra 1992: 105). In industry he moved away from a simple demand-led perspective and called for rationalization through shorter labour days, more shifts per day, and greater balance between heavy and light industry (cf. N. Chandra 1992: 109–13).

Thus, on the eve of Stalin's disastrous policy turn in 1929, a reasonably coherent policy alternative was in place. The state would *gradually* encourage the growth of a collective sector through preferential treatment, such as credit allocation and the concentration of advanced machinery (such as tractors) on the collective farms. In this way, "[t]he peasantry would be won to mechanized collectives by their demonstrated superiority in securing peasant interests" (Selden 1988: 42).

From 1927 to 1929, the state faced a growing grain procurement crisis. The crisis emerged in 1926, when the state cut purchasing prices for grain by 20 per cent, attacked private peasant trade and cut back on the provision of industrial goods to the countryside. All peasants (not just kulaks) responded by growing different crops and selling in unofficial markets (Selden 1988: 40). Bukharin's response to this situation was to call for the import of grain so that adequate supplies could be built up, which would lead to lower prices and thus compel the private sector to dehoard. This would have involved a foreign exchange requirement of around 100 million roubles, but at this time Soviet export revenue varied from around 771 million to 924 million a year, and so was affordable (N. Chandra 1992: 117). Stalin, by now the most powerful leader in the Party, rejected the import solution in favour of a more brutal strategy.

Stalinist collectivization and industrialization

Having eliminated many of his opponents from high political office, Stalin undertook the task of rapid collectivization from 1929. In September 1929, 7 per cent of rural households were collectivized; by March 1930, 59 per cent of peasant households were in large-scale collective farms. During this period, land, livestock and households were forcibly put into collectives, while a wage system was supposed to provide remuneration. A war on the kulaks became a war on the peasantry in general, and the collectivization drive met with widespread resistance. Peasants slaughtered much of their livestock and resented being forced into collective farms with the result that output fell drastically. Many who resisted were murdered by the state. Food shortages and an increase in state procurement of grain led to famine. An estimated 5.5 million people died in the period 1927–38 (Wheatcroft et al. 1986).

These changes in agriculture coincided with an increase in the industrial output targets set out in the first Five Year Plan, introduced the previous year (Cohen 1973: 330). The collectivization programme was "justified" on the grounds that it would provide a surplus for industrial investment. But the collectivization drive can be considered a failure on economic as well as moral grounds. Selden (1988: 45) points out that

> The state did squeeze the countryside of the agricultural surplus, but costly and inefficient collective agriculture required substantial state subsidies in both the short and long run . . . Far from providing a surplus that fuelled Soviet industrialization, following collectivization the net resource flow was *to* the countryside.

Grain production fell slightly in 1929 (compared to 1928), and quite significantly from 1931 to 1935 (compared to 1930), and losses in livestock were enormous. The state therefore procured less than planned (although still in sufficient amounts to starve peasants), from a far lower output, and had to provide extra inputs to offset losses in animals (Nove 1969: 186). It is true that collectivization did provide industry with a labour force through the impoverishment of the rural sector (Ellman 1975), but a more feasible alternative would have been lower investment drives utilizing both the urban unemployed and urban and rural underemployed (N. Chandra 1992: 132–6).

The first Plan and its successors gave priority to heavy industry so that the Soviet Union could catch up with the West. In 1931 Stalin maintained that "We are fifty or a hundred years behind the advanced countries. We must catch up this distance in ten years. Either we do it or we go under" (cited in Hosking 1990: 150). Plan targets were constantly revised upwards, and although targets often proved to be wildly optimistic, significant growth was achieved. However, sustained growth in heavy industry was achieved partly at the expense of neglected light industries such as textiles, construction and consumer goods, which led to massive shortages (Hosking 1990: 152).

Moreover, the development of the productive forces took precedence over the development of socialist relations of production (Corrigan et al. 1978). Propaganda campaigns were launched to promote increased labour productivity, such as the Stakhanov campaign[5] (Hosking 1990: 158). Workers suffered poor working conditions and low wages (Hosking 1990: 155). There were high rates of labour turnover, and so the state responded in 1932 by introducing internal passports, which restricted freedom of movement. Late arrival for work could lead to instant dismissal, and workers arbitrarily terminating employment could be sentenced to imprisonment. In practice these measures were rarely carried out as managers were anxious to retain scarce workers. Nonetheless, "the very existence of such legislation speaks volumes about the party's attitude towards the class in whose name it claimed to rule" (Hosking 1990: 157). Furthermore, millions were employed in forced labour camps (Davies 1995).

Although there were some improvements in living standards, the Stalinist era of industrialization – and the purges that followed it – was particularly brutal. The Soviet Union moved rapidly to large-scale, heavy industrialization, but the alternatives offered a route which was certainly more humane, and in the long run more economically feasible.[6]

In the 1930s the Stalinist system of economic organization was established. Despite later reform attempts (particularly by Khrushchev in the 1950s and Gorbachev in the 1980s) the system was still in place when the Soviet Union collapsed in the 1990s. The state "imposed upon the economy its own priorities, by ever tightening control over resource allocation, physical output, credit" (Nove 1969: 190). This Stalinist system proved to be effective at "extensive" industrialization, which depended on drawing new resources into industry, but it was far less effective at "intensive" industrialization, which depended on technological development, increasing skills, and using resources more efficiently (Kilmister 1992: 246). This social and economic system is examined on pp. 49–53 below.

Chinese industrialization

Industrialization in Communist China has taken a similar form to that in the Soviet Union, but there have also been some important differences. While the Chinese Communist Party established a one-party state in 1949, introduced a centrally planned economy and gave priority to heavy industry, some attempts were made to prioritize "class struggle" and supposedly overcome hierarchical relations within the workplace and beyond. Chinese industrial and agricultural development has been regarded as a struggle between two positions: first, to prioritize economics and develop the productive forces; second, to "put politics in command" and develop socialist relations of production (Schuurman 1968). This analysis contains a certain amount of truth, and in some periods priority was given to economics, whilst in others "class struggle" was emphasized. However, a simple binary divide is too simplistic and throughout Communist China's history there have been elements of both positions. Moreover, attempts to implement socialism in the workplace have often been limited by the continued dominance of the Communist Party, whose promotion of class struggle has often been rhetorical.

These points are highlighted through an examination of five key periods in Communist China's history: (i) the period of revolution and consolidation, 1949–53; (ii) the first Five Year Plan and collectivization, 1953–57; (iii) the Great Leap Forward and its aftermath, 1958–65; (iv) the Cultural Revolution and beyond, 1965–76; (v) the post-Mao period, 1978 to the present.

Revolution and consolidation, 1949–53

The Chinese Communist Party (CCP), led by Mao Zedong, established state power in 1949. It inherited a war-torn and overwhelmingly agrarian society. China had been divided by indirect foreign control, the territorial ambitions of local warlords, by Japanese imperialism and by the conflict between the Communists and Nationalist Kuomintang (KMT). The latter was defeated by 1949 and its leading cadres fled to Taiwan (see Chapter Seven).

The Communists had relied heavily on sections of the peasantry for its support. China was an overwhelmingly agrarian society in 1949, and so the Communists faced similar, but in some ways greater problems than the Bolsheviks had in 1917. Both were Marxist parties leading revolutions in backward societies. A major task was to develop the productive forces, while at the same time attempting to develop socialist relations of production. This was an even more daunting task for the Chinese Communists because since the 1920s they had lacked substantial support among the working class, who were supposed to be their natural allies. On the other hand, the existence of the Soviet Union initially guaranteed that China would not be isolated.

The Communists took a pragmatic approach to development in the immediate aftermath of revolution. A land reform was implemented which abolished the landlord class and redistributed land. Private ownership and some inequalities were maintained, but the reform still constituted a radical transformation of the agrarian social structure. The holdings of landlords (2.6 per cent of households) declined from 28.7 per cent of crop land to 2.1 per cent; the poor and landless peasants (57.1 per cent of housholds) doubled their holdings from 23.5 per cent to 46.8 per cent of crop land. Rich peasants (3.6 per cent of households) held 6.4 per cent of crop land, compared to 17.7 per cent before the reform, while middle peasants (35.8 per cent of households) now held 44.8 per cent of crop land. In addition, tools and livestock were redistributed (Blecher 1986: 45, 49).

The land reform, along with the end of civil conflict, helped to promote economic recovery. Grain output increased from 113 million tons in 1949 to 164 million in 1952 and cotton production tripled. The gross value of agricultural output increased by 50 per cent in these three years (Blecher 1986: 48).

In the towns nationalization proceeded at a relatively slow pace. Foreign firms were nationalized with compensation, while the national bourgeoisie was to some extent actively fostered by the state. Although subject to close state regulation, the number of private industrial firms increased six-fold from 1949 to 1953. By 1952, the urban economy was composed of a state sector which accounted for 56 per cent of gross industrial output; a state capitalist sector of private capital operating under state contracts or state–private joint ventures, which accounted for 27 per cent of output, and purely private firms which accounted for 17 per cent of output (Blecher 1986: 51).

By the early 1950s, the economy had largely recovered from the ravages of war and the CCP was ready to construct a new stage of socialist development.

The first Five Year Plan and collectivization

The first Five Year Plan (1953–57) was strongly influenced by the "Soviet model". This period was characterized by highly centralized planning, government control over the regions, priority to heavy industry and Soviet aid and technical assistance. Large industrial complexes were established in cities, such as the Anshan steel centre which by 1957 produced two-thirds of China's steel (Blecher 1986: 55). By 1956, the state sector accounted for two-thirds and the state capitalist sector one-third of industrial output. The private sector had been eliminated (Blecher 1986: 55). During the period of the Plan, industrial output grew faster than the target of 14.7 per cent a year (Blecher 1986: 56). Within the workplace, a strict system of one-person management was established. Like the Soviet system, workers were allocated specific tasks and payment was – in theory at least – linked to productivity (Lockett 1980: 462).

In agriculture, there was some concern over perceived increases in inequalities. Some poor peasants had been forced to borrow money, rent land or even sell land or labour power to richer peasants. In an attempt to avoid the return of capitalism in the countryside, mutual aid teams were established, which were composed of voluntary associations of several households, which exchanged labour or resources with each other. This reduced the dependence of poor peasants on rich ones and helped to raise production levels. In addition to a fixed tax on agriculture, in 1953 fixed quotas on state grain purchases were established and private grain merchants outlawed. Rural credit co-operatives were also established as an alternative source of credit supply. From 1955, the collectivization of agricultural land was gradually increased. By 1956, around 90 per cent of peasant households were in co-operatives (Maitan 1976: 30).

So, by 1957 industrial production had increased substantially (albeit from a low base) and peasants had joined co-operatives without the bloodshed that had occurred in the Soviet Union. Nevertheless, there were still problems concerning inequalities between town and countryside, between party members and non-members, and within workplaces. Moreover, relations with the Soviet Union had deteriorated and by 1960 there was open hostility between the two countries.[7] There would be no more Soviet aid. Criticism of the Party was encouraged (but also limited)[8] and it was in this context that Mao launched the Great Leap Forward.

The Great Leap Forward and its aftermath

Mao argued that the Great Leap Forward was a new strategy based on "walking on two legs" (Corrigan et al. 1978: ch. 4). By this he meant that industrial priorities should be maintained, but not at the expense of the countryside, in which both agriculture and rural industry should be promoted. This would resolve the problem of regional disparities and promote a "virtuous circle" in which agricultural output would help to finance industry, while industrial outputs could be used as agricultural inputs to further boost production in agriculture (Blecher 1986: 70).

People's Communes were created, which were often made up of as many as 5,000 households. Although these Communes were reduced in size from 1959, the average size (1,600 households) was still far greater than that of the co-operatives (around 160 households) (Blecher 1986: 70). The Communes included township governments and local party units, and provided social services such as childcare, health-care, education, food and sometimes housing. At the height of the Great Leap, there was even public ownership of consumer goods, including "free grain" in massive dining halls. Industries, such as the infamous backyard steel furnaces, were also established in the countryside.

In industry, hierarchical management was replaced by some (limited) attempts to radically restructure the division of labour. Emphasis was placed on the Two Participations, by which workers participated in management and managers worked on the shopfloor. In practice however, this strategy was largely rhetorical and was more a strategy to mobilize labour rather than abolish the division of labour within the factory – if indeed this was feasible (Lockett 1980: 465).

The initial optimism of the Great Leap Forward eventually gave way to the realization that its economic and social effects were an unmitigated disaster. In 1959, grain output fell back to 1953 levels, and in 1960 it fell to 1950 levels. Industrial output fell by 38 per cent in 1961. The backyard steel furnaces were a disaster. Peasants produced 3 million of a national 11 million tons of steel in 1958, but it was all but completely useless. Not surprisingly, national income declined by 50 per cent between 1960 and 1962 (Blecher 1986: 72–4; Selden 1988: 14). The cost to the population was enormous, as foodgrain consumption slumped in the late 1950s and early 1960s. This situation was worsened by excessive grain procurement by a state which in practice gave the Communes little meaningful autonomy, and continued to prioritize the need for rapid industrialization (Riskin 1987: 138). In 1960 there was a net population decline of 10 million (Selden 1988: 17).

> The most important reason for the failure of the Great Leap was the desire to impose an excessive pace of work – a pace which in any case could not be kept up for long – and in the ignorance or neglect of economic and technical factors which could not be brushed aside by what was a pure effort of will. (Maitan 1976: 46)

The withdrawal of Soviet technicians and bad weather conditions are often cited as major reasons. However, the former worked largely in the non-farm sector, and the floodings of 1960–61 were in part a *consequence* of the Great Leap policies, which involved ill-designed and ill-executed irrigation policies (Nolan 1988: 49–50).

Mao assumed much of the blame for the disasters of the Great Leap Forward and in 1962 it was abandoned. Communes were reduced in size and (controlled) private plots were re-introduced. Although the economy made a slow recovery, the long-term problems of peasant differentiation, industrial development, and town/country and regional disparities still needed to be addressed.

The Great Proletarian Cultural Revolution

The Cultural Revolution was launched in 1966 as an attempt by Mao and his followers to win mass support for eliminating "capitalist roaders" (those who allegedly favoured a return to capitalism) from the Party. The immediate impact of the revolution was to plunge the country into chaos and industrial production fell sharply. The People's Liberation Army (PLA) was sent into the factories to restore order from 1967, and the Party gradually restored control. Nevertheless, although the Commune system in agriculture was maintained (albeit with smaller production teams), important changes were made in industry.

Factory managers were accused of being capitalist roaders and management was passed into the hands of Revolutionary Committees. These were made up of representatives of Cultural Revolution cadres, members of the PLA, and workers' representatives. In practice, the committees quickly disappeared, and although they were revived in 1970 they had greatly reduced powers and were controlled by the Party.

Some attempts were made to alter the division of labour within factories, and workers were eager to eliminate tight management controls. Experiments were made with cadre participation in manual work, worker participation in management, job rotation, decentralization of managerial work and the establishment of "Three-in-One" innovation teams, made up of technicians, cadres and workers. These practices have led some observers to argue that China had made substantial progress towards abolishing the division of labour and establishing socialist relations of production (Bettelheim 1974; Andors 1977). In practice however, the changes were limited as cadres successfully resisted undertaking manual work and workers' representatives were closely vetted by the Communist Party (Lockett 1980: 471–4). As Littler (1985: 53) argues,

> in so far as experiments in work organization were implemented, they failed in their own terms. The division of labour was not radically altered, and worker participation, leading to a new system of worker control, was not extensively introduced.

Modernization in the post-Mao era, 1978 to the present

Mao died in 1976 and, following a two-year period of uncertainty, a new era of reform was introduced in 1978. From this time, more emphasis was placed on the development of the productive forces, and to this end some "capitalist" practices were re-introduced (White 1993). Agriculture was decollectivized, some private industry was established, the rural collective sector was developed, prices were reformed, and there was closer integration with the international economy (Nolan 1995b).

These reforms did not, however, lead to the introduction of capitalism in China as they were closely managed by the Communist state. There was a gradual increase in the proportion of goods sold at free market prices, but by 1990 these still accounted for less than half the goods sold (and many goods still lay outside the market mechanism). The rural collective sector was community-owned, and clear private property rights were not established. The distribution of agricultural land was determined by the village, and was relatively equal, and land was not allowed to be bought and sold. The state continued to give preferential credit to the public sector, and control the activity of private enterprise. Although China increased its trade with the rest of the world, the "open door" policy continued to be controlled by the state, through for instance trade restrictions and subsidies to loss-making exporters (Nolan 1995a, b). Special economic zones (SEZs) in parts of China encouraged foreign investment, and capitalism was effectively established, although even here there were still attempts by the state to control transnational corporations.[9]

In this period the Chinese economy experienced high rates of growth, increasing per capita consumption, including consumer goods, more light industries, and better living conditions (Nolan 1995a). These positive features appear to outweigh the negative ones, such as pervasive corruption, environmental degradation and the perceived increase in relative inequalities (White 1993: chs 6 & 7; and pp. 136–40 of this volume). On the other hand, there is the greater problem of the sustainability of the reform process, and whether it represents a *qualitative* shift to a more dynamic economy. This point is taken up below.

Social relations and state socialism

This section looks more closely at the relationship between agency, industrialization and development, by briefly examining the social relations of production, living standards and gender.

Relations of production

The Communist regimes in the Soviet Union and China both claimed to be states that represented the interests of workers and peasants. In theory, central planning was supposed to be the mechanism by which the productive forces and socialist relations of production would simultaneously be built. In practice, the implementation of the plan showed the reality of hierarchy, conflict and exploitation within the system.

Conflict occurred between three different groups in the Soviet Union – central planners, enterprise managers and workers (Ticktin 1973: 23). The worker was separated from direct access to the means of production, and so was effectively compelled to work for the enterprise in order to gain access to use values. Unemployment was eliminated in 1931, and so unemployment benefit did not exist. The state guaranteed work, so that removal from work in a particular enterprise occurred only in exceptional circumstances. Moreover, the state was obliged to find alternative employment in such cases (Filtzer 1986: 259–60; Arnot 1988: 33–4). The worker received a wage for his or her labour, which was administratively determined by the central planning apparatus. In addition to this basic wage, workers could recieve bonuses. However, wage differentials were relatively low, and, more importantly, the wage alone did not guarantee access to particular goods. Such access depended on "position in the hierarchy, access to privileged, closed supply channels, access to foreign currency, place of residence, influence ... chance or foreknowledge, corruption and the bartering of skills on the black market" (Arnot 1988: 36). So, money alone did not guarantee access to goods; hence the common experience of queues. Moreover, the social wage was vital – access to health, education, transport, and subsidized food were determined by the state, whilst housing, holiday facilities, and cultural amenities were determined by the enterprise.

The existence of full employment and a guaranteed social wage meant that there was limited scope for providing workers with incentives. Enterprise provision of housing and so on could be used as one method of increasing worker productivity, but the enterprise had very limited room for manoeuvre because most decisions were taken by central planners. Moreover, managers were reluctant to force the pace of work in factories (see below) and so were more likely to reward specific workers as a result of the development of informal personal relations.[10] Thus, "the Soviet workforce [was] controlled neither by the stick of unemployment nor the carrot of increased wages" (Arnot 1988: 37).

Managers in the Soviet Union had an interest in extracting a surplus from workers because this led to the possibility of career advancement and more money. However, these managers had little control over the surplus and so could not guarantee that success in terms of plan fulfilment would lead to more productive activity through reinvestment. Conflict therefore existed between those setting plan targets at the centre and managers implementing it at enterprise level. Managers therefore underestimated the productive capacity of enterprises so that plan targets set by the centre could be achieved with existing capacity. As a result, the potential surplus was underestimated, which in turn exacerbated supply difficulties. Each manager anticipated supply difficulties, and so overestimated the supplies needed for production – in particular labour supplies – with the result that the Soviet Union eventually faced an acute labour shortage. Thus each individual manager created the very problem that they were trying to avoid, but this was irrelevant to them, for what was rational for the individual manager was bad for the system as a whole. Thus

> The centralized control and allocation of the surplus product in the hands of an unproductive ruling stratum meant that the producers had an interest not in maximizing but in minimizing the surplus that they produced. Since neither the worker, nor the enterprise, nor the association, nor even the ministry, had any rights to the surplus produced they could only reliably expand the resources at their disposal by inflating their production costs, and could only protect themselves from the exactions of the ruling stratum by concealing their productive potential. (Clarke 1993: 26)

The result of this conflict was an acute difficulty in raising labour productivity once the initial extensive phase of industrialization (based on the mobilization of labour and resources) was exhausted. By the 1960s, a declining rural and increasingly ageing population limited the opportunities for recruiting labour into industry, and so increased reliance was placed on increasing labour productivity. However, in the period of the Ninth to Eleventh Five Year Plans (the 1970s and 1980s), productivity growth failed to match planned targets or wage increases (Arnot 1988: 68–9).

Although predominantly rural China has not faced this difficulty of labour shortage, it has displayed some similar characteristics to the Soviet Union. The state enterprise is the institution which guarantees a wage and access to limited use values, and labour is similarly hoarded as a fixed element of production in excess of current needs (Walder 1986: ch. 1). The hiring and firing of labour is largely unavailable to enterprise managers and so (limited) incentives and discipline are established through informal mechanisms, whereby a manager may guarantee wider access to goods.

The Cultural Revolution in theory represented an attempt to abolish both the limited incentives and clientelist ties available to workers, and so bonuses were abolished and wages frozen. However, in giving little priority to developmental issues, fundamental basic needs such as limited housing space were neglected. In this context, the scope for instrumental–personal ties was actually *widened* rather than reduced:

> With housing shortages becoming more acute, the wage freeze and abolition of bonuses creating more hardships for certain age groups, and shortages of commodities and foodstuffs continuing, competition for access to these goods and resources was intensified. Enterprise officials, with their ability to satisfy (selectively) requests for new apartments, extra ration coupons, loans, and relief payments, became the logical targets for this competition. (Walder 1986: 210)

Thus, the Cultural Revolution attacked the symptoms rather than the causes of industrial inefficiency in China.

The post-1978 reforms have certainly been more wide-ranging and in some respects successful, but they have also been subject to the contradictions of state socialist social relations of production. Much of the industrial growth since the late 1970s has come from the explicitly capitalist sectors, such as the Special Economic Zones and rural industries, and growth in the state sector has largely been a product of a new round of extensive industrialization, such as the building of new plants and the employment of more workers (Smith 1993: 68). While industrial output grew by an annual average of 12.4 per cent from 1979 to 1988, investment in fixed assets in state industries grew by 15.2 per cent over the same period (Smith 1993: 69).

Thus, social relations in both the USSR and China cannot be defined as socialist. Conflict existed between the state elite, factory managers and immediate producers, with the result that the system was both hierarchical and in many ways inefficient.

Living standards

Despite the limitations of Stalinism, some long-term advances were made in living standards. For example, life expectancy in China increased from forty-one years in 1952 to sixty-three by 1980 (Dreze & Sen 1989: 205). Adult literacy stood at 69 per cent for predominantly rural China in the late 1980s, compared to only 43 per cent for India (Dreze & Sen 1989: 204). In the Soviet Union, living standards improved by at least 100 per cent between the end of the war and the mid-1970s, and important advances were made in housing, education and health-care (Halliday 1991: 88). Moreover, many of the improvements were distributed relatively equally, at least compared to many capitalist countries in the Third World.

On the other hand the costs of "socialist" development in both countries were enormous, and sections of the peasantry (in the USSR in the 1930s, and in China from 1959 to 1962) were the main victims. Although workers enjoyed substantial negative power in the context of full employment, they were still subject to harsh working conditions and in some cases forced labour, particularly in the earlier stages of industrialization. Soviet per capita consumption actually declined in the period from 1928 to 1940 (Nuti 1979: 250), and in the long run improvements in living standards began to dry up. On the eve of the Gorbachev reforms the Soviet Union's developmental performance, measured against the improvements made by other nations, was declining. The USSR declined from 56th place in 1976 to 70th in 1982 in terms of per capita standard of living. By the late 1980s the USSR ranked only 50th for low infant mortality rates and 32nd for life expectancy (Sakwa 1990: 22).

Gender

The position of women in both societies showed some advances, but these remained limited. Both Communist leaderships accepted Engels' position that women's emancipation would come from their entry into paid employment. Under Lenin abortion was made legal and attempts were made to socialize housework and childcare, but most of the improvements were reversed under Stalin. In the Stalinist years, women made up a high proportion of the industrial labour force – as much as 40 per cent by 1937 (Atkinson et al. 1978: 125).[11] However, the mobilization of women as industrial workers did not challenge their position as domestic workers, responsible for childcare in the home, and they were largely excluded from the high-status jobs which guaranteed higher wages, greater access to goods, and possible entry into politics (Wolfe 1978: 23–34). Indeed, Stalin actively encouraged women to carry out housework and produce children. Abortion was made illegal in 1936 and tax incentives were granted to families that had children (Rai 1992: 82). Given the shortage of consumer goods that existed, domestic work (both in the home and queuing for food) was a particularly time-consuming activity (Atkinson et al. 1978: 131).

Molyneux (1991: 49) is therefore correct to assert that

52

Communist Party officials came to assume – or found it convenient to do so – that the oppression of women consisted almost entirely in their exclusion from paid employment. This, however, ignored both the question of women's inferior position in a segregated, hierarchical workforce, and the stringent demands of their new combined duties.

In China, the 1950 Marriage Law outlawed bigamy, made divorce available to both women and men, and gave women equal rights to property (Rai 1995: 182). The state also established nurseries, communal eating places and so on. However, the Chinese Communists shared with their Soviet counterparts the belief that emancipation would come primarily from the modern thrust of industrialization. This view left aside the hierarchical gendered division of labour within factories, and, except for the disastrous years of the Great Leap Forward, largely left the countryside untouched. As a result there was little change – and more importantly little attempt at change – to the patriarchal village, in which the female partner left her village once married and went to live in the isolated village of her male partner. This practice intensified the traditional preference for boys, as girls were a poor economic investment for parents (Blecher 1986: 153). One possible effect of the single-child policy of the 1980s was an increase in the practice of female infanticide (Kane 1995: 200–1). This policy, introduced by the state but interpreted by the provinces in different ways, has been particularly oppressive, and in extreme cases has led to forced abortions (Mu 1996: 113). Thus, the almost exclusive focus on paid employment in the industrial sphere as a means to liberation led not only to a neglect of the rural sector, it ignored the ways in which the Communist state intensified gender inequalities.

Conclusion

Socialist industrialization was a painful process that had beneficiaries and victims. Contrary to the claims of Communist Party leaders in the USSR and China, social relations of production were hierarchical and exploitative. Does this mean, then, that the convergence thesis (Kerr et al. 1962) is correct and that all industrial societies are inevitably hierarchical? The claim of Kerr and his co-authors is that societies of ostensibly different political ideologies converge on the basis of similar levels of technology. Thus, it is not socialist or capitalist ideology that is determinant in explaining the organization of work (and the wider society) but the level of technology. Communism is thus regarded as a utopia because it attempts to abolish the division of labour, in an unfavourable context of complex industrial technology.

The claim being made, then, is that the USSR and China were closer to the Western model of hierarchical industrial organization. However, it is one thing to accept that Soviet and Chinese industrialization occurred in the context of unequal social relations, but quite another to suggest that they were similar to

Western societies. As should be clear from the discussion in this chapter, socialist industrializations occurred under, and were therefore constrained by, very different social relations of production from those existing in advanced capitalist societies.[12] There were some similarities between socialism and capitalism but these were rooted in the political decisions made by Communist Party leaders, rather than technology *per se*. The early Soviet leadership, particularly Lenin and Stalin, were impressed by capitalist methods of scientific management as a means to increase labour productivity. This position was a reflection of the fact that classical Marxism shared with pro-capitalist ideology "the idea of the neutrality of science and technology, which implies that the work methods and division of labour employed under capitalism may be used just as well under socialism"[13] (Bayat 1991: 192; cf. Corrigan et al. 1978; Kiely 1995a). The effects of such measures were very different in the USSR than in capitalist societies however, precisely because of the non-capitalist social relations that existed in the former, and the comparative lack of (positive and negative) incentives that existed in the context of full employment and the absence of a labour market (Arnot 1988).

The problem of the convergence thesis, then, is that it regards technology as an independent, determinant variable, when in fact "a given technology – including machinery – reflects or embodies the relations of production in which it develops" (Leys 1984: 175). Nevertheless, the level of technology may still operate as a *constraint*, affecting attempts to implement new experiments in industrial organization. The limits of the Cultural Revolution can thus be seen in this way. Even if we charitably ignore the chaos in the country and factional in-fighting within the Communist Party, the conditions for a genuine transformation of the division of labour were not favourable. The room for manoeuvre faced by a technologically backward, socialist country is extremely narrow, because such societies

> are faced not just with new technologies but with older technologies, in which the form of the technology has been closed off by a series of decisions and technical developments which, in combination, constitute sunk costs – so that unwinding them, making a series of different choices, becomes an impossible cost burden. (Littler 1985: 53)

In addition, the effect of the Cultural Revolution was to slow down production and thereby increase workers' dependence on managers for access to scarce resources awarded by the latter on the basis of patron–client relations (Walder 1983: 71–2).

Socialist industrialization thus met with some success in developing the productive forces, but at the cost of any real commitment to genuine emancipation. Furthermore, long-term growth was constrained by the existence of non-capitalist social relations. Nevertheless, despite some superficial similarities between capitalism and the USSR and China, there were important differences as well.

The negative experiences of socialist developing societies leads one to ask some very difficult questions concerning the relationship between technology and emancipation. It is not sufficient for socialists to evade these questions by simply claiming that the USSR, China and others were not socialist. I return to those questions concerning socialism, technology and the division of labour in the final chapter.

Notes

1. I am aware of Marxist attempts to characterize these societies as state capitalist (Cliff 1974). Such approaches identify the former Soviet Union as capitalist, either on the basis of its incorporation into the world economy – a neo-Smithian analysis based on exchange relations rather than the social relations of production (Brenner 1977; Kiely 1995c: chs 2–5) – or through a superficial account of some characteristics common to "East" and "West" – such as the existence of wage labour. However, wage labour is not unique to capitalism, and the social relations of production in "socialist" societies remained very different from those in capitalist societies. In particular, enterprises lacked the capacity to hire and fire labour, and lacked meaningful independence from central planners. Cliff's theory of state capitalism therefore fetishizes the capitalist mode of production (Kiely 1995c), and assumes the universality of capitalist rationality (Clarke 1992: 6).

2. This does not necessarily mean that all societies pass through a similar stage of development (Kiely 1995a), and that therefore capitalism was the "next stage" for Russia. Nevertheless, relative backwardness did constitute a significant constraint on the Bolsheviks, and indeed in later state socialist countries.

3. There were uprisings throughout Europe, some of which failed to develop further, and others – most notably in Germany – which were brutally crushed. The issue of Soviet isolation is a contentious one, especially for Marxists. Many "Trotskyists" (cf. Cliff 1974) imply that Stalinism emerged because of Soviet isolation, but this argument is both too optimistic and pessimistic. It is pessimistic because it ignores the domestic alternatives that existed in the Soviet Union, not all of which relied on socialist revolution spreading to the West. It is optimistic because it is unclear how much, say, a socialist Germany in 1919 could have aided the Soviet Union, given the fact that it had just been devastated by four years of war.

4. The idea that Trotsky was a super-industrializer, whose economic strategy was not greatly different from Stalin's, has ironically been taken up by many so-called Trotskyists, possibly on the evidence presented by his most famous biographer (cf. Deutscher 1970).

5. Stakhanov was a coalminer who easily fulfilled his output targets. However, figures were manipulated and Stakhanovites were given preferential treatment, which entailed some workers undertaking some of the work of the favoured few. Some Stakhanovites were lynched by fellow workers (Hosking 1990: 158).

6. The argument that Stalinism was necessary to defend the Soviet Union in war ignores the fact that Stalin's policies had decimated the population. Moreover, within six months of the Nazi invasion in 1941 over half of Soviet industrial capacity had been lost, but the Nazis were still defeated.

7. This dispute, which erupted in 1960–61, was over socialist construction within the USSR and China, and rivalry over leadership of international Communism. The Soviet Union withdrew aid, and even sent troops to the Soviet–Chinese border.

8. The Hundred Flowers Campaign was launched by Mao in 1957 to encourage criticism of the Communist Party. Once criticism became too great the campaign was toned down and eventually abandoned. Nevertheless, the campaign helped to pave the way for the Great Leap Forward.

9. Cf. Chapter Seven.
10. This does not mean that there were no incentives to work in the Soviet system. The propaganda campaigns, such as Stakhanov, were resisted but also had some impact on the population. Moreover, recent research suggests that for all the limitations of the Soviet system of work organization, there was still some positive commitment to work, as an end in itself – as opposed to the (Western) capitalist view of work as a means to an end (cf. Clarke 1995: 10). Nevertheless, my comments on the limitations of the system as a means of mobilizing worker productivity remain valid.
11. I am grateful to my former student, Nicola Brelsford, for drawing my attention to some of the references on women in the Soviet Union.
12. It should also be mentioned that despite important similarities, advanced capitalist societies also show important levels of differences in terms of work organization, labour relations, politics and so on (cf. Open University 1985).
13. As Chapter Two makes clear, this is a major weakness in the position of Gavin Kitching. The final chapter returns to the questions of capitalism, socialism and the development of the productive forces.

Part III
Late industrialization

Chapter Five

Late industrialization and the global economy

My principal concern in this chapter is to examine the problems and opportunities faced by late industrializers in the global economy. I emphasize the specific conditions faced by late industrializers, stressing the crucial role of global factors in influencing development paths in the Third World, and how these have changed since the rise of the early developers.

These questions are examined in three sections. The first section provides a broad overview of the international division of labour from the period of early European colonial expansion until 1945, and shows how various parts of the periphery were incorporated into the world economy. The second section outlines the changes in the global economy in the period of decolonization since 1945, and documents the move towards industrialization in the Third World. The third section examines some of the theoretical approaches to the character of Third World industrialization. This section shows that there are specific opportunities and constraints faced by late industrializers, and examines debates concerning "dependent" and "independent" industrialization, and the related question of the role of transnational corporations in this process. I criticize both excessively globalist and state-centric accounts of Third World industrialization, which tend to dismiss this process as in some way distorted. Finally, as a precursor to the next chapter I suggest that while any convincing account of processes of late industrialization needs to take account of global factors, this should not be at the expense of analyzing how local factors also influence the process.

European industrialization and the international division of labour in the colonial era

European industrialization went hand in hand with the creation of a global capitalist economy. From the early sixteenth century, emerging European nations such as Spain, Portugal, and England expanded their commercial interests through a form of "mercantile imperialism", which had largely adverse effects in the rest of the world. With the coming of the industrial age in nineteenth-century Europe, new relationships emerged between the nascent

59

industrial powers and the rest of the world, which in some respects hindered the industrialization of the latter. This section provides a brief historical overview of these relationships, and shows how the industrialization of *core* countries led to the emergence of a specific international division of labour.

The period from the early fifteenth century saw the expansion of Spain and Portugal into the New World. Britain, France and the Netherlands later followed. This era of mercantile imperialism had the effect of drawing new territories into an emerging world trading system. Europeans traded and plundered goods such as tobacco, potatoes, spices, and precious metals.

The effect of this new pattern of international trading relationships varied from region to region (cf. Stavrianos 1981). In the Americas, contact with Europeans led to a massive decline in the indigenous population, and many died as a result of imported diseases or were simply killed. Parts of West Africa were then drawn into a triangular trade based on African slaves for the Americas, New World sugar, cotton and tobacco for Europe, and European textiles and guns for Africa (Williams 1987). In India, taxation systems and discrimination against Indian textiles had the effect of hindering industrial development (Mukherjee 1974). Similarly, Britain used its military and commercial dominance to force the opium trade on the inhabitants of China (Stavrianos 1981: 315–20). In other parts of Asia (now Indonesia, Malaysia and the Philippines), the Dutch East India Company extracted remittances, dividends and spices worth around £60 million from 1650 to 1780 (Bernstein & Crow 1988: 16).

Although a number of writers (cf. Frank 1969; criticized by O'Brien 1982) have exaggerated the relationship between the effective plunder of the periphery and the industrialization of the core, it is hard to deny the devastating consequences of mercantile imperialism on the former, or that its exploitation at least *contributed to* the industrial development of parts of Europe. A simple causal connection – i.e. the underdevelopment of Latin America caused the development of Europe – fails to take account of the fact that the initial colonizers were Spain and Portugal, both of whom went into relative decline with the emergence of the industrial era. Moreover, historical research shows that trade flows between the periphery and core did not substantially increase during the period of industrial "take-off" in the latter (Solow and Engerman 1987). These observations suggest that the most important causes of the industrial revolution were the changing social relations of production emerging in parts of Europe, but not in Spain and Portugal, as outlined in Chapter Three (cf. Brenner 1977; Kiely 1996: ch. 1). Having said that, it is still true that the profits made from mercantile imperialism could be, and sometimes were, used to boost industrial development, as well as luxury consumption. Thus, European industrial development was ultimately caused by the *qualitative* transformation in the social relations of production, but it was also boosted by the *quantitative* contribution of the profits of merchant capital. The revenues acquired from India in the late eighteenth and early nineteenth centuries were

60

the equivalent of between one-quarter and one-third of gross domestic capital formation in Britain (Mitchell 1988).

As Europe industrialized, its relations with the rest of the world underwent new changes. By the mid-nineteenth century, Britain was the most powerful nation in the world and for a brief period it attempted to maintain its dominance through "free trade imperialism". The pro-free-traders argued that as Britain was ahead of its rivals in terms of productivity and technology, it could maintain this advantage through a system of open trade and thereby undercut any potential competitors (Gamble 1985: 54). It was partly on this basis that Britain's influence in the newly independent Latin American nations grew. Britain and other European powers traded manufactured goods for raw materials and unprocessed food, a divsion of labour that mutually benefited both industrialists in Europe and powerful landowners in Latin America (Skidmore and Smith 1992: 41–2).

However, other nascent industrial powers such as France, Germany and the United States were not prepared to tolerate the maintenance of the British-dominated system. As well as protecting their own infant industries from foreign competition, the new powers began their search for new areas of influence. While the US established a largely informal empire in its own backyard – although this did not preclude cases of formal colonization too (Kiernan 1981) – European powers searched for new areas of commercial opportunity. The precise motives for the European colonial drive during the mid to late nineteenth century are a matter of controversy, and need not detain us here, but it is the case that the search for new investment opportunities, markets and raw materials was an important factor (Bernstein et al. 1992a).

The British and French extended their influence in much of Asia after India was formally colonized in 1857–58, and this was followed by the unprecedented scramble for Africa. In 1876, European powers ruled about 10 per cent of Africa; by 1900, they ruled about 90 per cent of it (Bernstein et al. 1992a: 176). The effects of colonialism in Africa largely depended on the interests and actions of the colonial power within a particular territory. The weakness of the colonial state and fear of unrest in British West Africa meant that the colonial authorities were reluctant to inaugurate radical changes in systems of labour control (Phillips 1989). On the other hand, settler capitalism in much of British eastern and southern Africa led to sweeping innovations, based on land reforms. However, the effect in both cases was to limit the potential for rapid industrial development, particularly among the indigenous population, which suffered from discriminatory policies on issues such as taxation, land ownership and access to credit (Kennedy 1988: ch. 3; Stavrianos 1981: 235–45, 294–8).

African industrial development was likewise hindered by all the colonial powers, who were more interested in the raw materials that the region had to offer. For instance, with the development of the motor vehicle industry in the industrial world, parts of the Belgian Congo were converted into giant rubber plantations, utilizing forced labour in extremely harsh conditions (Nzula 1979: 23–5). Similarly, the British Gold Coast was converted into a basic mono-crop economy, exporting unprocessed cocoa for mass consumption in Europe (ibid.: 26–7).

These developments were widespread throughout the colonial world and Latin America. Although there was some development of indigenous industry, especially from the 1930s (Kennedy 1988: 56–9; Skidmore & Smith 1992: 53–5; Kemp 1983: 74–80), this was mainly limited to light industry serving the domestic market and was not on a level that could effectively compete with the industries of the core capitalist countries. Up to 1945, then, both the output and the exports of most of the periphery focused on unprocessed foodstuffs and raw materials. So, in this era colonial policy and the power of national landowning classes in Latin America acted as a constraint against widespread industrial development.

Third World industrialization since independence

After the Second World War, political leaders in the Third World favoured development strategies based on rapid industrialization. Raw material production was regarded as a legacy of the colonial era, and industrialization was regarded as essential to raise the living standards of the masses. Moreover, many Latin American nations in the 1930s had begun to industrialize, partly in response to unfavourable world market conditions. Industrialization was therefore deemed to play a leading role in nation-building in the developing world. It would promote economic growth, raise living standards and increase the power of new states in the world system. To what extent, then, have Third World nations successfully industrialized?

Over the last seventy years, there has been a shift away from the concentration of industrial production in the "advanced" capitalist or First World. Until the late 1920s, Western Europe, North America and Japan accounted for over 90 per cent of the world's industrial production (Jenkins 1992a: 16–17). Since then, there has been some move away from the colonial division of labour outlined above, so that by the 1980s, the First World's share had fallen to around 60 per cent (Jenkins 1992a: 17). This decline was the consequence of the rapid industrialization of the Communist world. From 1948 to 1984, its share of the global distribution of industry increased from 8.4 per cent to 25.4 per cent (Gordon 1988: 31–5).

The Third World's share actually *declined* slightly, from 14 per cent to 13.9 per cent (Gordon 1988: 31–5). However, Third World industrialization is far from irrelevant. In absolute terms, industry grew throughout the Third World for much of the post-war period, but not as fast as it did in the Communist world. Industry's contribution to GNP largely increased in Third World countries until the reversals in the debt-ridden 1980s: from 1960 to 1985 it increased in Bangladesh from 8 per cent to 14 per cent, in Thailand from 19 to 30 per cent, and in the Ivory Coast from 14 to 26 per cent (Kitching 1982: 7). Between 1965 and 1983, industry in the low-income[1] countries increased its share of GDP from 29 to 34 per cent; in middle-income (lower) from 24 to 33 per cent, and middle-income (upper) from 35 to 37 per cent (Colman and Nixson 1986: 275).

Moreover, with the growth of industry there have been important shifts in social structures. Industrial employment in low-income economies accounted for 9 per cent of the population in 1965, and had increased to 13 per cent by 1981; the corresponding figures for lower-middle-income countries were 13 per cent and 17 per cent, and for upper-middle-income countries the increase was from 21 to 28 per cent (Colman and Nixson 1986: 279).

Furthermore, in *parts* of the Third World, there have been periods of unprecedented industrial growth. The 1930s saw rapid growth in Latin America and more recently the newly industrializing countries of East Asia have emerged, successfully exporting manufacturing products to the First World. The high-growth regions of East and South-East Asia increased their share of world manufacturing from 1.67 per cent in 1975 to 3.26 per cent in 1985 (R. Chandra 1992: 35). South Korea increased the value of its exports (which are overwhelmingly in manufacturing) from $4 billion in 1975 to almost $44 billion in 1985; while Taiwan's export values (also mainly manufacturing products) increased from almost $4.5 billion to over $50 billion over the same period (Gereffi 1990: 15). Such figures have led some writers to claim that there is a new international division of labour (Frobel et al. 1980; Harris 1986), which has supplanted the old colonial-based structures of the world economy.

Nevertheless, it is still a fact that the Third World as a whole has been largely unsuccessful in increasing its share of world industrial production, and its share of manufacturing exports. In the 1980s, the exports of manufactures from the First World to the Third World were approximately 3.6 times greater than the flow from Third to First World (Colman and Nixson 1986: 300–1).

So, to summarize:

(i)   industry in the Third World has expanded since independence;
(ii) despite this expansion, the share of the Third World *as a whole* in the global distribution of industry has remained static since the late 1940s;
(iii) *some* Third World nations – the NICs – have expanded rapidly.

Explaining Third World industrialization

This section attempts to make sense of the three observations listed above, and in doing so to provide an introduction to some of the debates concerning the status of late industrialization in the Third World. Three principal issues are addressed in this section: first, the question of whether late industrialization can be described as dependent or autonomous, "distorted" or "genuine"; second, the related question of the impact of transnational corporations in the Third World; and, third, the question of the relationship between the "global" and the "local" in late industrialization.

Industrialization in the periphery: dependent or independent?

By the early 1970s, it was clear that the industrialization of parts of the Third World had undermined the old colonial international division of labour. The new question that concerned development theorists, particularly those influenced by Marxism, was the status of these processes of industrialization. This was important for radical development thinkers because many had argued that the old colonial division of labour had been based on the exploitation of the poor South (periphery) by the rich North (core). Some writers had argued that it was unlikely that the Third World could industrialize substantially if it was to remain an integral part of the world capitalist system (Frank 1969; Thomas 1974; for critical surveys see Brewer 1990: ch. 8; Webster 1991: ch. 4; Kiely 1995c: ch. 3).

The record of post-war industrialization and economic expansion in the Third World showed that such a view was inadequate. Writing in the early 1970s, Bill Warren (1973: 6–7; cf. Schiffer 1981: 519) argued that by historical standards post-war industrial growth in the periphery was very significant, with growth rates higher than those in the First World. Moreover, this expansion had occurred precisely at a time when links between the Third and First Worlds were strong, and so constituted a major challenge to Frank's thesis. For instance, Warren (1973: 6) cited statistics showing that the annual average rate of growth in manufacturing from 1951 to 1969 was 7.8 per cent for Brazil, 13.8 per cent for Zambia and an unprecedented 16.9 per cent for South Korea, and that these were not isolated examples.

Some radical thinkers responded by claiming that a modified version of dependency remained useful. The most extreme position, taken by Andre Gunder Frank, was that industrialization in the Third World was not genuine, and was highly dependent on the "advanced" capitalist world. The high rates of growth in East Asia based on the export of manufactured goods to the First World was dismissed as "in no way significantly different from the old raw materials export-led growth which underdeveloped the Third World in the first place" (Frank 1983: 355).

Others were less inclined to take such a dogmatic viewpoint, but still argued that late industrialization was weaker than the figures suggested. The case that late industrialization was in some way dependent or distorted was best made by Bob Sutcliffe (1972: 174–6). He put forward a hypothetical model of independent industrialization, based on the following factors:

(i)   that industrial production was primarily for the domestic market;
(ii) that it was led by local investment;
(iii) that the domestic industrial structure was diversified;
(iv) that it was based on the utilization of an independent technological capacity.[2]

By these criteria, Sutcliffe argued that the record of post-war late industrializers, including the "successes" in East Asia and Latin America, was not good. The East Asian industrializers were dependent on export markets, and more especially the import of technology, to promote industrial growth (Sutcliffe 1972: 192). Latin American industrialization was often led by transnational corporations, or relied on the import of expensive foreign technology. Moreover, industrial technology was capital-intensive and so created little employment, and production was largely for a limited internal market of high-income consumers (Sutcliffe 1972: 185–7).

For these reasons, Sutcliffe was pessimistic about the prospects for, and the actual course of, industrialization in the periphery. However, Warren responded to the claims of Sutcliffe too, and argued not only that the post-war record of economic growth in the Third World was good, but that the potential for *independent national capitalist development* was even greater. He argued that independence had helped to promote industrialization as it broke the monopoly of the colonial power and led to national pressures for higher living standards. Moreover, the independence era coincided with the expansion of productive capital (transnational corporations), which further promoted industrial development (Warren 1973: 13–16).

Referring explicitly to Sutcliffe's four criteria for independent development, Warren argued that the prospects in each case were favourable. Although domestic markets were limited, and there was substantial unemployment, he pointed out that these factors existed primarily for reasons *internal* to Third World societies, such as agricultural stagnation and inefficient state policy, and not because of (alleged) foreign domination of the economy (Warren 1973: 17–35). He also showed that investment by TNCs in the Third World accounted for a comparatively small amount of domestic capital formation, that it complemented national capital, and was subject to state control (Warren 1973: 39). Moreover, whilst TNCs exported capital in the form of repatriated profits, it was also true that some investment went to the receiving country and this could act as a stimulant to further economic activity – for instance through greater demand stimulated by wage payments to employees, to local suppliers, and so on. This argument applied equally to financial dependence – it was absurd to claim that the drain of surplus away from the Third World caused by TNC repatriation of profits created balance of payments problems, because this argument ignored the initial inflow of foreign investment which could be used for further capital accumulation (cf. Weiss 1990: 129).

Finally, Warren (1973: 29–32) argued that the original source of technology was not important, and that Third World states could benefit from importing technology. Research and development expenses that led to technological innovation in the first place were met by First World companies and states, and so Third World states could "leap" years of expensive and time-consuming research by importing new technology, and "learning by doing" (ibid.: 30–31).

These, then, are the basic arguments of the pessimistic/dependent versus optimistic/independent positions. For all the disagreements of the two sides, they share a conception of an ideal, ahistorical national capitalism (cf. Bernstein 1982). The pessimists tend towards the view that late industrialization fails to conform to the requirements of this model, while the optimists believe that the world economy is actively promoting such a model. Both positions point to important aspects of the relationship between developing countries and the global economy – the pessimists focus on the constraints while the optimists emphasize the opportunities, but in measuring such factors against an ahistorical model of capitalist industrialization, they fail to specify how these factors impinge on any national capitalist economy (or local space) at a particular point in time.[3]

Thus, contrary to the claims of Sutcliffe, the nationality of capitals is not really the issue. Indian capitalism was until recently far more "national" than Canadian capitalism, but its rate of capital accumulation far lower (Kitching 1987: 36). Similarly, Sutcliffe's argument that the import of technology is likely to lead to inappropriate development for the periphery based on capital-intensive production neglects the fact that "capitalist firms, whether foreign or national, will adopt the technique that maximizes profits ... It is thus unlikely that local firms using locally devised techniques would make very different choices" (Brewer 1990: 276; cf. Jenkins 1987: ch. 4).

Moreover, the pessimists' argument that late industrialization only benefits a small proportion of the population

> embodies a conceptual distinction at the core of dependency theory, which is that an understanding of "genuine" or "national" development as a process which delivers the goods of increased social welfare, more egalitarian income distribution, full employment, and so on (to the benefit of the majority), virtually *excludes capitalist development by definition*.[4] (Bernstein 1982: 227)

One advocate of the dependency approach, Hart-Landsberg (1984: 185–8), has argued along these lines in his assessment of South Korean industrialization. In particular, he has pointed to the country's dependence on exports, foreign capital, uneven development, and lack of production for basic needs. Whilst it may be correct to characterize these problems as important factors in the Korean industrialization process,[5] it is far from clear how such problems differ from *any* process of capitalist industrialization – without recourse to a Eurocentric, idealized norm of capitalist development that has never existed. For as Barone (1984: 195) has argued, South Korean industrialization may in some senses be dependent, but it is still "successful industrialization". Of course we may ask for *whom* it is successful, but that is true of all industrializations.

On the other hand, Warren's arguments also contain an implicit ahistorical norm of capitalist development, so that he fails to pay attention to the specificities of capitalism within particular nation-states (Brewer 1990: 283). In effect, we are left with the view of a benign imperialism promoting a "normal capitalism" that hardly differs from the British experience of two hundred years ago. Warren therefore wants to have it both ways, correctly arguing that capitalism and industrialization have taken place in the Third World, and (more problematically) that this is in some sense independent. What is missing from Warren's account is "any (explicit) theorization ... of the nature of international and national capitalist economy in the present period" (Bernstein 1982: 229).

These debates – and the problems associated with them – have similarly influenced discussions concerning the developmental role of transnational corporations.

TNCs and the Third World

A transnational corporation is a company that controls production in more than one country (Jenkins 1987: 1–2). TNCs differ from other international companies such as the old British East India Company which controlled trading activities, but did not directly control productive activities. By the early 1990s, there were around 37,000 TNCs controlling over 200,000 foreign affiliates worldwide, which generated sales of more than $4.8 trillion in 1991 (UNCTAD 1994b: 86). The combined sales of the world's largest 350 TNCs totalled nearly one-third of the combined GNPs of all "advanced" capitalist countries (*New Internationalist* 1993: 18). The top 100 firms controlled about one-third of world foreign investment stock (UNCTAD 1994b: 86). Pepsico, the largest beverage company, has more than 500 plants employing 335,000 workers in over 100 countries. The top five TNCs in the consumer goods, automobile, airlines, aerospace and electronic components sectors accounted for over 50 per cent of worldwide sales in those sectors in 1992. TNCs also control a high proportion of world trade, much of which is between branches owned by the same parent firm. This accounts for around a third of all world trade (*New Internationalist* 1993: 18; UNCTAD 1994b: 87).

Although historically most direct investment flows in manufacturing have been between "advanced" capitalist countries,[6] some productive capital flows were directed towards the periphery from the late nineteenth century. Most of this investment was however in raw material production, but after the Second World War there was a major expansion of direct foreign investment in manufacturing in the periphery. From 1950 to 1984, the proportion of US direct foreign investment flows in manufacturing to the Third World increased from 15 to 37 per cent (Jenkins 1987: 7). TNCs from other countries have also increased their levels of investment, and by 1993 there was an estimated $80 billion of direct foreign investment (DFI) in developing countries, including the NICs (UNCTAD 1994b: 9). Investment by TNCs has been encouraged by the activities of Third World states, which have often provided incentives to would-be investors such as tax holidays, no duties on imports, and a developed infrastructure (R. Chandra 1992: ch. 6).

What then is the developmental impact of TNCs in the Third World, particularly those in manufacturing? The arguments can be divided into two camps, the apologists and the critics, which broadly coincides with the views of the optimists and pessimists discussed above.

First, the pro-TNC position is taken by both neo-liberals and some Marxists. Writers such as Warren (1980) and Vernon (1977) argue that DFI by TNCs constitutes a net gain for the receiving country. This is so for the following reasons:

(i)   DFI increases the capital stock in a country, and therefore the income of that particular country, including foreign currency earnings;
(ii)   DFI develops important linkages in the economy, such as the development of local suppliers and sales to intermediate goods industries;
(iii) DFI provides Third World countries with technology so that they can compete with advanced capitalist countries;
(iv)   DFI leads to intensified competition, and therefore economic efficiency, both within a country and within the world economy;
(v)   DFI provides employment for labourers within the Third World;
(vi)   by increasing incomes, the local population increases its consumption;
(vii) in promoting economic growth, TNCs may also promote long-term political stability.

On the other hand, critics of TNCs argue that:

(i)   DFI does not automatically lead to an increase in income for a particular country, as capital outflow may exceed inflow (Frank 1969: 162–3), and TNCs may transfer price (Lall 1980: 111). Intra-firm trade is therefore not "hands-off" trade between companies competing with each other and thereby minimizing costs, but is based on transactions where "the price is merely an accounting device and the two parties are trying to maximize joint profits" (Lall 1980: 111). This takes place when two subsidiaries of the same parent company trade with each other and so are in a position to manipulate the prices paid for those goods. This practice enables them to evade tax payments to particular nation-states and avoid other forms of state regulation;
(ii)   linkages with the local economy are rare as TNCs produce and import the required inputs (Girvan 1971: 47–51), rather than obtain them from domestic suppliers;
(iii) the technology acquired from direct foreign investment is inappropriate – for example, it may be capital-intensive and so create few jobs in labour-abundant economies (Hymer 1982);
(iv)   TNCs exploit their monopoly position in domestic economies, and so do not create competition and greater efficiency;
(v)   few jobs are created by TNCs, and even when they are they tend to be highly exploitative (Frobel et al. 1980);
(vi)   even if TNCs do increase incomes in Third World nations, this leads to the consumption of inappropriate products, which may be unhealthy or even fatal (Muller 1974);

(vii) TNCs do not promote political stability in the Third World, and may actually undermine the sovereignty of nation-states through the promotion of military takeover (cf. Sampson 1974) or evading certain state controls, such as those relating to the environment (cf. Smith 1992: 286–7).

The problem with these alternative positions is their tendency to take a few select examples, and construct from these their own particular over-generalized theories. TNCs are regarded as all-powerful promoters of development on the one hand, or as agents of underdevelopment on the other. Both sides can cite examples which back up their particular claims, but neither side effectively discusses the *specific conditions* in which the developmental effects of TNCs occur.

Let us return to the seven issues addressed above.

(i) Capital stock and income

In at least some sectors, TNCs raise the capital within the country in which they invest. About a third of all funds comes from foreign borrowing, mainly involving capital raised locally in the host country, while half or more of the total is made up of the reinvested profits of the subsidiaries (Jenkins 1987: 96). There is also an increasing tendency for TNCs to supply franchises to local capital, and so not invest directly at all – a point I return to below. So, the neo-liberal and Warrenite case that TNC investment raises income in a particular country is at least an exaggeration, as TNCs take advantage of cheap credit opportunities (especially in high-inflation Latin American nations) *within* the Third World.

On the other hand, the pessimists' argument that TNCs underdevelop the Third World is weak for three reasons. First, not all funds are borrowed from within the Third World country – the fact that TNCs do not always bring funds from abroad does not mean that they *never* do. Second, as argued above the drain of surplus argument does not account for the capital that does remain in the periphery and is used for productive investment. Third, there is little convincing account of why such capital exports occur in the first place. Of course some is remitted to help pay for share dividends, but this does not differ from the activities of TNCs operating in the First World. Moreover, profit remittances from the most "underdeveloped" regions of the world (sub-Saharan Africa and parts of southern Asia) are very small, for the simple reason that TNC investment in these areas is low in the first place. The extent of profit remittances from some parts of the Third World, particularly Latin America, have been high but this is more likely to be the result of long-term unprofitable opportunities, rather than the conscious underdevelopment of a particular region.[7] Furthermore, TNCs are not the only source of such capital export. Accurate statistics are hard to come by in what is often an illegal activity, but the practice of exporting money to Swiss bank accounts or rich property markets in the First World is very common. This is true not only of infamous dictators, but of less well known figures in the private as well as public sector. As Jenkins (1987: 154; cf. Kiely 1996: chs 1 & 6) states,

Whatever else it may have done, the current debt crisis of countries such as Mexico should have dispelled the illusion that the local bourgeoisie patriotically invests in the national economy while foreign capital "drains surplus" from the country.

Finally, it is true that profits may also be remitted through transfer pricing (Murray 1981). In the 1970s, there were a number of important studies of transfer pricing, which was shown to be particularly common in the pharmaceutical industry (Lall 1978). On the other hand, the focus on the pharmaceutical industry was one-sided and too many generalizations were made from this one sector (Lall 1984: 13). In particular an unwarranted comparison was made between the high price of an innovator (the TNC) and the (lower) price of an imitator (often a local company). The point, however, is that the high price was often a result of the original innovation and the surplus profits that accrued from this (short-lived) dominance of a local market, rather than only being a product of deliberate price manipulation. Moreover, as taxation rates are often lower in the periphery, it is not clear why TNCs should deliberately single out Third World nations to transfer price (Corbridge 1986: 172). Given the types of state formation in parts of the Third World, it may be *easier* for TNCs to transfer price in the Third rather than the First World, but this is more a question of the character of Third World states, rather than of TNCs themselves. Again, this is not to say that transfer pricing is irrelevant, but its extent might be overestimated, particularly as an explanation for the "underdevelopment" of the Third World.

(ii) Linkages

Both sides in the debate are prone to make sweeping generalizations about linkages, claiming that TNCs simply shut off or open up new possibilities for increased local economic activity. In fact, the expansion of linkages will depend on factors such as the economic sector in which TNCs operate, and state regulation of TNC activity – which may or may not require some levels of local inputs (Sklair 1994: 169–70). TNCs are notorious for closing off linkages in mining industries and in labour-intensive manufacturing in export processing zones,[8] and importing the required technical inputs. However, the experience of some labour-intensive manufacturing and extractive industries cannot be extended to TNCs operating in all industries, and even in these sectors some linkages may develop – for instance, Japanese companies in the Mexican maquiladoras[9] have encouraged their suppliers to move with them, rather than simply import supplies as was the common practice with US companies (Sklair 1993: 237). Furthermore, faced with similar situations to TNCs, it is far from clear that local capital would behave any differently. If there are important local linkages available then capital, be it foreign or local, will take advantage of them. As Lall (1978: 223) argues:

> The extent of linkages created in particular LDCs depends upon the stage of development of indigenous industry, the availability of local skills and

technology, institutions and government policies, changes in demand and technology in world markets and their political attractiveness to TNCs.

(iii) Technology

The debate on technology was largely covered in my discussion of dependent and independent industrialization above, where I stressed that there was little reason to believe that local capital (in the same sector) would behave any differently from TNCs in its choice of techniques (cf. Kirkpatrick et al. 1984: ch. 4). Thus, questions of appropriate technology do not depend on the "nationality" of that particular technology, but rather on the place of that technology within capitalist social relations.[10] Capitalist firms, be they local or foreign, are forced through competition between capitals to introduce the most advanced techniques in order to lower production costs and increase profits (Shaikh 1978; Weeks 1982). This is not to deny that some regulation of this accumulation can be made, or that capital may adapt to local conditions, but these points apply to both local and foreign capital, and depend crucially on the capacity of Third World states to direct the activities of the capitalist class.

(iv) Competition

The perfect competition model assumed by neo-liberal apologists for TNCs (that is, competition between many small producers, which makes companies price takers rather than price makers) does not exist. However, neither is it correct to claim, as do many critics of TNCs (Baran and Sweezy 1966), that we have entered an era of monopoly capitalism which has completely eliminated competition and destroyed the expansionary character of capitalism (cf. Olle and Schoeller 1982; Weeks 1982). Competition does exist, not in the sense of a level playing field between producers with equal capacities, but in the sense of a competitive accumulation of capitals and their constant search for surplus profits (Jenkins 1987: 48). Competition in many sectors therefore involves large firms with substantial control over production, marketing and distribution, but still competing with each other.

These points apply both at the level of the global economy and within particular nation-states. A TNC may invest in a particular country in order to take advantage of the opportunities for surplus profits, but these are eroded by the entry of other TNCs attempting to follow suit. Such a scenario does not conform to the neo-liberal utopia of perfect competition, because these firms, "in a position of leadership both in the economy as a whole and within individual sectors ... are able to structure the pattern of industrial development, consumption and distribution" (Jenkins 1984a: 33). Competition thus takes place between a handful of oligopolistic market leaders rather than a multitude of industrial producers competing on a level playing field.

In some sectors, such as the Latin American automobile industry, the problem is that there is *too much* competition, which has led to the development of a high-cost, comparatively inefficient industry. From the 1950s, there were widespread investments by most of the automobile TNCs from Europe and later the United States. The result was a high level of model diversity: by the late 1970s, Argentina produced 47 models of passenger cars, Mexico 37 and Brazil 68 (Jenkins 1984a: 61–2). For Latin American states, this open door approach to foreign investment was justified on the neo-liberal grounds that the resultant competition would reduce prices. However, the size of the automobile sector created a situation in which "the output capacity of the industry was far in excess of existing volumes of production, and [so] the resulting unutilized capacity increased production costs" (Jenkins 1984a: 64–5). These high costs were intensified by the protective tariffs of Latin American states, which enabled TNCs to pass on the high costs of production to the consumer, a point that neo-liberals emphasize in their critique of protected industrialization. However, the ultimate cause of high consumer prices was the oligopolistic competition of the TNCs and the excessive *production costs* that resulted from their strategies[11] (cf. Jenkins 1984a: ch. 3).

(v) Employment

It is undeniable that TNCs provide employment for workers in the periphery, and in many cases they pay higher wages than local capital. However, TNC investment may lead to the displacement of workers, who are employed in local companies which are put out of business when TNCs set up shop in a particular country. Moreover, the higher wages paid by TNCs are unlikely to be as high as wages paid to workers in similar jobs in the First World, and these may be more than offset by higher productivities in TNC subsidiaries (Vaitsos 1976). Finally, in some sectors (especially labour-intensive ones like textiles and industrialized agriculture) TNCs pay low wages and their employment practices are very harsh. As already mentioned, in export processing zones some TNCs take advantage of gendered inequalities and exploit young women in terms of poor working conditions, low wages and little job security (Mitter 1986).

Once again, none of these comments should be taken as a simple apology for or condemnation of the activities of TNCs. Critics are correct in their seemingly contradictory claims that TNCs utilize capital-intensive techniques and exploit workers in labour-intensive industries, but too often a rigid model substitutes for serious analysis of how this varies from sector to sector, and how TNCs *may* sometimes be more progressive than local capital (but of course the opposite may also be true). This last point is important because it should not be forgotten that local capital is just as likely as TNCs to take advantage of cheap labour in EPZs.

(vi) Inappropriate products

The arguments over inappropriate products are particularly complex, and relate to wider debates over the issue of cultural imperialism. For the apologists, the goods produced by TNCs are seen as extending choice to consumers in the Third World (Balsubramanyam 1980: 52), while the critics point to ways in which such "choices" are in fact manipulated by the marketing strategies of the companies (Barnet & Muller 1974: 172).

There are relatively straightforward examples of aggressive marketing by TNCs having harmful effects among consumers in the Third World. Perhaps most infamously, Nestle was accused from 1970 onwards of the promotion of powdered milk for babies in areas where potential customers did not have access to clean water (Muller 1982), leading to serious health consequences or even death for the babies. Similarly, some drug companies have flooded Third World markets with a vast array of high-price brand names, rather than promoting one basic, and cheap, generic drug. Moreover, some products banned in the First World have been sold in the Third World, while others are tested in the Third World before they are made available in the "advanced" capitalist countries, with their more stringent controls (Gereffi 1983). For instance, hydroxyquinolines, some of which were withdrawn from the US market in the mid-1970s, are still available over the counter in many Third World countries for the treatment of diarrhoea, even though far more effective and cheaper remedies are available (Sklair 1991a: 158).

Even in these cases, however, the problem cannot be reduced to TNCs simply imposing their will on passive Third World countries. The fact that these practices occur at all[12] tells us that we need some understanding not only of TNC practices (in some sectors), but also of states in at least part of the Third World.

The other question that needs to be addressed is how far we can generalize from these relatively clear-cut examples. When the health of people is so directly undermined, it is easy to criticize the role of TNCs. However, other writers have denounced the role of TNCs in introducing alien products into very different cultures. Thus Hamelink (1983: 15) argues that

A cultural system which would be adequate for the poorest people in that system would mean a set of instrumental, symbolic and social relations that help them to *survive* in meeting such fundamental needs as food, clothing, housing, medical treatment and education. Such needs are not met if they are identified with the consumption of Kentucky Fried Chicken, Coca-Cola, Aspro, or Peter Stuyvesant cigarettes.

The problem with statements like this is, who is to decide what people's true needs are? At their worst, views such as these are based on a romantic vision of Third World cultures which are regarded as somehow representing "authentic" responses to Western materialism. However, such "authenticity" may only exist in the heads of condescending intellectuals in the First World (Warren 1980: 225; Tomlinson 1991: 120–21), rather than consumers in the Third. Cultural imperialism can operate on more than one level.

On the other hand, these comments should not be taken as a populist endorsement of consumer sovereignty in the Third World. There are specific reasons why some consumers in the Third World are in a more vulnerable position than they are in the "advanced" world, such as lower levels of education and lack of controls over advertising (Jenkins 1988: 1366). Nevertheless, Tomlinson (1991: 122) is right to argue that

> we are simply not in a position to deny the attractions consumer culture may have for other cultures unless and until we have established a coherent critique of our *own* consumer culture.

A challenge to the idea of the autonomous sovereign consumer would emphasize the following points. First, consumption is obviously linked to income, and its highly unequal distribution. Second, it operates in an environment in which people have little control over their lives, in terms of choice of work (if they have a job), public decision-making and so on. These factors may encroach on consumption patterns – for instance, fast food may be consumed not for its quality but simply because of lack of time, a car may be bought not for the purposes of enjoyment but because it is impossible to live without one. That is, "needs" can be created not by the specific use-value of a commodity, but by other imperatives. Third, those with greater control have the market power to at least influence consumption patterns (cf. Williamson 1988; Tomlinson 1991). Consumption is thus an activity which takes place in a particular social context, in which TNCs have played a leading role in influencing a global standardization of tastes.[13]

(vii) TNCs and the state

Once again, there are specific examples of TNCs undermining the weakness of Third World states or even playing a part in the overthrow of governments. The activities of ITT in Chile in the build-up to the successful and extremely bloody military coup is one example (Petras & Morley 1974). In addition, there were cases of earlier involvement between food TNCs and US-backed coups in Central America (Pearce 1982).

TNCs have also taken advantage of the weaknesses of states in the Third World. They have sometimes had to concede to local demands for state nationalizations, but have often retained effective power through their control of international distribution and marketing networks (Elson 1988: 268–72). Furthermore, they have ignored weakly enforced environmental regulations, with sometimes tragic consequences. The chemical leak from a Union Carbide pesticides factory in Bhopal, India, which killed over 2,000 people and maimed an estimated 200,000 is the most telling example (Smith 1992: 286).

Certainly, then, TNCs are powerful, and at times can behave in ways that undermine the sovereignty of states. However, it would be wrong to draw the conclusion that TNCs *always* undermine states, or *always* support military governments in preference to democratic ones. Some states in East Asia have been very successful in regulating the activity of TNCs (see Chapter Seven). Becker and Sklar (1987: 8) rightly argue that TNC subsidiaries "have no cause to object to local democratic governance, so long as its presence is compatible with the stable economic environment that corporate planning requires". This of course does not mean that TNCs are *always* democrats – in fact they are largely *indifferent* to systems of government, unless they threaten investment opportunities. Moreover, states and TNCs may have mutual interests based on the expansion of capitalist industrialization within a particular country, although this does not preclude the development of conflicts – for instance over the distribution of these benefits, as in Brazil in the 1970s. The TNC–state relationship is therefore based neither on automatic domination by one over the other, or indeed conflict between the two. Jenkins (1984a: 203) best describes the relationship as one "consisting of islands of conflict within a sea of cooperation and mutual accommodation".

It should be clear, then, that the developmental effects of TNCs in the Third World are not uniform, and that they vary in time and place. Their effect will depend on a number of factors, such as the sector in which the particular company operates, the role of the Third World state in regulating TNC behaviour, and the local social relations within which TNC investment occurs.

The discussion so far suggests that the independent versus dependent dichotomy is not a particularly useful one. We are left with one view that suggests that independent industrialization is *impossible*, which on the other hand is challenged by the conviction that such development is *inevitable* (cf. Gulalp 1986). Similarly, we are presented with the views of TNCs as either "a knight on a white charger coming to the rescue of Third World countries, or as the evil genius behind all their problems" (Jenkins 1987: 194). Both views are excessively concerned with analyzing the "national economy" as an economic unit – the pessimists to show that global factors have made national development impossible, the optimists to show that national development is unproblematic in the face of benign global factors.

Without denying the necessity of analyzing specific nation-states (cf. Bienefeld 1994), the discussion so far suggests that an alternative approach is required. What is needed is a more precise theorization of the relationship between the international or global economy and specific national economies (the local) (Sklair 1991a). TNCs are then analyzed not as institutions in themselves, but as part of an underlying structure of which they are a leading part (Jenkins 1984a: 40). The question then becomes one of examining how global factors influence local ones, and how the influence of localities reflects back and impinges on the global order.

The global, the local and late industrialization

In assessing the position of the Third World in the global economy, the emphasis should be placed less on the strategies of specific TNCs (although these remain important), and more on the nature of global capital flows. For it is here that we begin to get a broader explanation for the hierarchies that exist in the global order, and the problems faced by specific countries in the Third World in overcoming them.

The first point to make is that of the $150 billion total global direct foreign investment in 1991, over two-thirds went to the "advanced" capitalist countries

(*New Internationalist* 1993: 19). The share of the direct foreign investment made by specific First World countries going to the Third World has generally fallen over the last twenty years – from 27 per cent (1975) to 19 per cent (1984) for West Germany; from 73 per cent to 52 per cent for Japan; and from 19 to 16 per cent for the UK (Jenkins 1992a: 35). These figures also overestimate Japan's investment levels to the "Third World proper", as much of this investment is actually to the newly industrializing countries in East Asia. In the 1980s, this picture of capital investment concentrating in the First World intensified. Direct foreign investment in Latin America and South and South-East Asia fell by 25 per cent from 1981 to 1985 (Gordon 1988: 51). From 1984 to 1987, the Third World's share of new global direct foreign investment was 21 per cent, compared with 27 per cent over the 1981–83 period (Stopford and Strange 1991: 18). The direct foreign investment that does go to the Third World is highly concentrated, with just ten nations[14] accounting for 68 per cent of total DFI in the Third World in 1991 (*New Internationalist* 1993: 19).

The early 1990s saw a partial reversal of these trends, so that by 1993 developing countries as a whole received $80 billion (double the amount they received in 1991) and therefore around 40 per cent of the proportion of world DFI flows (UNCTAD 1994a: 77; *Financial Times* 19 April 1993). However, these figures need to be treated with considerable caution. Of the new investment that went to the Third World from 1991 to 1993, China accounted for nearly three-quarters of the increase in DFI in 1992 and over half in 1993, while the share of the least developed countries (mainly in sub-Saharan Africa and parts of Asia) continued to decline (UNCTAD 1994a: 78–9). Moreover, much of the foreign investment in China was from TNCs in the East Asian region (UNCTAD 1994a: 80). These factors suggest that the supposed increase in the proportion of DFI received by developing countries is more a reflection of the emergence of Pacific Asia as a force in the global order, rather than the end of unequal flows of capital investment.

Statistics on DFI flows do not take account of all the strategies utilized by TNCs, which may include forms of collaboration with local capital in the Third World, such as franchises, licenses, and subcontracting agreements (Gilpin 1987: 256). For example, some TNCs in the First World do not own factories, but instead rely on overseas production contractors that actually manufacture the products. This practice is common among companies in labour-intensive sectors such as clothing and footwear, including such brand name leaders as Nike and The Gap (Mitchell 1992; cf. Chapter Nine). Local capital in the Third World may also enter into licensing agreements with well known brand names from the First World, so that TNCs may obtain money without any initial investment in the local economy. This practice is common in the fast food and soft drinks industries (Clairmonte & Cavanagh 1988).

Although data on such practices is not easily available, these forms of investment have not substantially altered the Third World's share in global levels of industrial production, or the First World's dominance of the global trade in manufactured goods. In 1988, the EEC's consumption of imports from the Third World, as a percentage of total consumption, stood at 2.83 per cent; for the USA and Canada the figure was 3.42 per cent, and for Japan it was 1.43 per cent (Jenkins 1992a: 34).[15]

These figures show that it is not so much a problem of TNCs exploiting the periphery (the claim of much dependency-influenced work), and more a question of why so much capital investment stays within the First World (cf. Kay 1975). The basic reason for this pattern of investment is the tendency for capital to centralize and concentrate in existing areas of accumulation, which gives early developers a *relative* advantage over potential late industrializers (Murray 1972; Brett 1983: 91–117). As Mandel (1983: 502) states,

Under capitalism, it is mainly the possibility of overtaking competitors in the use of up-to-date production techniques and/or labour organization, i.e. enjoying a higher productivity of labour, which determines the rhythm of development of both firms and nations. *Cumulative growth* becomes possible once a certain threshold of accumulation of capital, industrialization, technical training of workers, engineers and scientists, etc. is passed.

Early industrializers thus enjoy certain advantages over late developers, based on successive waves of technological innovation. Early developers secure economies of scale – that is, they utilize methods of production which enable them to produce goods more efficiently than their potential competitors. These include: (i) the exploitation of mass production techniques (e.g. specialization of labour, machinery and knowledge); (ii) access to credit and to cheap inputs; (iii) substantial infrastructural facilities; and (iv) the organization of Research and Development facilities.

Thus potential late industrializers confront regions in the First World that (i) monopolize technology and skills; (ii) have highly trained workforces; (iii) have established markets; and (iv) have sophisticated research facilities (Kiely 1994: 147–8). Long-term profitable opportunities are therefore greater in these existing areas and so it is not surprising that TNCs concentrate their investments in these areas. This problem for potential late developers is made worse by the fact that local capital in the Third World is also inclined to take advantage of these profitable opportunities, and so the (often illegal) export of capital is an endemic problem (Griffin 1978).

Of course these advantages for early developers are only tendencies, which can be and are amended by some limits to expansion in the centre, and by the actions of states in the periphery. Nevertheless, given a situation of more or less unhindered market forces in the global economy, the result is likely to be an intensification of uneven development, rather than a situation of perfect competition between free and equal producers.

Thus, the concentration of the most advanced production techniques in the "advanced" world ensures that lower labour costs in the periphery are more than compensated for by higher productivity levels in the former – in Marxist terms, profitability is maintained by the extraction of relative surplus value in the First World, rather than extraction of absolute surplus value in the Third World.

None of these points imply that there are no attractions for capital investment in the periphery. First, TNCs must consider the location of particular raw materials in extractive industries, such as oil or bauxite. Second, they may invest in countries to secure access to markets, which may otherwise be protected by state policy. This accounts for the wave of investment by automobile TNCs in Brazil from the 1950s, as well as expansion by Japanese TNCs from the 1970s (including into the First World). Third, capital may invest in the periphery in order to take advantage of cheap and more easily controlled labour.[16] There are some industrial sectors where there are obstacles to increasing relative surplus value through technological innovation. Therefore, cheaper labour costs in labour-intensive industries such as textiles and electronic components gives the Third World a competitive advantage in these sectors, especially in countries with decent infrastructures, communications systems, some labour skills and close proximity to mass markets (such as parts of East Asia and the Caribbean).

It is precisely in these sectors that there has been some capital relocation[17] from First to Third World. However, the figures above show such relocation to be the exception rather than the rule, and there is evidence of protectionist practices by First World governments in precisely these sectors (Cline 1982). Moreover, whilst the barriers to entry into labour-intensive manufacturing are not based on technology, there are still barriers at the brand-name merchandising and retailing levels (Gereffi 1994a: 219).[18] Nevertheless, there has been some (limited and low value) industrialization in the periphery based on the inducement of low labour costs.

The other major countervailing tendency to the global concentration of capital is the action of nation-states. The previous two chapters showed how state intervention increased in all industrializations after the British case, and this became more pronounced as the agglomeration tendencies outlined above intensified (Gerschenkron 1962). The basic purpose of state intervention is to eliminate the constraints and draw on the opportunities existing in the world economy at a particular point in time.[19] States have therefore played a crucial role in late development in attempting to regulate the potential disequilibrium of a global economy based on unhindered market forces. As Myrdal (1957: 53) suggested many years ago, "if the forces in the capital market were given unhampered play – capitalists in underdeveloped countries would be exporting capital". Thus through strategic state intervention some late industrializers have successfully acquired up-to-date technology through both foreign and local investment, limited the export of capital, and so developed competitive advantages in the global economy (cf. Hewitt & Wield 1992, and the next two chapters).[20] The success and failure of such instances of "dependency management" (Gereffi 1992: 2) depends on specific factors operating in the global economy at a particular time, but also the historical and social forces that influence the patterns of state formation within particular spaces (Kiely 1994, 1995a). The local therefore reacts back on and influences the global.

Conclusion

This chapter has attempted to show how the conditions that have faced late industrializers in the periphery are different from those of nineteenth-century industrializers.[21] The general constraints (unequal competition and protectionism, the contradictory effects of TNC investment, and capital export) and opportunities (already developed technology, potential foreign investment, international credit and potential markets) existing in the world economy will influence the industrialization prospects of peripheral countries in specific ways. This will depend on factors occurring at the global level at a particular time, but also on events within Third World countries themselves.

Chapters Six and Seven examine specific cases of late industrialization, and show how different countries reacted to these constraints and opportunities in formulating industrialization strategies. In examining such strategies I also return to the questions of social and political agency and the relationship between industrialization and development.

Notes

1. The categorizations low income, middle income (upper) and middle income (lower) are taken from the World Bank and were first used in the *World Development Report 1989*. In this report the categories referred to countries with per capita GNP in 1987 of less than $480, more than $480 but less than $1,940, and more than $1,940 but less than $6,000. The categorizations in the text refer to 1983, and are therefore used retrospectively.
2. Sutcliffe's definition of industry requires some clarification here. In order to exclude economies with high-earning mineral or energy sectors, Sutcliffe (1971: 16–26) had earlier argued that any genuinely independent industrialization requires that at least 60 per cent of industrial output should be in manufacturing.
3. In this sense such views mirror the ahistoricism of technicist cases for industrialization outlined in Chapter Two. As the relationship between industrialization and development will vary in time and place, so too will the relationship between global and local factors.
4. The argument here should not be misunderstood. Whilst I largely agree with Bernstein's criticisms of most variants of dependency theory, it is still true that some capitalisms may better fulfill certain needs than others. Indeed, this was a major part of the argument in Chapter Two. Nevertheless, Bernstein's claim that dependency theory rests on an ahistorical account of an idealized capitalism which does not exist (and never has existed) is sound. Having said that, it is true that *some* versions of dependency theory are useful in that they attempt to examine specific historical and social reasons for the varieties of "actually existing capitalisms" (see Palma 1978; Larrain 1989: ch. 6; Mouzelis 1980; Kiely 1995a). My disagreement with dependency theory here is its recourse to purely external/global factors to explain dependence, and its implicit model of a "normal" capitalism, in which all others are somehow dependent or distorted because they deviate from that

norm. On this point, see Phillips 1977; Bernstein 1979, 1982. There is nothing wrong with comparison (Mouzelis 1980, 1988; Gunnarsson 1985), so long as it is not done on the basis that A is the norm, and B, C, D, etc. regarded as simple deviations from this norm.

5. We should bear in mind however that compared to many other late industrializers, Korea's problems may not be so bad – although this is not to downplay state repression, working-class exploitation, environmental degradation or female oppression. This case is addressed in detail in Chapters Seven and Eight.

6. The implications of this point are enormous, not least for Lenin's theory of imperialism (cf. Lenin 1977b) and the crude theories of underdevelopment (espoused by the Third International, Baran, Frank, many varieties of Trotskyism and Third Worldism) that were influenced by this theory. In fairness to Lenin later writers have to some extent mis-interpreted his theory, but this probably reflects the ambiguities in his thesis. The reputation of Lenin's theory among many Marxists is out of all proportion to its value as a coherent piece of work. The fact that capital flows have concentrated in the First World undermines the view that the First World developed simply by underdeveloping the Third World, and that capital had to flow to the Third World because there was a surplus of capital in the "monopolistic" core countries. Excellent critiques of the Leninist legacy, from various political standpoints, can be found in Emmanuel 1974, Warren 1980: chs 3–5, Olle and Schoeller 1982, Kitching 1982: ch. 6, and Thomas 1985.

7. This point relates to the uneven development of the global economy, and the (unequal) competitive conditions that arise from this. TNCs may invest in some of the more advanced parts of the Third World to take advantage of the surplus profits that can be obtained through the cheaper costs of these companies compared to local capital. However, in the long run competition tends to eliminate these surplus profits. The potential for new sources of surplus profits are limited by the fact that, historically at least, the wage goods sector in much of the periphery has had very low productivity, largely because such goods have been produced under non-capitalist conditions. For a fuller account, see Jenkins 1987: 97–101. These problems operate at a global level too, and I examine them below.

8. Export processing zones (similar to the earlier free trade zones) can be defined as special economic areas within nations which allow for more or less unrestricted trade between the zone and the rest of the world. The absence of regulations means that firms are basically exempt from at least some items of government legislation such as taxation and restrictions on working conditions. It has been estimated that EPZs employ around 2 million workers worldwide, although this figure excludes the cases of the Special Economic Zones in China (Gereffi & Hempel 1996: 22).

9. The maquiladora system is the system of export-oriented production in Mexico. Although larger and less territorially-specific than official EPZs, they display the same basic characteristics.

10. Technology must therefore be understood in the context of particular – and in this case capitalist–social relations. This case has been made in more detail in Chapter Two.

11. This point is true historically of the Latin American automobile industry, but it should be borne in mind that there have been significant changes – notably the rise of exports and the development of a low cost, basic car for a mass market in the late 1980s and 1990s (cf. Gereffi & Hempel 1996: 25).

12. Although it is true that the comparative weakness of state structures in parts of the Third World makes it easier for these practices to occur there, TNCs attempt to secure their interests throughout the world. For instance, drug companies have recently won a victory against Canadian consumers when the Canadian state repealed its system of compulsory licensing, which had allowed local companies to produce cheap copies of brand-name drugs. See Snider in *New Internationalist* 1993: 11.

13. I use the word influence rather than determine because I reject the notion that consumers are simply passive victims of global capitalism (cf. Adorno 1991; Strinàti 1995). Standardization of tastes should be seen as a tendency, subject to enormous counter-tendencies which TNCs, for all their efforts, are unable to control. This is probably best exemplified by the case of popular music, which is far more diverse and unpredictable than the standardization thesis allows. Furthermore, many forms of popular music are characterized by an ideology of distrust if not open hostility (on the part of both artists and consumers) towards the owners of the music industry (cf. Frith 1983, 1988).

14. In 1991 these were Singapore ($2.3 billion), Mexico ($1.9 billion), Brazil ($1.8 billion), China ($1.7 billion), Hong Kong ($1.1 billion), Malaysia ($1.1 billion), Egypt ($0.9 billion), Argentina ($0.7 billion), Thailand ($0.7 billion), Taiwan ($0.5 billion) – *New Internationalist* 1993: 19. Sub-Saharan Africa's share of global direct foreign investment in the late 1980s was around 1 per cent (Stopford and Strange 1991: 18).

15. These figures do not tell the whole story, as some fail to break down manufacturing by sector or even refer to industry as a separate category. Nevertheless, the evidence remains overwhelming that investment in the most dynamic sectors of industrial production is still concentrated in the First World. The figures also show that "moral panics" in the First World about Third World workers "stealing" the jobs of First World workers are wildly inaccurate. The decline in manufacturing employment in the First World is a result of technological innovation displacing workers, the shift to services (many of which are closely linked to manufacturing) and in some cases competitive pressures in the world economy (mostly, but not exclusively, between First World countries). The figures in the text clearly show that industrial relocation to the Third World has had a minimal impact on job losses in the First World, although it may have had some effect in labour-intensive sectors such as clothing. In fact, the First World trade surplus with Third World countries actually enhances job opportunities in the "advanced" capitalist world (Jenkins 1992a: 34). Claims made by some radical writers (Frobel et al. 1980; Peet 1986; Harris 1986, 1991) that there is a new international division of labour in which industry increasingly relocates to the Third World are similarly mistaken (cf. Jenkins 1984a: ch. 5; 1984b; Gordon 1988; Kiely 1994).

16. This factor of "super-exploitation" (Frobel et al. 1980; Frank 1981) has achieved the status of an almost religious dogma among a number of neo-Marxist dependency writers. In fact, the argument that capital is attracted to areas of capital scarcity and labour abundance (and low cost) is fully compatible with the neo-liberal theory of comparative costs (see Jenkins 1984b; Kiely 1994). It is also compatible with opposition by the British Conservative Party to "interventions" in the labour market, such as the European Union's Social Charter. The basic argument of Conservative politicians such as John Major is that the natural price of labour is determined by the supply and demand for labour, and so artificial interventions will price workers out of jobs. The problem with this thesis, as with all market equilibrium arguments, is that it does not conform to the rather obvious reality that the world is composed of high-wage areas with comparatively low levels of unemployment, compared with low-wage areas with high levels of unemployment. The reason for this supposed anomaly is that wages are not an independent variable, but are influenced by other factors such as labour organization and, most crucially, levels of labour productivity, which in turn are determined by the processes of cumulative development and hence economies of scale outlined in the text.

17. This may take the form of direct investment, or in the case of TNCs, it may be through the subcontracting agreements detailed earlier.

18. This point relates to the theory of global commodity chains, developed by Gereffi and Korzeniewicz (1994), which is examined in more detail in Chapter Nine.

19. This is the central theme of the next three chapters, which critically discuss the role of the state (and markets) in the development process.

20. However, many state interventions have been detrimental to the industrial (and agricultural) development of Third World nations. These questions are taken up in detail in the next three chapters.
21. In practice of course these constraints must be periodized, and in Chapter Nine I will examine some of the constraints and opportunities that exist for late industrializers at the end of the twentieth century.

Chapter Six
Import substitution industrialization

The previous chapter suggested that while global factors may strongly influence the development of a particular industrialization strategy, any convincing account of industrial development in the periphery must also examine local factors within a particular nation-state. This chapter examines one such local strategy: that of import substitution industrialization (ISI). The first section outlines an ideal-typical model of import substitution industrialization. I then investigate two concrete cases of ISI: Brazil and India. Finally, I conclude by briefly introducing neo-liberal criticisms of ISI, an issue taken up in later chapters.

ISI defined

Late industrializers in the Third World adopted an ISI strategy – in Latin America from around the 1930s, and from the 1940s and 1950s in the rest of the periphery. Although such a strategy did not preclude export promotion (see below), it is only a slight exaggeration to claim that ISI was *the* development strategy from the 1950s to the 1970s.

An ideal model of ISI was based on the following premises:

(i) the promotion of a domestic industrial base to serve the home market;
(ii) a consequent reduction in the widespread dependence on the import of expensive manufactured goods, and export of relatively cheap unprocessed goods;
(iii) the protection of domestic industries through tariffs or import controls.

The theoretical rationale for ISI strategies therefore was to draw on the opportunities offered, and eliminate the constraints established, by the world economy. The state was to have a central role in this process. First, it would boost industrial development by offering certain incentives to potential investors – for instance, by developing infrastructure and offering tax holidays. Second, it would directly protect domestic industry from cheaper imports through the imposition of high tariffs or quantitative import controls. Third, it would reinforce this protection through the indirect mechanism of state subsidies (cf. Shapiro & Taylor 1992: 433–5).

Advocates of ISI also hoped that it would involve substantial progress from the production of light industrial goods to heavy and high technology industries. Following Raj and Sen (1961), we can distinguish three different stages. In the early stages of ISI, foreign exchange (generated through the export of traditional goods and reinforced by savings made on limiting the import of light industrial goods) would be used to import investment goods and raw materials, in order to manufacture consumer goods – what is sometimes referred to as *primary* import substitution. This would then be followed by a strategy of importing capital goods to make more consumer goods, but also produce some relatively simple industrial machinery and intermediate goods. Finally, the aim was to develop the production of capital goods. The second and third strategies together constitute a process of *secondary* import substitution (Gereffi 1990: 17).

It is important to note that such a scenario was based only on a model of ISI, and in the real world the question became one of the *degree of emphasis* placed on a particular strategy (Colman & Nixson 1986: 281). Thus for instance, a strategy of ISI does not automatically exclude industrial development based on export promotion (Bradford 1990; cf. Chapter Eight).

Moreover, although there are certain common patterns to be found in the different experiences of national ISI strategies, their specific results and outcomes depended on the concrete social structures in which such policies were implemented. This relationship between the general and the particular is explored below, through a consideration of ISI in Brazil and India.

ISI in Brazil

Over the last forty years, Brazil has emerged as one of the largest economies in the world, with a significant industrial base. At the same time, in terms of its distribution of income and wealth, it is one of the most unequal societies in the world. Here I examine Brazil's transition to an industrial economy, emphasizing that there was a particular social and political basis to this industrialization process. Also, some of the reasons for the degree of inequality are suggested. My discussion is divided into three periods: 1822–1930; 1930–64; 1964 to the early 1990s.

Background: 1822–1930

Brazil won its independence from Portugal in 1822. A monarchy was established, but different regions had considerable autonomy, and slavery was maintained as the central form of production. Sugar was for many years the principal export but by the nineteenth century rubber and especially coffee were dominant. By 1901, Brazil accounted for three-quarters of the world's supply of coffee (Skidmore & Smith 1992: 153).

The monarchy fell in 1889 and slavery was abolished in three stages between

1871 and 1889. However, these changes did not break the power of the ruling class in the Brazilian countryside, and land ownership remained concentrated in the hands of a small but powerful minority. These landowners were happy for production to be based on agriculture, and for manufactured goods to be imported. As a result,

> industrialisation, in so far as it did take place, occurred in the pores of the old system, and was completely subordinated to the agrarian economy. Thus food, drink, clothes and textile production emerged, linked to the various agrarian sectors, and not integrated among themselves. (Munck 1984: 212)

Nevertheless, the period from 1889 to 1930 did see some significant social and political changes. A new constitution was established in 1891 and Brazil became a federal Republic of twenty states with a Constituent Assembly, whose governors were elected by a very limited suffrage. However, the more powerful regions such as São Paulo continued to have virtual autonomy, and were led by local colonels (the *coronelismo*). Nevertheless, the partial centralization of the state and the establishment of a (limited) parliamentary system were to have enormous consequences for later political and economic developments.

In the social sphere the abolition of slavery led to the development of new classes who were to challenge the dominance of the agrarian elite. Some industrialists emerged out of the development of light industry and infrastucture. A small but militant working class also emerged, both in town and countryside. Between 1887 and 1920, 1.7 million workers were imported from Portugal, Spain and Italy, with a further half-million following in the 1920s (Hewitt 1992: 70). Despite their conflicting interests on many fronts, the nascent bourgeoisie and proletariat shared an interest in winning a political voice and in the promotion of industry to boost living standards. The interests of both classes therefore conflicted with those of the landowners.

Furthermore, there was growing unrest within the army, particularly among younger army officers, known as the *tenentes*. They were concerned at indiscipline and lack of training in the army, and the archaic nature of Brazilian society. They shared the belief of the newer classes that Brazil needed to "modernize" and build the nation (Skidmore & Smith 1992: 162–3).

Conflict within the Republic was exacerbated by the necessity for some industrialization during the First World War, when industrial imports from the advanced capitalist countries were effectively cut off. The world economic crash of 1929 also hit Brazil hard, as coffee export prices plummeted.

These factors led to a crisis in the Republic, and in October 1930 a coalition of forces led by defeated presidential candidate Getulio Vargas took power in a coup. Although sections of the army played a crucial role in the takeover, it was left to Vargas and his civilian supporters to undertake the task of modernising Brazil, through industrial development and the centralization of the state apparatus.

1930–64: populism[1] and industrialization in Brazil

Vargas reduced the autonomy of the regions and gradually undertook the task of incorporating and subordinating different sectors of Brazilian society. This process was formalized from 1937 with the establishment of the New State (*Estado Novo*), which was influenced by the example of Fascist Italy. The New State suppressed independent working-class organizations and banned strikes, controlled the media and treated dissidents harshly. The authoritarian state also promoted substantial industrial development. From 1933 to 1939 industrial production grew by an average of 11.2 per cent a year, and in the war years national steel, mining and motor companies were established (Munck 1984: 214). On the whole, the Estado Novo period was

> characterised by the ending of the old republic's extreme regionalism, the transformation of the army into a national institution and, above all, the spectacular centralisation of the state and its increased interventionism in the economy and polity. (Mouzelis 1986: 27)

However, the effects of the so-called revolution of 1930 were limited. Although the period from 1930 to 1945 did see a significant growth of industry, in practice the process was restricted. A deliberate, conscious ISI strategy had not yet been established, and the prime reason for the promotion of industry remained the unfavourable world market conditions for traditional Brazilian exports (Furtado 1970). In the Industrial Census of 1940, over 49,000 industrial establishments were registered, and of these more than 34,000 had been established since 1930. However, 56 per cent of these establishments employed less than five workers (Munck 1984: 214).

Moreover, the movement towards industrialization was further constrained by the continued power of the landowning class in the countryside. In effect, Vargas' so-called revolution was based on a compromise between the aspirations of the new industrial classes and the old landowners. Although Vargas was forced out of office in 1945, he returned in 1950 before committing suicide in 1954. However, the legacy of his rule lived on as it laid the foundations for a specific pattern of class rule in Brazil, based on populism. In this context, populism can be defined as "a mode of vertical inclusion/ incorporation of the lower classes into the political arena during the transition from oligarchic to post-oligarchic parliamentary politics" (Mouzelis 1986: 91–2). Although populist appeals to "the masses" were less common in Brazil than in Argentina and Mexico (Roxborough 1987), the state carried out a number of measures designed to incorporate but also to subordinate the working class. These included the creation (and control) of trade unions, and laws designed to provide some job stability and compensation for dismissal from work (Munck 1987: 117; Kucinski 1982: 22–6). Although in practice these laws were largely rhetorical, and were accompanied by more directly repressive measures designed to curb militancy, more concrete legislation also introduced, for example, an eight-hour working day and paid holidays. Along with the promise of higher living standards through industrial development, these measures were reasonably effective in winning working-class support, at least until the late 1950s (Spalding 1977: 181).

It was in this context that a more deliberate ISI strategy was established after the Second World War, and reached its zenith during the rule of President Kubitschek (1956–60). In this period the state set about building a domestic industrial base through a system of tariff protection and import controls, such as the law of similars which limited imports of items already produced in Brazil or regarded as luxuries (Hewitt 1992: 75). It also invested in key industrial sectors such as steel production and oil refining and in infrastructure such as roads, buildings and hydroelectricity. Incentives were also provided to private capital, including foreign investors, and it was in this period that transnational corporations began to undertake substantial manufacturing investments in Brazil. DFI increased from $52 million in 1954 to $139 million in 1956. TNC investment was particularly high in motor vehicles, chemicals, and some machinery, as well as in consumer goods production (Munck 1984: 217).

The rationale for this deliberate policy of ISI was to reduce dependence on expensive manufactured goods and create a diversified industrial structure that would "lead to a process of self-sustaining growth sufficient to overcome secular backwardness and bring about a rise in incomes and living standards" (Kemp 1983: 139). In the short term, this strategy appeared to be working as manufacturing output soared – between 1957 and 1961 it rose by 62 per cent in real terms, while motor industry production grew by over 500 per cent and electrical equipment by 300 per cent (Hewitt 1992: 74). Moreover, it was in this period that industry displaced agriculture in terms of value added (Munck 1984: 219).

However, the boom failed to resolve substantial economic and social problems. Rapid industrial growth was bought at the cost of state spending growing faster than state revenues, and continued balance of payments problems. ISI was intended to reduce dependence on the export of cheap agricultural goods and the import of expensive industrial goods. However, in the short term[2] it led to a new form of dependence – the need to import machinery and raw materials to supply the new industries (Hewitt 1992: 74). Hence the boom had not resolved some long-standing economic problems.

This situation was intensified by tensions within the populist "alliance" (Schelling 1992: 251–5). Labour became disillusioned with the effects of industrialization as industrial employment failed to keep pace with the number of people entering the labour market. This problem was a reflection of both the capital-intensive nature of many new industries, and the massive rural–urban migration in response to continued inequalities within the countryside (Schelling 1992: 258–60). Indeed, the situation was intensified by the increase in the number of rural labourers who owned no land. According to the Brazilian Institute for Social Action and Education, 12 million rural people have either no land or an insufficient amount on which to live (Oxfam 1991: 32). The result was a labour surplus and therefore high unemployment and urban poverty. The labour surplus also served to keep wages down, as well as limiting the development of the internal market for industrial goods. This fuelled labour unrest throughout the 1950s, and in the early 1960s there were demands for redistribution of land in the countryside and the nationalization of industry (Munck 1987: 116–19). On the other hand, industrialists demanded government spending cuts and wage controls as a way to remedy the economic problems of the early 1960s. Faced with a perceived radicalization of populist government, the military took power in 1964.

1964 to the early 1990s: from military rule to "indebted democracy"
Under the military, the state was centralized further and labour organizations were once again subject to government control. In the aftermath of the coup, politicians, labour leaders, intellectuals and dissident army leaders were arrested or subject to state surveillance. This control intensified when, following a period of heightened labour militancy and social unrest in 1967–68, the military violently suppressed strikes in the São Paulo area. Thus,

> A pattern was set: an authoritarian government resorting to dictatorial measures to carry out its version of rapid economic development. It was a growth strategy based on repression of labor unions, avid recruiting of foreign investment, and high rewards for economic managers. (Skidmore & Smith 1992: 181)

From 1968, Brazil experienced a massive economic boom, based on the expansion of the industrial sector and the commercialization and mechanization of some sectors of agriculture. From 1968 to 1974, gross domestic product grew by an average of 10 per cent a year (Kucinski 1982: 47). The social basis of this "miracle" was a triple alliance of local capital, foreign capital and the state (Evans 1979: 236–49). Foreign capital was especially active in the most advanced industries, the state played a crucial role in the development of infrastructure and as a producer (for instance in oil, steel and electricity), while local capital was largely concentrated in the more labour-intensive sectors, or entered joint ventures with TNCs.

After 1964 some measures were taken to encourage the promotion of exports (exchange rate devaluations and state incentives to exporters) and to subject domestic firms to foreign competition (tariff reduction). However, this period represented a modification of ISI strategy, rather than a substantial shift in policy. The claim made by some neo-liberals (Balassa 1981) that Brazil followed free market principles from 1968 cannot be substantiated – the economy still focused on the domestic market and the economic role of the state actually *increased* in this period (Hewitt 1992: 79–80). In 1974, 19 of the largest 20 and 45 of the largest 100 domestic firms were state-owned (Munck 1984: 223). In 1974, the net assets of the 300 largest companies in Brazil were distributed as follows: state enterprises accounted for 32 per cent, Brazilian private capital 28 per cent, and TNCs 40 per cent. Corresponding figures for 1966 (before the miracle) were state enterprises 17 per cent, Brazilian private capital 36 per cent and TNCs 47 per cent (ibid.).

Although Brazil achieved rapid rates of economic growth in this period, its record in terms of social development indicators was poor. The miracle partly rested on the intensification of the exploitation of the labour force. The real value of the minimum wage, which affected 25 per cent of rural and 45 per cent of urban workers, fell by 25 per cent between 1963 and 1973 (Munck 1984: 221). In the countryside, the partial move towards mechanized crops such as soya and extensive activities such as cattle-breeding had the effect of increasing mass urbanization, without increasing formal employment. The result was an increase in urban poverty and shanty-towns (favelas). Infant mortality rates in the major towns actually worsened – in São Paulo from 62 per 1,000 in 1960 to 93 per 1,000 in 1973 (ibid.). Between 1964 and 1974, 75 per cent of the increase in Brazilian income went to the richest 10 per cent of the population, while the poorest half got 10 per cent. As well as this relative[3] decline in social development, there may have also been an absolute decline in living standards for the poorest 80 per cent of the population in the period from 1960 to 1976 (Sader & Silverstein 1991: 20). In the mid-1970s, Brazil had a rating of 68 out of 100 in the Physical Quality of Life Index,[4] far below other, less industrialized Latin American nations (ibid.). Furthermore, the opening up of the Amazon rainforest to industrial development, particularly mining, logging, iron and aluminium smelting and industrialized agriculture, led to an increase in landlessness, and a consequent increase in rural poverty and further urbanization, as well as environmental problems that have had an impact at the global as well as the local level (Oxfam 1991: 51–8, 77–9).

By 1974, the fragility of the miracle began to be exposed as Brazil faced a massive increase in its oil import bill. The OPEC price rises of 1973–74 hit the country badly, as the boom had focused so strongly on the development of the motor car. Brazil ran a large deficit on its balance of payments, which was financed by heavy government borrowing, and paid for both oil imports and new industrial investments. Encouraged by low interest rates and easy access to international credit, the government decided to borrow money for new projects, and in the long run pay back its debt through increased export earnings which would derive from these new projects.

However, in practice the country met with limited success in breaking into export markets,[5] and had to borrow to finance interest payments on the debt, as by 1980 total external debt reached a figure of nearly US$60 billion (Humphrey 1988: 233). By 1980, Brazil's total foreign debt payments represented 259 per cent of total export earnings (Sader & Silverstein 1991: 21). The situation worsened considerably when interest rates on the original debts increased, and by the early 1980s the country was paying out over 10 per cent of the total debt in interest payments alone (Sader & Silverstein 1991: 31).

From 1980, Brazil experienced a sustained recession. From 1980 to 1983, GNP per capita fell by 13 per cent and real wages by 25 per cent (Hewitt 1992: 89). Inflation soared and interest rates increased in order to attract investors to finance the debt. These factors facilitated a reduction in productive activity as capital found it more profitable to speculate in gold and dollars. Furthermore, whilst capital was exported to pay off interest on loans, this was insufficient to reduce the actual debt, which continued to increase in the 1980s.

Although the 1990s saw a slight economic recovery and a move to civilian democracy, there is a consensus that Brazil's experiment with ISI has failed. As Hewitt (1992: 94) states, "[t]he crisis of the 1980s was seen by many not as a short-term problem but as a crisis of a development model which could no longer be sustained." Through ISI Brazil underwent substantial industrial development, but it is also clear that industry is largely of a high-cost, low-productivity and low-quality nature. Moreover, the country's record of human development is poor. Between 1950 and 1980, the urban population increased from around 19 million to over 95 million. Urban employment failed to keep pace with such rapid growth, and urban poverty, homelessness, poor quality housing and crime are pervasive. From 1960 to 1980, the share of national income going to the bottom 50 per cent of the population fell from 17.7 per cent to 13.4 per cent, and the figure worsened in the 1980s. Over the same period, the top 5 per cent of landowners increased their share of land from 67.9 per cent to 69.3 per cent. In 1980, literacy stood at 68 per cent, 44 per cent of households lacked piped water and 57 per cent lacked sewerage (Cammack 1991: 54). Clearly, there is no straightforward correlation between indus-trialization and development.[6]

ISI in India

Independent India can also be regarded as a case study of ISI, albeit one with important differences from Brazil. The Congress Party that led the country to independence in 1947 was a cross-class coalition of social and political forces, and included a strong "socialist" current. On the other hand, the most powerful currents in the Congress were semi-capitalists, rich farmers and a petty-bourgeois state elite – groups of people who had the most to lose from any meaningful socialist transformation. The postcolonial state was therefore based on compromises, in which industrial (and especially foreign) capital was subject to strict controls, but at the same time was fostered by state activities.

The experience of both industrial and agrarian capitalist development in India is mixed. Industrial output has substantially increased since independence, and the growth of indigenous heavy industry has been particularly striking, but at the same time industries have generally been marked by low-productivity, high-cost production. Agricultural growth increased with the onset of the "Green Revolution" from 1967 onwards, but its impact has been uneven. Most importantly, the increases in industrial and agricultural output have failed to resolve the problems of uneven development and massive poverty (Sen 1990).

Industry and agriculture in the colonial period

British colonialism[7] did not encourage the development of industry in India. The development of the textile industry in Britain gradually led to the displacement of Indian producers of finished goods. After the American civil war threatened supplies, India became a major exporter of raw cotton. In addition it supplied other primary products for the "motherland" such as tea and jute. By 1910 India had the largest merchandize export surplus after the United States, but

> America's exports reflected rapid and massive economic development, whereas India's exports of raw materials reflected its subordination as a "captive" source of supply within Britain's imperial trade system. (Bernstein 1992b: 53)

The surplus that was generated from agriculture was mainly consumed by wealthy elites, used to finance the colonial state bureaucracy, or exported back to Britain. In fact the British attempts to "modernize" agricultural systems of production largely backfired. The *zamindar* system of agriculture under the Mogul Empire, based on taxes in kind, was replaced by a system of annual fixed rents payable in money. Peasants therefore suffered in times of bad harvests or when crop prices fell, as they were forced to produce cash crops to pay rents. Landlords found it more profitable to live off the rents of the peasants, rather than raise productivity through innovation, and the impoverished peasantry could not afford to innovate. The result was the emergence of a "parasitic landlordism" (Moore 1966: 344) in which a wealthy rentier class lived off the surpluses produced by a poor producing class and in which there was little incentive to accumulate.

Although at certain periods – such as the First World War – there was some industrial growth, on the whole colonial India remained a technologically backward society. In 1947 it had one of the lowest per capita incomes in the world; 75 per cent of the population worked in agriculture and produced 50 per cent of the income, while organized industry employed about 2 per cent of the population (Kemp 1983: 72). Life expectancy at this time averaged 33 years, and in 1943 the Great Bengal Famine led to 3 million deaths (Sen 1990: 8).

India at independence

The Congress Party that led India to independence in 1947 was both representative, and independent, of a diversity of social groups in India. It represented the educated middle class, professionals, small business people, small landlords and rich and poor peasants, and was led by intellectuals of middle-class origin (Sen 1984: 103). Its mass support came from small peasants but, given their degree of self-isolation, it was this sector that also had the most difficulty in self-organization. The consequence was that "at independence, Nehru and his Congress party were confronted with a situation in which the state had considerable leverage, free from any dominant class hegemony, to plan and determine India's future social development" (Sen 1984: 103; cf. Bardhan 1984: ch. 5).

As early as 1938, a National Planning Commission was established under Nehru's leadership. In 1944, the Bombay Plan emphasized a crucial role for state planning, with investment priority to be given to heavy industry (Kemp 1983: 88). Much of the inspiration for these policies came from the Soviet Union, and some emphasis was placed on "socialism" after independence. In practice, however, Indian socialism took the form of a state capitalism based on planning, heavy industry and the creation rather than elimination of social classes.

Planned industrialization, 1947–66

From 1947 to 1951, Congress lacked a clear strategy, but from 1952 Nehru emerged as the dominant figure and imposed his will on the direction of Indian development. The first Five Year Plan (1951–55), published in 1952, controlled private enterprise through the framework adopted under the Industries (Development and Regulation) Act 1951. The expansion and creation of new industries required the granting of a licence from central government, and the state played a leading role in the expansion of investment. The plan envisaged a total investment of 35 billion rupees,[8] of which 20 billion would come from the public and 15 billion from the private sector (Rothermund 1993: 130). Although the plan fell short of this target (a total of 31 billion rupees was invested), the target of increasing the national income by 11 per cent was surpassed, and in fact it increased by 18 per cent (ibid.).

The second Plan (1956–60) also focused on the development of industry and put forward a four-sector model based on investment goods, industry, agriculture and cottage industries and services, health and education. One-third of investment was allocated to investment goods while the other three sectors were allocated the remaining two-thirds. The third plan (1961–66) continued this pattern, but also increased the role of the public sector.

In this period industrial growth expanded. Taking the industrial production index to be 100 units in 1950, the figure had increased to 200 by 1960 and 280 by 1964 (Rothermund 1993: 133). Expansion was most rapid in the heavy industry sector, and the country rapidly developed (among others) indigenous steel and machine tools sectors. Between 1951 and 1969, there was a 70 per cent rise in the consumer goods industries, a 400 per cent rise in intermediate goods and a 1,000 per cent increase in the capital goods sector (Vanaik 1990: 28–9). On the whole, the public sector concentrated its industrial investments in high-cost, low-return heavy industries, while the private sector focused more on the development of consumer goods production. In so doing, it enjoyed the protection of the state from foreign competition. Private capital was therefore relatively unthreatened by state capital, and indeed benefited from the development of an industrial infrastructure. By 1966, the private sector contributed around 80 per cent of the output of organized industry (Harriss 1989: 75). Sen (1984: 160) is therefore right to claim that the state sector "developed because the bourgeoisie was weak".

In the same period, agricultural output expanded, but this was largely a result of an extension of the amount of land under cultivation rather than an increase in productivity. Sweeping land reform was usually resisted by rich farmers, many of whom controlled systems of government within the local states in the countryside. State policies in both industry (where the private sector was regulated but not eliminated) and agriculture (where radical change was largely averted) "reflected both the relative unity and freedom of the state elite and the constraints imposed by the propertied classes of town and country" (Vanaik 1990: 28).

However, by 1966 it was clear that the period of sustained economic growth had come to an end. Harriss (1989: 75–6) has attributed the slowdown in growth to the contradictions of the development strategy during the period from 1951 to 1965. First, growth had been accompanied by an increase in indebtedness; second, there was the expense of importing technology from abroad; third, there was little expansion of industrial employment; fourth, real wages stagnated; and fifth, there was a lack of structural transformation in agriculture. Revenue had been raised by indirect taxation, deficit financing and aid. Indirect taxation is regressive in its impact on income and so had the effect of limiting the development of the internal market, a problem reinforced by low wages and wage and agricultural stagnation. Aid constituted a vital source of finance, particularly in the second Five Year Plan, but these flows declined in the 1960s (Rothermund 1993: 137). Deficit financing therefore reached unsustainable levels and inflation increased. These factors together increased the pressure for an increased reliance on, and more independence for, the private sector.

Neo-liberal interpretations of the recession emphasize the crowding out of the private by the public sector (Bhagwati & Srinivasan 1975). On the other hand, Marxist interpretations point to the contradictions of class–state relations, and the conflict between the state's promotion of "socialist development" and the growing power of indigenous class forces (Bardhan 1984). As Harriss (1989: 76) argues, the factors outlined above

> reflect the inability of the government to raise resources domestically at the expense of property incomes, and by the mid-1960s the state was unable to sustain increased development expenditure because of resource constraints.

Industrial development from 1966 to 1985

The recession of the mid-1960s was exacerbated by the political uncertainties following Nehru's death in 1964 and border conflicts with China and Pakistan. Drought in 1965–67 had the effect of pushing up prices, which further increased following a devaluation of the rupee in 1966. These factors exposed the weaknesses of the agrarian sector, where slow rates of growth existed alongside the continued slow development of the industrial sector.

Planning was suspended in 1966 but resumed three years later as part of the "left turn" of the Congress Party. Although some measures such as the nationalization of major banks were introduced, the radicalization of Congress under Indira Gandhi was largely rhetorical, and "she never seriously tried to change the prevailing social order" (Rothermund 1993: 146). In fact under Mrs Gandhi, Five Year Plans became "a kind of commentary on the economic development that took place regardless of the plans" (ibid.: 147).

In the period from 1966 to 1985, industrial development remained locked in a cycle of high-cost production. Textiles actually declined, while iron and steel and car production continued to utilize outdated technology and hardly expanded. In 1960 manufacturing contributed 14 per cent of Gross Domestic Product, and by 1985 this figure had increased to only 17 per cent (Bernstein 1992b: 63).

However, in this period there was some important development in agriculture. Under the "Green Revolution" a package of biochemical inputs was introduced to promote an increase in agricultural productivity. These inputs – High Yielding Variety seeds, water, fertilizer – were of potential benefit to all farmers regardless of size of landholding (Byres & Crow 1988). The effects of this "revolution" varied from region to region, and were most far-reaching in the north where wheat production increased. On the other hand, in the eastern states productivity remained low. Nevertheless, substantial productivity increases ensured that by 1975 India was self-sufficient in wheat (Bernstein 1992b: 57).

It is a matter of contention whether the increase in agricultural productivity caused by the Green Revolution also led to a general increase in economic growth, and an increase in social development. In the period after 1967 both central and state governments have often paid more to farmers than recommended by the Agricultural Prices Commission. This effective subsidy to rich farmers *may* have led to a diversion of potential resources away from industry and so affected economic growth adversely[9] (Byres 1974). The Green Revolution also may have affected social development adversely by increasing the differentiation of the peasantry, and in doing so enriching some and impoverishing others. The main reason for this increase in social differentiation is that the effects of the new technologies were not resource neutral as opposed to scale neutral (Bernstein 1992b: 57–8). Those farmers who owned far more resources were in a more favourable position to benefit from the purchase of the new technologies than smaller producers with only limited (or no) direct access to land. Whether this process of differentiation has led to an *absolute impoverishment* of small farmers is questionable, but it is also true that increases in agricultural performance have not, on their own, alleviated mass poverty in the countryside, particularly among those dependent on casual wage labour (Ghosh & Bharadwaj 1992; Harriss 1995a: 129–30).

Indian economic development from 1947 to the early 1980s was very contradictory. There was substantial development of indigenous industry and some expansion of agricultural output, and an increase in some social development indicators such as life expectancy (Sen 1990). On the other hand, industrial and agricultural output was often inefficient, its effects were uneven and massive inequalities persisted.

Conclusion: ISI assessed

The two case studies addressed in this chapter show that the relationship between industrialization and development is far from straightforward. Both Brazil and India can be regarded as examples of highly uneven development, based on substantial rates of industrial growth existing side by side with high levels of poverty.

Neo-liberals believe that these problems are a result of misguided government policies. Import substitution industrialization is regarded as being both economically inefficient and socially undesirable (Lal 1983). It encourages the promotion of inefficient and high-cost industries rather than the development of dynamic, low-cost production which will promote economic growth, full employment and an increase in living standards. Neo-liberals therefore put forward an alternative development strategy in which market forces play the leading role. They argue that such policies have been adopted in East Asia and have led to both economic growth and development. The next chapter critically outlines their case and this is followed in Chapter Eight by a detailed assessment of late industrialization strategies.

Notes

1. Populism here is used in a different way from my discussion in Chapter Two. Briefly, in that chapter I referred to populism as a development strategy based on small-scale production. In this chapter, populism refers to a political strategy utilized by political elites to both incorporate and subordinate different interests in society, particularly the potentially subversive working class.
2. The question of the short-term inefficiencies and potential long-term dynamics of ISI is discussed in Chapter Eight.
3. The use of the term relative refers to the fact that it is possible for the poor to experience an increase in living standards even when the distribution of income between rich and poor worsens. For example, a country with GNP of 100 units may have an income distribution where the poorest 50 per cent only get 10 per cent of the total income. With economic growth, the GNP may increase to 200 units, and the income of the poorest 50 per cent may be 8 per cent. Income distribution has worsened, but the poorest 50 per cent are still better off after economic growth – before, the bottom 50 per cent shared 10 units; afterwards, they share 16 units. This hypothetical example should not be taken as an endorsement of a simple "economics first, distribution later" type of argument (but on the other hand, neither should a "distribution first, economics later [if at all]" argument be accepted). The point here is that in the years of the Brazilian miracle, living standards for the poorest 50 per cent fell in both relative and absolute terms.
4. The PQLI is an attempt to quantify social development (out of a mark of 100) on the basis of high literacy rates, low infant mortality rates and high life expectancy.

5. There were some exceptions, but these were largely in low-cost goods produced by labour-intensive industries.
6. Neither is it the case that there is no correlation, as I argued in Chapter Two.
7. The British formally colonized India following the "Mutiny" of 1857–58. Before then, the British East India Company had strongly influenced the development of the social structure of parts of India, particularly in Bengal.
8. All references to billions are to the US billion (one thousand million).
9. This contention rests on a number of assumptions concerning the actions of (some) peasants if they would not have been granted high administered prices by government. In the absence of high prices, producers may have cut production levels, thus forcing up prices or reducing surpluses available to the government. These problems have been discussed in the context of socialist development strategies in Chapter Four, and I return to these questions in Chapter Eight.

Chapter Seven
Export oriented industrialization

This chapter examines another strategy utlised by late industrializing countries – export oriented industrialization (EOI). This is discussed through an assessment of the industrialization experiences of the "four tigers" – Hong Kong, Singapore, South Korea and Taiwan – and the special economic zones in China. Industrialization in these four countries[1] has been very successful in the last thirty years. From 1960 to the mid-1980s, they each experienced annual average growth rates of around 8 per cent, compared with 7 per cent for Japan, and 3 per cent for the United States and the European Community (Wade 1990: 34). In terms of manufactured exports, together they accounted for around 8 per cent of the world markets compared to 0.4 per cent for Mexico, and over half of all developing country manufactured exports in the mid-1980s (ibid.). In the 1970s, the export growth rate in South Korea averaged 37 per cent a year; while on a per capita basis, in the late 1980s Hong Kong's and Singapore's manufacturing exports were around 50 per cent greater than those of West Germany (Edwards 1992: 109; Drakakis-Smith 1992: 141–2). As growth rates fell for many countries in the recessionary 1980s, the tigers maintained relatively high growth of around 7 per cent a year (Wade 1990: 34). Moreover, as well as experiencing rapid rates of industrial growth, the tigers also scored comparatively well in terms of social development.

It is not surprising, then, that EOI (or a certain interpretation of it) has been hailed as *the* success story for the developing world, and a model for others to follow. This chapter examines EOI in three sections. First, I give an overview of an ideal-typical model of export oriented industrialization. I then look at EOI in the four tigers, and in the special economic zones in China. The final section provides a brief preliminary assessment of EOI.

EOI: an introduction

Neo-liberals argue that EOI and ISI are mutually exclusive, and that development should be based on the former. ISI is regarded as counter-productive because it leads to the state protecting monopolistic, high-cost industry, and therefore distorting the market-based efficient allocation of resources. This scenario is contrasted with a strategy of export promotion in which domestic firms are forced to be efficient because they compete with foreign firms, rather than benefit from the protection of the state. Firms therefore have to cut costs in order to survive in a competitive environment.

Export oriented industrialization is therefore said to be based on the following features:

(i) industrial production is oriented towards the world market, rather than the protected domestic market;

(ii) industrial production takes place in a context of (more or less) free trade, so that firms have to be efficient or suffer the consequences.

Neo-liberal advocates of EOI argue that such a strategy is far more productive because it allows nation-states to exercise their *comparative advantage* in the world economy – that is, it allows countries to concentrate on those goods that they produce most cheaply, and exchange these for the products of other countries' comparative advantage (Balassa 1981).

In practice, EOI involves a set of policies designed to promote development based on market forces. These include exchange rate devaluations to make exports cheaper, the liberalization of trade and elimination of subsidies to force firms to be competitive, and the elimination of other "distortions" to the market place, such as minimum wages and price controls (Balassa et al. 1986).

Neo-liberals argue that as well as promoting greater economic efficiency (i.e. growth), EOI also leads to more equitable income distribution (i.e. development). Competition forces a particular country to exercise its comparative advantage, which in the case of labour-abundant countries will mean the use of labour-intensive technologies. This allows the country to compete in the world market through cheap labour costs. The use of such technology will lead to greater employment creation compared to the use of capital-intensive technologies utilized under ISI, and therefore a more equitable distribution of income.[2]

This, then, is the basic neo-liberal theory of export oriented industrialization. The question of EOI in practice now requires some consideration.

EOI in South Korea

Since 1945 South Korea[3] has developed from a relatively poor, war-devastated colony of Japan into a major producer and exporter of manufactured goods. Moreover, contrary to common misconceptions, it has diversified away from the production of labour-intensive goods such as textiles, into heavy and high-technology industries such as shipbuilding, computers and motor vehicles. This manufacturing success story has also found success in terms of human development. South Korea has a highly educated population, a high life expectancy and a relatively more equal income distribution than many developing countries (Edwards 1992: 97).

To faciliate clarity, my historical outline of Korean industrialization is divided into four parts: (a) Japanese colonialism to independence; (b) from independence and partition to 1961; (c) the miracle from 1961 to 1979; and (d) the post-1979 period.

Korea as a Japanese colony

In 1910, Korea (or Chosen, as the Japanese called it) became a Japanese colony. Under the ruling Yi dynasty (1392–1910), Korean society was characterized by rural poverty and backwardness. The aristocracy organized the estates, but had no real ownership rights, while the king owned the land but had no real control over its management. Thus, "while both sides engaged in frequent struggle over the distribution of the collected surplus, neither side had a clear interest in pursuing greater wealth through investment or innovation" (Hart-Landsberg 1993: 99).

Japanese colonialism was extremely authoritarian, but it also laid the basis for later industrial development. There were important changes in land ownership, so that increasing amounts of land became privately owned and exchange relations were extended. Between 1910 and 1918, the Government-General (the Japanese colonial state in Korea) transferred land ownership to Japanese and Korean landowners. In addition, all land formerly owned by the Yi dynasty was declared the property of the Government-General, which made it the largest landowner in Korea. These reforms led to the (absolute) impoverishment of the Korean majority, who were forced into tenant farming and paid very high rents (Hamilton 1986: 12; Hart-Landsberg 1993: 102–3). However, in purely economic terms the land reforms were a success and agricultural output rose by 74 per cent between 1910 and 1940 (Edwards 1992: 103).

Under Japanese rule, there was also some development of industrial production. By 1940, 213,000 Koreans were working in industry (excluding mining), and the net value of mining and manufacturing grew by 266 per cent from 1929 to 1941 (Cumings 1987). By the late 1930s, manufacturing constituted 29 per cent of total output, a very high figure for a colony (Edwards 1992: 103). Although most of this industry was concentrated in what was to become North Korea, it still had an impact in the South. Industrialization established a comparatively advanced infrastructure and a proportionately larger urban population compared to most of the colonial world.

So, although Japanese colonization of Korea was repressive, by "modernising" agriculture and developing industry, it did help to lay the foundations for later industrialization.

1945–61: from independence and partition to military coup

The defeat of Japan in the Second World War ended Korea's status as a colony. However, it also left a question mark over the future of Korean government. Two administrative districts were planned – the North was to be controlled by the Soviet Union and the South by the United States. However, social unrest, especially over land reform, followed and, when combined with superpower intervention, led ultimately to the Korean civil war (1950–53). The Soviet Union and China supported the People's Republic in the North, while the United States (through the United Nations) supported the government in the South (Halliday & Cumings 1988). The war ended in 1953 and a supposedly temporary partition (at the 38th parallel) was agreed, which survives to this day. South Korea was therefore effectively established, with a civilian government backed by the United States.

The war had a significant impact on industrialization in South Korea in three particular areas: land reform, nationalism and US aid. A land reform was implemented in 1953 in which tenancy was abolished and so farmers became owner-occupiers. This reform had the effect of boosting industrial development by forcing the former landlords to diversify into commercial and industrial sectors of the economy, rather than live off the rents obtained under the old system of land ownership. Furthermore, the existence of a relatively egalitarian structure of land ownership[4] allowed the state to pursue a policy of squeezing agriculture, so that the agrarian surplus could help to finance industrial development (Wade 1983). Thus, in the 1960s state manipulation of prices fixed the terms of trade between agriculture and industry against the former (Hamilton 1986: 39–40). These policies in turn had the effect of supplying a labour force for new industry as some people left the countryside in search of better living standards in the towns. Between 1967 and 1972, 7 million Koreans stopped working on the land to find industrial employment (Hamilton 1986: 156).

In terms of the militarization of society, the 1950s saw a conscious effort by the state to develop the Korean nation, and in doing so protect it from the threat of Communism. As part of this strategy, much emphasis was placed on industrial development. From 1953 to 1958, domestic industry was promoted through a strategy of import substitution. Large private companies or *chaebols* were developed with the active support of the state (Amsden 1989: 39–41). Although much of the industrial growth in the 1950s came from light industries such as textiles, food and clothing, there was also some important growth in heavier industries like chemicals and petroleum products (Edwards 1992: 107).

Building the Korean nation also meant that in practice all potential opposition to the state was suppressed. The government led by Syngman Rhee was highly authoritarian. Before the war, there was a massive purge of "subversives", with as many as 90,000 people being arrested in an eight-month period in 1948–49 (Edwards 1992: 105). In the 1950s, labour was controlled through the Federation of Korean Trade Unions, an organ of the ruling party (Bello & Rosenfeld 1992: 30). These actions were justified by recourse to a crude anti-communist rhetoric.

However, capital too was subject to state controls, as political connections played a crucial role in gaining access to cheap property, scarce foreign exchange, and other sources of "illicit wealth accumulation" (Hamilton 1984:

40). In particular, state distribution of formerly Japanese-owned property to individuals with close connections to the political elite played a crucial role in the development of a capitalist class in Korea (Koo & Kim 1992: 123–4).

Hostility to Communism was fully supported by the United States, and in the Cold War climate of the 1950s (and beyond), South Korea was a major recipient of US aid. From 1946 to 1978, South Korea received almost $6 billion in US economic aid, compared with $6.89 billion for the whole of Africa and $14.8 billion for Latin America. Only India, with a population seventeen times that of South Korea, received more ($9 billion). US military aid to South Korea and Taiwan from 1955 to 1978 (that is, *after* the Korean war) totalled $9 billion, compared to $3.2 billion for Latin America and Africa combined (Cumings 1987: 67). Although we should be careful not to overstate the contribution of aid to South Korean industrialization,[5] *in the 1950s at least*, it played an important role, accounting for five-sixths of the value of Korea's imports. From 1953 to 1962, US aid totalled approximately 75 per cent of South Korea's fixed capital investment and 8 per cent of its GNP (Hart-Landsberg 1993: 44). Aid therefore helped to develop infrastructure in the 1950s and so contributed to (but hardly *caused*) later industrial developments.

By the late 1950s, as US aid fell, economic growth declined. The economy faced similar problems to those of the import-substituters discussed in the previous chapter – namely, a limited domestic market, small amounts of manufactured exports, and an over-reliance on imports. These factors helped to undermine the government, and after a period of unrest from the late 1950s, the military took power through a coup in May 1961.

The miracle, 1961–79

The military takeover in 1961 intensified the centralization of state power that had occurred in the 1950s. Under General Park, some lip-service was paid to elections,[6] but this did not stop a concentration of power in the hands of the President, and the suppression of opposition. In May 1961, the already tightly controlled trade unions were dissolved. Although this ban was eventually removed, they were still subject to strong state controls through the Labour Union Law and Labour Disputes Adjustments Law (Bello & Rosenfeld 1992: 30–31). In 1971 the facade of elections was removed and Park increased his control over state legislators and effectively abolished presidential elections.

Park's presidency also saw an unprecedented expansion in economic growth. This boom was led by an increase in manufacturing output and exports. In 1961, South Korea's top six export earners were basic ores, iron ore, fish, raw silk, vegetables and swine. By 1976 they were clothing, footwear, fabrics, electrical machinery, plywood and telecommunications equipment (Hart-Landsberg 1993: 59). From 1960 to 1983, the contribution of manufacturing to GDP increased from 14 to 30 per cent (Wade 1990: 44). The ratio of value added in light industry to value added in heavy industry moved from 4 to 1 in about fifteen years (around 1962–77). It took Japan 25 years (1910–35) to achieve a similar ratio, while Britain, the United States and Germany took around 45–55 years just to move from a ratio of 2 to 1 (Wade 1990: 45–6).

According to some observers (World Bank 1983), exports were given a substantial boost by the devaluation of the national currency, the *won*. In 1961, it was devalued by 50 per cent, from 65 to 130 won to the US dollar (Amsden 1989: 65). Further devaluations in 1963 and 1971–72 had the effect of making Korea's exports at least potentially cheaper, and therefore more competitive, in the world market.[7] For some neo-liberal observers, this policy was part of a strategic shift to an industrialization strategy based on "market friendly interventions" (World Bank 1993).

Nevertheless, the state continued to play an active role in the promotion of industrial development. It continued to subsidize industries, and plan national development strategies in alliance with the chaebols. This was carried out through institutions like the Economic Planning Board, the Ministry of Trade and Industry, the Economic Secretariat and the Ministry of Finance. The state used these organizations to direct national planning, regulate foreign borrowing, control some prices, directly invest in some sectors, and promote exports and control imports.

Import controls were combined with a specific strategy of export promotion. For instance, successful firms – i.e. those that met export targets – were rewarded by the state by being granted access to restricted licensed imports, and were allowed to recover losses made on the world market through sales in the protected domestic market. This practice occurred not only in heavy and high-technology industries, but also in those labour-intensive sectors in which South Korea was said to have a comparative advantage, such as textiles (Amsden 1989: 66; 1993).

A further crucial mechanism of state control was the nationalization of banking in 1961. The state was able to set interest rates and credit ceilings, and make budget decisions at each individual bank (Hart-Landsberg 1993: 57). Moreover, direct control enabled the state to loan money to industries in the most favoured sectors of economic development. Thus in the 1970s, faced with increasing labour costs, the state focused its attention on the encouragement of heavy industries such as chemicals, shipbuilding and iron and steel (Amsden 1989: chs 11 & 12). Through its control of credit, the state encouraged a movement in Korea's export profile, and the share of heavy and chemical goods in merchandise exports rose from 14 per cent in 1971 to 60 per cent in 1984 (Hart-Landsberg 1993: 60). This policy also further stimulated the growth of the chaebols. Between 1972 and 1979, the average number of firms owned by the ten largest chaebols grew from 7.5 to 25.4. In the same period, the ten largest chaebols achieved a 47.7 per cent annual average rate of growth in terms of assets, while the average rate of growth of GNP was 10.2 per cent (Koo & Kim 1992: 136).

The state also assumed control over private access to foreign capital. An amendment to the Foreign Capital Inducement Law in 1962 ensured that the

Economic Planning Board had the power to decide which enterprises would have access to foreign capital. The outflow of capital was also controlled through legislation which made any illegal transfer overseas of $1 million or more punishable with a minimum of ten years' imprisonment and a maximum sentence of death (Hart-Landsberg 1993: 57). Direct foreign investment was also closely regulated and majority foreign ownership discouraged, although there was some relaxation with the passing of the Foreign Capital Inducement Law in 1972, and in the early 1980s, when 100 per cent foreign ownership was permitted in some industries (Deyo 1989: 35).

Sustained industrial growth was accompanied by the continued suppression of labour. In the 1970s unemployment was low but labour was tightly controlled by both the state and dictatorial management practices within factories. Illegal strikes, often led by women workers in textiles factories, were brutally suppressed (Bello & Rosenfeld 1992: 34–5). Wages increased from the mid-1960s, but from a low base, and they failed to keep pace with productivity increases. Moreover, average hours of work were very high and working conditions often very dangerous (Edwards 1992: 117–18; Bello & Rosenfeld 1992: 24–5).

By the late 1970s, strains in the miracle became more visible as there was a heightening of social unrest and economic problems. In 1979, women workers took over a factory at Y. H. Trading Company as the president had run off to the United States with company assets. The state adopted a hostile response, and many of the workers were beaten by the police. This had the effect of inciting riots throughout urban Korea (Ogle 1990: 91–2). The same year saw a fall in exports, a rise in the price of oil imports, and an increase in the country's debt burden along with rising interest rates. Amidst a growing atmosphere of crisis, President Park discussed ways of dealing with the situation with Kim Jae Kyu, the head of the Korean CIA. Unfortunately for Park, there were obvious points of disagreement and Kim ended the discussion by killing the President. Students and workers then rioted, but the military under Chun Doo Hwan instigated another coup. Protests continued, most notably in the southern city of Kwangju, where students and Kwangju residents set up People's Committees. The military responded by entering Kwangju and killing many citizens. Kwangju was to become a focus for opposition throughout Korea in the 1980s.

Korea in the 1980s

In 1980, the economy threatened to fall into recession. National output fell by 5 per cent, and a deficit was run on the current account of its balance of payments. The country increased its borrowing to finance the external deficit, and together with an increase in interest payments, therefore faced an increase in its debt burden. Korea's deficit on its current account constituted more than 8 per cent of its GDP, and its external debt was more than 45 per cent of its GDP (Edwards 1992: 121, 123). However, by the late 1980s its gross foreign debt was less than 20 per cent of its GNP, which was almost completely offset by investment held overseas (ibid.).

Some measures of economic liberalization were carried out such as an increase in the share of the manufacturing industries open to foreign investment, the privatization of the ownership of city banks, and the abolition of preferential interest rates applied to strategic industries (Koo & Kim 1992: 141). A stand-by agreement with the IMF was signed in 1983 which led to cuts in government spending.

On the other hand, the state played an important role in expanding investment and bailing out "lame duck" companies during the economic downturn. The government also intervened in order to scale down the operations of the chaebols, and encourage the development of the small and medium-sized business sector. However, the chaebols sold off some of their firms but bought others (Koo & Kim 1992: 142). Liberalization encouraged further concentration of capital as the chaebols bought holdings in the newly privatized banks (Edwards 1992: 122). Finally, although by the late 1980s South Korean trade officials were asserting that the country's import liberalization ratio had reached 95 per cent for manufactures, the reality was somewhat different. The country's Automatic Approval list (i.e. the list allowing imports without quantitative restrictions) had many exceptions such as special laws and import area diversification and surveillance measures. According to Luedde-Neurath (1988: 78–9), in 1982 these controls accounted for over $10 billion out of $14.2 billion of AA classified imports (i.e. those imports supposedly not subject to quantitative restrictions).

The 1980s also saw a period of sustained labour unrest, particularly from 1987 to 1989, when there were over 7,000 labour disputes, and many independent unions were established (Bello & Rosenfeld 1992: 40–42). Labour unrest eventually paved the way for a process of (limited) political liberalization, culminating in direct presidential elections in 1992 (Berry & Kiely 1993).

South Korean industrialization has been very successful in a number of ways. Contrary to the Western stereotype of Korea as a passive victim, simply serving the needs of Western capital (most commonly used by the left[8]), the real story is one of sustained industrial growth and successful diversification into some heavy and high-technology industry. Furthermore, this industrial growth has also gone hand in hand with social development, which *may* suggest that South Korea is a relatively clear confirmation of the Kitching thesis, although we should not ignore the negative features detailed above. Furthermore, does this case uphold or challenge the neo-liberal thesis? These questions are considered in Chapter Eight. For the moment, I return to an outline of some of the other cases of EOI.

EOI in Taiwan

Taiwan is in many ways an even bigger success story than South Korea. From 1953 to 1982 it experienced an annual average rate of growth of 8.7 per cent

(Castells 1992: 41), and its share of manufacturing increased from 12 per cent in the early 1950s to 33 per cent by the early 1980s (Harris 1986: 46). Its record in terms of social development is equally impressive. Taiwan has one of the most egalitarian distributions of income in the developing world (although this was partly undermined in the 1980s), has high rates of literacy and of participation in higher education, and a very low rate of infant mortality (Bello & Rosenfeld 1992: 177).

I consider the history of Taiwanese industrialization in four parts: (a) the era of Japanese colonialism; (b) the nationalist era from 1945 to 1958; (c) export oriented industrialization from the late 1950s to the early 1970s; and (d) technological upgrading and liberalization in the 1970s and 1980s.

Japanese colonialism, 1895–1945

Japan took over the Chinese province of Taiwan after defeating the latter in war in 1895. The pattern of colonialism in Taiwan was not dissimilar to that in Korea, in that the colonial state acted in a very repressive manner but at the same time laid the foundations for later industrial development. It introduced a land reform that granted land rights to local rather than absentee landlords, and promoted agricultural development through investment in infrastructure and technology such as fertilizers and better seeds (Amsden 1985). There was also some industrial development from the 1930s onwards, in light industries such as textiles, food processing and plywood, but also in heavier sectors such as shipbuilding (Wade 1990: 74). In addition there was some development of local entrepreneurship, and important social developments such as some improvement in health-care and education.

The result was that "[b]y the time of retrocession in 1945 Taiwan was probably the most agriculturally, commercially and industrially advanced of all the provinces of China" (Wade 1990: 74).

The nationalist era, 1945–58

After Japan was defeated in 1945, Taiwan was returned to China. At this time, there was conflict over who was to rule the mainland between the nationalist Kuomintang (KMT), led by Chiang Kai-shek, and the Chinese Communist Party. The latter had emerged as the clear victor by 1949, and so from 1947 onwards defeated nationalists fled to Taiwan. The KMT had few ties with the local population of around 6 million people, but it faced little sustained opposition to its rule.[9] These factors were significant because they enabled a KMT-dominated state to impose its will on the population,[10] and therefore play a central role in directing economic development, unhindered by the pressure of powerful vested interests (Wade 1990: 75).

The first important measure introduced was a radical land reform, which transferred formerly Japanese-owned land to tenants, and redistributed land above a ceiling of 3 hectares to the tenants. The result was that "almost overnight the countryside in Taiwan ceased to be oppressed by a small class of large landlords and became characterized by a large number of owner-operators with extremely small holdings" (Amsden 1985: 85). The state maintained the class of small peasants by providing an advanced infrastructure and new technologies, which ensured that productivity would increase. Furthermore, by maintaining relatively stable prices and cheap credit, it ensured that farmers were unlikely to be forced to sell their land in the face of high interest payments on loans. This state promotion of agriculture helped to secure an annual average growth rate for agriculture of 4.8 per cent from 1953 to 1962, and 4 per cent from 1963 to 1972 (Bello & Rosenfeld 1992: 186).

On the other hand, a surplus was extracted from agriculture and used to finance industrial development. This was achieved, first, through an overvalued currency and multiple exchange rates, which together acted as a kind of export tax on agriculture, as imports for industry were cheapened and export revenue from agriculture reduced. Second, the domestic terms of trade were biased against agriculture, through land taxes, the compulsory procurement of rice by the state at below market prices, and a rice–fertilizer barter scheme (Wade 1990: 76–7). Through the latter scheme, which lasted until 1972, the state was able to control around 40 per cent of the marketable supply of rice, which in practice meant that it could release its stock onto the market whenever the price threatened to go too high.

These policies resulted in a kind of "virtuous circle" in which "a self-exploitative peasantry, working long hours to maximize production per hectare, and a super-exploitative state, ticking along effectively to exact the fruits of the peasantry's labour, operated hand in hand in Taiwan to great advantage" (Amsden 1985: 87). Agricultural development, facilitated by a land reform and a particular relationship with the Taiwanese state, provided to industry a labour force, a surplus, foreign exchange, demand for industrial outputs and a market for consumer goods.

In the early 1950s, industrial development focused on labour-intensive industries such as plastics, fibres and, most importantly, textiles. Industry was developed through primary import substitution – domestic industry was protected through quantitative import controls, high tariffs and overvalued exchange rates. The public sector played the leading role in manufacturing, accounting for 57 per cent of industrial production in the early 1950s, and also dominanted the financial sector (Bello & Rosenfeld 1992: 232). Between 1952 and 1958 manufacturing output doubled and the process of primary import substitution was largely completed. By 1957 consumer goods constituted only 7 per cent of total imports (Wade 1990: 77–8).

Aid from the United States played an important part in the financing of industrial development in the 1950s. Like South Korea, Taiwan was a favoured recipient of large amounts of US aid because of its anti-communist credentials – in this case Taiwan was seen as a bulwark against communist China. Between 1945 and 1978, Taiwan received $5.6 billion in US economic and military aid (Cumings 1987: 67). In the 1950s, the quantity of economic aid equalled 6 per cent of GNP and 40 per cent of gross investment, and financed over 30 per cent of the imports of intermediate and consumer goods (Wade 1990: 82). Aid also helped to bring inflation down from 3,400 per cent in 1949 to 9 per cent in 1953 (Amsden 1985: 91).

EOI from 1958 to the early 1970s

From as early as 1954, the state gave some encouragement to potential exporters through the granting of export subsidies, but it was from 1958 onwards that a substantial package of economic reforms was put in place. The multiple exchange rate system was gradually abolished and in February 1960 the Nineteen Point Programme was introduced, which eased import controls and reduced tariffs (Cheng 1990: 154–5). Furthermore, a tariff and tax rebate system was implemented, by which exporters could gain refunds on customs duties for imported goods, or a local producer could sell inputs to the exporters at the lower world market price and then claim the amount of tariff duties that the exporter would have paid for the input to be imported (Bello & Rosenfeld 1992: 241).

In this period, there was also a substantial move towards the development of the private sector. By 1970, the state sector, which had dominated industrial production in the early 1950s, accounted for around 20 per cent of industrial production (Wade 1990: 88). Foreign investment was encouraged through the granting of tax incentives, the allowance of 100 per cent equity holdings and profit remittances, and in 1965 the world's first Export Processing Zone was established at Kaohsiung (Wade 1990: 54; Stallings 1990: 77). However, the rate of foreign investment in Taiwan was comparatively small – in the late 1960s and early 1970s it never exceeded 4.3 per cent of Gross Domestic Capital Formation (Huang 1989: 104). The domestic private sector developed in a quite distinct way in this period. Unlike South Korea, Taiwan's industries were overwhelmingly small. Workplaces employing fewer than thirty workers made up more than 90 per cent of Taiwan's manufacturing enterprises, and 80 per cent of the labour force were employed in these firms (Bello & Rosenfeld 1992: 219). In 1976 only 176 firms (including state and foreign firms) had more than a thousand employees, and between 1966 and 1976 the number of manufacturing firms increased by 250 per cent, while the number of employees per firm increased by 29 per cent. In South Korea in the same period, the number of manufacturing firms increased by 10 per cent, and employees per firm by 100 per cent (Wade 1990: 67). Perhaps even more striking is the fact that small and medium-sized firms (i.e. those firms employing less than 300 workers) accounted for 65 per cent of manufactured exports in 1985 (ibid.: 70).[11]

These factors have led some neo-liberal writers (Little 1979; see Chapter 8) to claim that Taiwan developed on the basis of free market policies. They maintain that Taiwan industrialized by exercising its comparative advantage in cheap labour, and that it was able to do this because the government allowed market forces to operate in an unhindered way. The result was both rapid economic growth and a proliferation of small, efficient and flexible firms that responded effectively to changing world market conditions. On the other hand, the state continued to play a very active role in the economy, directing the flow of credit through its control of financial institutions, planning industrial growth, and continuing to invest in key strategic sectors of the economy (Haggard & Cheng 1987: 115–16).

The 1970s and 1980s: technological upgrading and liberalization

By the early 1970s, Taiwan faced a number of economic and political problems. Protectionism abroad, rising wages at home, competition from other NICs and, after the oil price rises, an increased import bill were all potentially damaging to the economy. Derecognition of Taiwan by the United Nations in 1971, and improved relations between the United States and China, further aggravated the country's problems.

The state responded by a process of planned upgrading of industrial development, so that the country would move from the export of labour-intensive goods (primary EOI) to higher-value-added goods based around heavy industry and/or high technology (secondary EOI). As early as 1961, the state had stressed the need to develop heavy industry, and some moves were made in this direction. Nevertheless, it was not until 1973 that there was sustained development of heavy and chemical industries. The sixth Four Year Plan of 1973–76 gave state support to relatively new industries such as petrochemicals, electrical machinery, and machine tools. Some of the heaviest industries, such as steel and shipbuilding, were directly owned by the state. There was also an increase in investment in infrastructure and in research and development activities (Wade 1990: 98). This technical upgrading has on the whole been a success. Exports have increased in sectors such as electronics, computers and machine tools, and niche markets found for its high-quality steel products. Only the automobile sector can be deemed a failure (Wade 1990: 99–108).

After a brief recession in the early 1980s, the economy recovered and high growth continued as Taiwan's good quality products successfully broke into new export markets. This decade also saw the start of political liberalization, as martial law was lifted and new trade unions were established. In 1992, elections were held, which were won by the KMT.

Taiwanese industrialization has in many ways been the most successful of all "Third World" industrializations. The country has experienced rapid industrial growth and at the same time considerable improvements in living standards. This raises a number of issues. At first sight, as with South Korea, its close correlation between industrialization and development appears to confirm the Kitching thesis. But this leaves aside a number of issues, such as political repression, gender inequalities, environmental destruction and continued uneven development. Furthermore, perhaps most problematic for Kitching is the fact that development has occurred on the basis of *relatively small-scale* industry and agriculture. These may have been maintained by a strong centralized state, but as I showed in Chapter Two, this is perfectly compatible with some neo-populist strategies, not all of which believe in small-scale and laissez-faire-based development. These factors lead on to other, closely related questions, which concern the type of government policies that have promoted both industrial growth and social development. In other words, is Taiwan a model of unrestricted market forces or of government intervention? I address these questions in detail in the following two chapters.

EOI in the city-states: Hong Kong and Singapore

Hong Kong and Singapore have similarly experienced rapid rates of growth of manufacturing output and exports, although there has also been a marked shift to growth based on services in recent years. From 1959 to 1976 Hong Kong's annual average growth rate stood at 8.9 per cent, while the export sector grew at an average of 16.9 per cent a year – twice the rate of growth of world trade (Schiffer 1991: 182). From 1965 to 1980, Singapore's growth rates averaged over 10 per cent a year, and by 1994 its GNP per capita stood at US$18,025 (Bello & Rosenfeld 1992: 289; *New Internationalist* 1995: 18).

Hong Kong's industrialization process has been strongly influenced by its status as a British colony[12] and its proximity to China. Until the Second World War, it served as a major port serving mainly Anglo-Chinese trade. This situation changed first with Japanese occupation from 1941 to 1945, and then with the Communist takeover in China in 1949. From 1945 to 1949, when it reverted to its traditional economic role, around 90 per cent of Hong Kong's exports were actually re-exports (Haggard & Cheng 1987: 107). Following the Communist takeover and intervention in the Korean war from 1950, the UN introduced trade sanctions against China, which devastated Hong Kong's trading houses and shipping companies. The revolution also led to a massive flow of refugees from the mainland. These factors together led to the economy entering a period of recession in the early 1950s.

However, some of the refugees were nascent industrial capitalists who brought with them both money and textile machinery, and thus "within a short space of time, refugee capital using state-of-the-art textile machinery had put to work refugee labour to produce the foundation of the colony's industrialization" (Henderson 1991: 170). Although clothing was the leading industrial sector, there was some diversification in the late 1950s into other labour-intensive industries such as cheap plastic products and wigs. By 1959, the amount of locally manufactured exports overtook the amount of re-exports originating from elsewhere in the region (Haggard & Cheng 1987: 107). This was followed in the 1970s and 1980s by a move into new sectors such as con-sumer electronics, including televisions, videos and personal computers, and watch assembly (Harris 1986: 56). There has also been a shift away from manufacturing, which now generates around 20 per cent of GDP, towards higher value services, which generate around 70 per cent (Henderson 1991: 170–71).

Small businesses dominate the manufacturing sector. In 1981, more than 90 per cent of manufacturing firms employed less than 50 workers, and large enterprises (employing more than 100 workers) accounted for only 22 per cent of manufacturing's contribution to GDP (Castells 1992: 47). The average size of manufacturing firms actually *declined* from 52 workers per firm in 1951 to 20 in 1981 (ibid.). Furthermore, in terms of export promotion, the contribution of foreign firms is relatively small (Henderson 1991: 171).

The small size of manufacturing firms has acted as a constraint on the growth of a well organized labour movement. Although there have been periods of labour militancy, particularly from 1945 to 1949, the state has taken a largely "hands-off" approach to labour, which reflects the particular form that industrialization has taken in the colony. Trade unions, when they do exist, are often little more than friendly societies, and labour relations in the small firms have taken on a paternalist character (Deyo 1989).

Singapore's rapid industrialization emerged out of its forced departure from the Federation of Malaysia in 1965,[13] when it was cut off from access to Malaysian markets and raw material supplies. The small size of the domestic market rendered ISI an unviable option, and so the People's Action Party government[14] took the decision to combine nationalist and authoritarian politics with an openness to foreign investment. Foreign capital was granted tax holidays, the right to 100 per cent ownership and profit repatriation, and the attraction of a tightly controlled labour force. In addition, the state invested heavily in infrastructure, which had already been developed when Singapore served as a port and military outpost of the British Empire.

Transnational investment was high in some of the leading sectors, such as oil refining (which had been established in the colonial era) and petroleum (Huang 1989: 99–100). In 1974, 43 per cent of DFI in the manufacturing sector went to petroleum and petroleum products, a reflection of the fact of Singapore's strategic location for both oil-producing and oil-consuming countries (ibid.: 103). However, after the oil price rises there was a considerable fall in investment in these sectors and an increase in investment in sectors such as textiles and electronics (Haggard & Cheng 1987: 106). By the mid-1980s, TNCs accounted for 70 per cent of the gross output, over 50 per cent of employment, and 82 per cent of exports in manufacturing (Bello & Rosenfeld 1992: 293). Recession in the mid-1980s, partly caused by a relocation of labour-intensive industries to lower-cost areas, was followed by the importation of cheap labour from neighbouring countries.[15] The long-term shift towards the service sector also continued (Harris 1986: 66).

As in the cases of Taiwan and South Korea, the major controversy concerning industrialization in Hong Kong and Singapore concerns the role of the state. The key question again is whether the state played a key role in promoting industrial development, or, insofar as there was intervention, whether this was irrelevant to industrial performance.

This question is perhaps most pertinent in the case of Hong Kong, which is still widely regarded as a model of free market development (Rabushka 1979). It is true that in the colony there is no economic strategy, no planning of output, no central bank and so on. These facts have led to the neo-liberal claim that in Hong Kong

> Government plays an important (but limited) role ... It enforces law and order, provides a means for formulating the rules of conduct, adjudicates disputes, facilitates transportation and communication, and supervises the issuance of currency. (Friedman & Friedman 1981: 55)

A full analysis of the role of the state in late industrialization strategies is reserved for the next chapter. It needs to be stressed immediately however that Friedman and Friedman's statement constitutes a massive understatement of the role of the state in Hong Kong. Schiffer (1991) has shown that from 1959 to 1976 around 70 per cent of household spending went on foodstuffs and housing, and that these sectors were subsidized by the state. In terms of foodstuffs, Hong Kong imported around 80 per cent of its total and 50 per cent of this was from China. This cheap food was produced at administered rather than market prices, the former being considerably lower than the latter. The effect was to subsidize the consumption of the Hong Kong labour force, which enabled employers to keep wages down. This of course was a vital strategy for the colony, as it was largely competing in the world market at this time on the basis of low-wage and therefore cheap labour-intensive products. The Hong Kong government also played a direct role in subsidizing foodstuffs through its active role in the distribution of foods, especially rice, vegetables and fish (Schiffer 1991: 183–6). The state was active in the public provision of housing, both directly and through the practice of rent controls. By the end of the 1970s, around 40 per cent of accommodation was in the public sphere (ibid.: 186). Household consumption is also subsidized through state spending on social services such as health and education.

Although taxation rates are low, the state has other sources of revenue. In particular, all land is owned by the state and leased to individuals. This is an important source of revenue, especially as land expansion has occurred through reclamation from the sea, or more recently the buying of land in the New Territories. Huge profits are also made from the constant demolition and reconstruction of buildings to create more shops, offices and hotels (Drakakis-Smith 1992: 167). From 1949/50 to 1975/76, non-tax revenues accounted for over 34 per cent of total government revenues (Schiffer 1991: 189).

Much the same can be said of Singapore, where state regulation of personal behaviour has often reached levels that are not incompatible with Stalinism.[16] The state has also played a crucial role through direct control of strategic industries such as shipbuilding, steel, engineering and petrochemicals. Taxation rates are similarly low in Singapore, but again state revenue is acquired through other means. The major mechanism, the Central Provident fund, set up in 1955, is a compulsory insurance scheme for both employers and employees.

Although ostensibly set up to act as a welfare and pension scheme, it generates such enormous amounts of revenue (as it takes such a high proportion of gross earnings) that it has acted as an instrument of public finance. By 1982, total Central Provident funds were the equivalent of two-thirds of all individual deposits in Singapore's banks (Harris 1986: 62).

EOI in the special economic zones in China

From December 1978, China began a shift in policy which involved some economic liberalization. The Maoist era, which paid lip-service to the development of socialist relations of production,[17] was effectively abandoned and more emphasis was placed on the development of the productive forces. In order to do this, some policies of "market reform" were implemented. These included more autonomy for enterprises, the abolition of the commune system in agriculture, some development of the private sector, and a greater openness to foreign trade (White 1993: 42–50). These policies have in practice been limited (Smith 1993), but more far-reaching has been the creation of special economic zones in Shenzhen, Zhuhai, Shantou and Xiamen. In addition there are a number of areas that have been granted special priority for investment, such as Beijing and the Guangdong province, which includes Shenzhen. The zones, and their surrounding hinterlands, are small compared to the whole of China. Guangdong, the most significant area, has a population of around 65 million people – as much as the population of the original four tigers, but not much more than one-twentieth of the population of China (Drakakis-Smith 1992: 150).

These special economic zones have been established to attract investment, including investment from transnational corporations. Typically capitalist incentives have been used, such as a cheap and controllable labour force, as well as a good infrastructure financed by the Communist state. When the zones were first established in 1979 there were strong controls by the state (Howell 1992), but these have been relaxed in recent years as the government attempts to finance budget and trade deficits through direct foreign investment. In terms of the building of Communism, the most significant development has been the (partial) destruction of the "iron rice bowl" as some workers in the zones are not allocated work and housing by the state-controlled Labour Bureaux, but are granted short-term contracts (usually of three to five years' duration) or are even just seasonal workers (Sklair 1991b: 201; Ip 1995).

In the early 1980s, levels of foreign investment were relatively small, and concentrated in the service sector and in oil exploration. However, from the mid-1980s there was a marked shift towards manufacturing investment, most of which originated from Hong Kong and located in the neighbouring Guangdong province. Most was in labour-intensive manufacturing, and was largely an attempt by Hong Kong businesses to escape rising wage costs in the colony (Smith 1993: 91). Capital investment into China has also taken advantage of extremely long working hours and few regulations relating, for example, to safety or the environment (Smith 1993: 95–6; Sklair 1991b: 206).

Since the early 1990s, the "miracle" has really taken off and China is now the second largest recipient of foreign investment in the world, after the USA (UNCTAD 1994a: 68). Although most of this investment remains concentrated in labour-intensive activity, optimists point to the partial shift away from the zones and into the mainland, and the upgrading of industrial activity in the zones themselves (ibid.). Critics on the other hand point to the exploitative nature of labour relations in the zones, as well as questioning the view that they represent a model for the rest of China to follow (Dwyer 1993).

EOI: a preliminary assessment

The major contention of neo-liberalism is that export oriented industrialization has been more successful than ISI, both in terms of economic growth and development (Krueger 1978). Furthermore, EOI represents a model that others can follow, because its success was "almost entirely due to good policies and the ability of the people – [and] scarcely at all to favourable circumstances or a good start" (Little 1979: 4). These good policies are said to derive from a hands-off approach by the government to the economy and an outward orientation which allows countries to exercise their comparative advantages (Balassa et al. 1986).

Critics of neo-liberalism dispute these claims. In pointing to the negative aspects of EOI in East Asia – long working hours, low wages, state repression, damage to the environment, the oppression of women, etc. – some writers question the idea that East Asia *should* be a model (Bello & Rosenfeld 1992). Other writers show how the state has intervened heavily in the economy and so question the neo-liberal claim that East Asia represents a model of development led by market forces (Amsden 1989; Wade 1990). Finally, the idea that East Asia *can* be a model has been questioned on the grounds that the success of the tigers rested on specific, historically contingent factors which are not easily repeated (Hamilton 1987; Kiely 1994). These questions are examined in the next chapter.

Notes

1. The terms country and nation are used throughout the text for convenience. In fact, the national status of all four original tigers is open to question, as the text below makes clear. Briefly, South Korea is a product of a "temporary" boundary created in 1954; Taiwan is regarded by Communist China as a province, while successive governments in Taiwan have considered themselves the rightful leaders of mainland China; and Singapore and Hong Kong are city-states, the latter of which remained a British colony until reverting to Chinese rule on 1 July 1997. At the time of writing, the precise status of Hong Kong within China remains unclear, although *in theory* it will have more autonomy than other regions of China. In practice, however, this situation may be very different.
2. The argument here should not be misunderstood. Neo-liberals are largely unconcerned

with social issues such as income distribution. One of the key ideas of neo-liberalism is that "individuals have the right to be unequal". However, their point is that state interventions designed to alleviate inequalities in the distribution of income can actually make things worse than a strategy based on market forces. This point is upheld as a general principle, as well as applying specifically to income distribution. See Lal 1983: 106–7.

3. In the text I frequently refer to South Korea as "Korea", and use "Korean" to mean "South Korean". This is purely for stylistic reasons.

4. This egalitarianism should not be exaggerated. The land reform actually brought little change to the size of land-holdings, and so inequalities persisted. However, these were not as great as in many Third World nations, and did not involve highly exploitative relations with private landlords and merchants.

5. In the 1960s, Korea relied less on aid, at a time when per capita incomes were still significantly less than in some Latin American countries (Jenkins 1990).

6. In 1963 there was a general election, and in 1969 a presidential election, both won by Park. There were question marks over the conduct of both elections.

7. I use the word "potentially" because devaluations are not necessarily an easy way to increase competitiveness. I am not arguing that exchange rate devaluations simply led to an increase in export performance. Indeed, for South Korea the 1961 devaluations were a disaster for import-intensive industries such as textiles, for the simple reason that devaluations make imports more expensive (Amsden 1989: 65–6). Thus the rise in competitiveness through cheaper exports *may* be more than offset by more expensive imports.

8. See for instance Frank 1982, a classic example of denying that the peoples of the Third World are capable of any meaningful action in the world system today.

9. After 1949, the KMT continued to see itself as the legitimate ruler of China, a situation that exists (albeit with some qualifications) to this day. It was therefore technically at war with the People's Republic of China, and so martial law was imposed on the domestic population of Taiwan. It was not fully lifted until 1987.

10. This was firmly established from the outset through the systematic repression of the population, which included the massive slaughter of thousands of people between 1947 and 1950.

11. Along with state surveillance, the small size of industries enabled the KMT to exercise close control over labour. Until 1987, unions in workplaces with fewer than 30 employees were prohibited. Strikes in all sectors were also illegal.

12. The British seized Hong Kong island in 1841, and by the Treaty of Nanking of 1842, it formally became a British colony. After further military action, the British acquired Kowloon in 1860. Finally, the New Territories were leased from China on 1 July 1898.

13. Singapore was occupied by the British from 1819 (Rodan 1989: 32–3). It became part of the Federation of Malaysia in 1957. However, following tensions between the Chinese minority, which held economic power, and the Malay majority, which held political power, Singapore was separated from the Federation in 1965.

14. The People's Action Party, led by Lee Kuan Yew, won elections in 1959, but then turned on its allies in the labour movement. Union leaders were arrested and the pro-PAP National Trade Union Congress was formed. Under Lee Kuan Yew a one-party state was established with rigid state control of the population.

15. The main sources have been Indonesia, Thailand, Sri Lanka, India, Bangladesh and the Philippines. In addition the PAP has attempted to maintain an "ethnic balance" and so recruit Chinese labour from South Korea, Hong Kong, Macao and Taiwan.

16. For example, vandals are caned, people who do not flush public toilets are heavily fined, no chewing gum is allowed, long hair for men is not allowed, and the media is subject to close state surveillance (Tellmann 1995).

17. See Chapter Four.

Chapter Eight
Late industrialization assessed

In drawing on the case studies in the previous two chapters, this chapter addresses the following questions. First, what is the relationship between culture and industrialization? Second, what was the role of the state in promoting industrialization? Third, what social and political factors help to explain the conflicting development experiences of late industrializers? Fourth, how did the world market help to shape the successes and failures of late industrializers? Fifth, what was the relationship between industrialization and social development?

The chapter therefore addresses the key questions of the book – the relationship between agency, development, lateness and industrialization. It also examines the claims of neo-liberals, who imply that successful late industrialization (and development) can be achieved by policies of limited government and an open door policy which embraces the world market.

Culture and industrialization

Some writers have argued that culture is a major factor in explaining the industrial successes in East Asia, and the comparative failures in Brazil (and the rest of Latin America) and India. East Asian societies are said to be based on a Confucian[1] heritage, which promotes the values of trust, loyalty and the belief in hierarchy and stability (MacFarquhar 1980). These values are said to be more conducive to rapid industrial development than the "Ibero-Catholic" heritage in Latin America, which has encouraged an elite culture of luxury, distrust of commercial activity and a resistance to meritocracy. Thus, according to Lawrence Harrison, Latin America has been dominated by a Hispanic tradition "that is anti-democratic, anti-social, anti-progress, anti-entrepreneurial, and at least among the elite, anti-work" (cited in Fishlow 1989: 118). Hinduism in India is also said to have a negative impact on economic growth. It has been claimed that the doctrine of karma (the belief that one's actions in the present life determines status in the next) leads to a fatalism which hinders economic development (Lal 1988).

Such views are, however, based on ahistorical stereotypes. If Confucianism is the primary reason for "economic take-off" in East Asia, then why did this not happen earlier when Confucian values were greater? What of the influences of Taoism, Buddhism and Christianity in South Korea in particular? How does the Confucianism thesis deal with the differences – for instance in political systems, work organization and state–business relations – that exist between the countries in the region (Whitley 1991)? Moreover, until recently Confucianism was regarded by many Western commentators as an *obstacle* to industrial development (Hamilton & Kao 1987). Finally, Confucianism is not a homogenous belief-system, divorced from wider historical and social change and conflicting interpretations within those societies (Kyong-Dong 1994). The notion that the Sinic East Asian societies are based on a Confucianist stability, unchanging hierarchies and unquestioning loyalty simply flies in the face of their turbulent and varied recent histories.

The "negative examples" of Brazil and India are similarly based on cultural stereotypes. The notion that an Ibero-Catholic tradition hindered economic growth in Brazil is not very useful in considering the high rates of growth in that country in the miracle years. The slowdown in growth and the move into recession in the 1980s similarly cannot be explained by such omnipresent cultural factors, but instead should be regarded as a product of wider factors such as the role of the state and the world market.

By isolating supposed cultural features of "backward" societies, these approaches reduce development to cultural stereotypes divorced from any convincing analysis (or awareness) of real historical processes. Previous closely related attempts to explain development purely in terms of psychological motivation (such as the "need to achieve" or "*n*" factor – McClelland 1966) ran up against all kinds of empirical difficulties – for example Japan was deemed to have a low need to achieve whereas India's *n* achievement rate was high (Larrain 1989: 99–100).

As regards Hinduism,

> One can raise questions regarding the existence of a monolithic ideology for India; the degree to which formal religious thought affects actual behaviour given the fact that such ideas are confined to a small elite; and why the pursuit of duty must have poor economic results (for instance, it could help investment by strengthening animal spirits). (Dutt & Kim 1994: 191–2)

Arguments that Indians were less responsive than the entrepreneurial British to economic incentives in the colonial era assumes that equal opportunities existed, which was patently not the case. Evidence in the colonial period shows that Indian capital was if anything more adventurous than British capital in terms of investment, with the British concentrating industrial investment in the low-risk jute industry while Indian industrial investment focused on higher-risk textiles (Morris 1967: 598–9). The postcolonial era of sluggish industrial growth can therefore hardly be explained by impressionistic reference to an alleged conservatism in Indian society.

Culturalist analyses can therefore be criticized for their tendency to homogenize, dehistoricize and stereotype cultures.[2] For culture to form an intrinsic part of the study of contrasting development processes, it must be sensitive to both historical processes and the changing interconnections between economics, politics and culture (Worsley 1984: 60; Portes 1976). Culture must therefore be seen as "historically situated and emergent, [with] shifting and incomplete meanings and practices generated in the webs of agency and power" (Ong 1987: 2). It is in this sense that I draw on culture on pp. 127–34 below.

The state and late industrialization

As the previous two chapters showed, neo-liberal theory places great emphasis on a limited role for government in the development process. One of the key justifications for this argument is that the more successful NICs in East Asia are seen as models of good government, allowing industry to flourish in a market-friendly environment. This is contrasted with the *dirigisme* of indiscriminate ISI, where the dynamic private sector is crowded out by a suffocating state (Lal 1983). Thus, Brazil (except in the outward-oriented period from 1968 to 1974) is criticized for its attachment to "too much government" and an inward orientation, while India is regarded as a bureaucratic "rent-seeking" society where self-serving state elites profit from state regulations, and where an over-regulated industrial sector continues to stagnate in the absence of competition (Krueger 1978; Balassa et al. 1986).

Neo-liberal thought initially contrasted this critique of state-led development with the successes of East Asia and claimed that rapid economic growth in the latter "was achieved not by economic tricks, but by sensible policies based on sound neo-classical principles" (Tsiang & Wu 1985: 329). Policies of limited government intervention in the economy and an outward-oriented trade strategy were said to lead to a low level of price distortion, which thereby promotes efficiency. Prices should be set by the "natural" laws of supply and demand, unhindered by the distorting effects of government subsidies, minimum wages or price controls. In a study of the performance of thirty-one developing economies in the 1970s (World Bank 1983), it was claimed that those with low rates of price distortion and an outward orientation to the world economy tended to perform far more effectively than medium or high distortion countries. The standard neo-liberal conclusion was reached that "countries applying outward-oriented development strategies had a superior performance in terms of export, economic growth, and employment" (Balassa 1981: 16).

This version of the neo-liberal perspective was undermined in two ways. First, the evidence that there was a strong correlation between low levels of price distortion and high economic growth was challenged. As the Bank's evidence itself makes clear, price distortions can only explain about one-third of the differences in growth rates between different countries (Jenkins 1992c:

193), while some of the classifications (such as free market Chile having a high level of price distortion) are questionable. Perhaps most importantly, the evidence itself does not confirm the proposition that trade policy in itself is a major determinant of economic growth (Evans 1991: 64). The relationship between price distortion, outward orientation and economic growth may be the result of a third factor, such as structural problems which slow down economic growth (Jenkins 1992c: 194). Thus, the strong inward orientation of many of the poorest economies in the world may be a *reflection*, rather than a *cause*, of slow rates of economic growth (Singer 1988). Second, as the previous chapter showed, East Asian industrialization processes had strongly interventionist states. A wide body of literature[3] has convincingly challenged the crude neo-liberal argument that East Asia is simply a model of development based on market forces.

My concern in this section, however, is to examine a more subtle version of the neo-liberal argument, based on the notion that interventions have been more market-friendly in East Asia than elsewhere, and that this explains the success of the former and failure of the latter. This will be done through an examination of the notion of "market-friendly intervention" (World Bank 1991, 1993).

I proceed in the following way. First, I outline the concept of market-friendly intervention and show how this is used to explain different industrialization experiences. Second, I return to my case studies to see if the "successes" can be regarded as market-friendly and the "failures" as market-unfriendly. I suggest that this distinction is too rigid, and hardly takes us beyond the previous neo-liberal arguments which denied that state intervention existed in East Asia. Third, I discuss the problems associated with the neo-liberal conception of the state.

Market-friendly intervention

The basic contention of the World Bank's report *The East Asian Miracle* (1993: 5) is that the East Asian miracle economies "achieved high growth by getting the basics right". This statement represents an important qualification to the older argument (World Bank 1983: 60–63) that East Asian success was due to a low level of price distortion in the economy – in other words, high growth was a result of "getting prices right". The Bank accepts that intervention did occur in the East Asian economies – the 1993 report lists a number of factors including targeting industries, subsidies, protecting domestic import substitutes, state banking, state-led R&D, export targets and close consultation between public and private sector (World Bank 1993: 5–6). However, the report argues that these interventions meet the criteria of market-friendly, as opposed to market-distorting, intervention.[4] In this development strategy,

> the appropriate role of government is to ensure adequate investments in people, provide a competitive climate for private enterprise, keep the economy open to international trade, and maintain a stable macro-economy. (World Bank 1993: 10)

Market-friendly intervention can take one of three forms (World Bank 1991: 5):

(i) States intervene reluctantly, preferring to "let markets work".
(ii) States apply checks and balances, subjecting interventions "to the discipline of international and domestic markets".
(iii) States intervene openly, and are "subject to rules rather than to official discretion".

According to the World Bank, the interventions in East Asia conformed to these basic principles. The key to the high growth (and equitable development) can be found

> in fundamentally sound, market-oriented policies. Labor markets were allowed to work. Financial markets, although subject to more selective interventions to allocate credit, generally had low distortions and limited subsidies compared with other developing economies. Import substitution ... was quickly accompanied by the promotion of exports and duty-free admission of imports for exporters. The result was limited differences between international relative prices and domestic relative prices ... Market forces and competitive pressures guided resources into activities that were consistent with comparative advantage and, in the case of labor-intensive exports, laid the foundation for learning international best practice and subsequent industrial upgrading. (World Bank 1993: 325)

So, to summarize: the earlier neo-liberal view (Balassa et al. 1986) that East Asian success was a product of sound policies of limited government has been altered so that proper recognition is given to the fact that the state was interventionist. The new view accepts the reality of state intervention, but argues that this did not fundamentally alter a policy of industrial development through market forces. State regulations were either insignificant or they cancelled each other out, and so the outcome was the emergence of an industrial structure that would have emerged through market forces anyway. This argument is similar to that proposed by Berger (1979: 64) who argued that

> the crux of the Korean example is that the active interventionist attitude of the state has been aimed at applying moderate incentives which are very close to the relative prices of products and factors that would prevail in a situation of free trade ... It is as though the government were "simulating" a free market.

Such interventions are contrasted with the distorting activities of states in much of the developing world (World Bank 1993: 351).

Assessing the concept of market-friendly intervention

The main problem with the World Bank's report is its tendency to isolate specific examples of state intervention, and to then show how these were counter-balanced by further interventions. For example, in South Korea and Taiwan the potentially damaging policy of import substitution was said to be cancelled out by policies of export promotion, with the result that a market-conforming structure emerged despite the interventions (World Bank 1993: 292–316). However, the effects of interventions cannot be adequately assessed in this way, and the effect of any particular state regulation must be analyzed through its impact on the economy as a whole. Singh (1994: 17) makes this point clear, arguing that the World Bank approach

> overlooks the effects of industrial policy on a country's balance of payments and its long-term rate of growth of domestic demand. By confining its attention only to the supply side effect of productivity growth and technical change ... *the East Asian Miracle* hypothesizes that "spillovers" of these activities will be confined only to the favoured sectors or their close sub-sectors within the two-digit industrial classification which they have analysed. However, to the extent that industrial policy helps to relieve the balance-of-payments constraint, most sectors will benefit from higher rates of growth of production and hence productivity ... and not just the favoured sectors. In other words, the spillovers will be universal.

Furthermore, the Bank's argument (1993: 316) rests on the mistaken assumption that the textiles industry was not protected by the state. In fact, despite the labour-intensive nature of this particular industry, it was still subject to heavy state protection from Japanese competition (Amsden 1989: 143). Therefore, the existence of a large textiles industry "is not proof that industrial policy did not work but in fact suggests that it worked really well, as this was one of the most heavily promoted sectors" (Chang 1995: 214).

The argument that protectionism was largely irrelevant because it was counter-balanced by the setting of export targets is similarly problematic. This claim ignores how protectionism alleviated potential balance of payments constraints and helped to promote technical change and hence productivity growth through the linking of import controls to export targets (Singh 1994: 20).

Similarly, the World Bank recognizes that South Korea and Taiwan were restrictive in their policies towards direct foreign investment, but argues that this was counteracted by a policy of openness to foreign technology acquisition (World Bank 1993: 21). However, as Lall (1994: 651) argues,

> There is no analysis in the study ... of the effects of different modes of technology import on the industrial development: different forms of openness were perceived by these countries to have different implications for the development of their own innovative capabilities, and this formed a crucial element of their industrial strategies.

In particular, in Korea and Taiwan the state policy of guiding the market was achieved far more easily by a reliance on domestic rather than foreign firms, and it facilitated the growth of substantial research and development activities[5] (Singh 1994: 21–2). These developments were clearly crucial to the ability of Korea and Taiwan to "unpack", utilize and build upon imported technologies, and in the long run to become internationally competitive and break into export markets (Lall 1994: 651). This contrasts sharply with the alleged failures of import substituters in Latin America (though not in India) which, in terms of its open door policy to foreign investment, was if anything more "market-friendly" than Korea and Taiwan (Jenkins 1990: 50).

Some "market-unfriendly" technological upgradings, such as Korea's heavy and chemical industry (HCI) drive, are recognized by the Bank. In this case however, the non-market-conforming interventions are criticized for their costs in terms of support for inefficient and expensive industries (World Bank 1993: 309). Closer empirical scrutiny of these costs shows that in fact the most targeted heavy industries (chemicals and machinery) accounted for a lower share of outstanding non-performing loans than outstanding total loans, and that 60 per cent of all non-performing loans were accounted for by the construction industry's over-investment in the Middle East (Amsden & Euh 1990). Furthermore, the drive can hardly be considered a disaster when one considers that by the early 1980s, heavy industries accounted for most of the country's export earnings (Amsden 1994: 631). It was in this period that the Korean economy was substantially liberalized, but only the most wishful of neo-liberal thinkers would attempt to argue that it was this process (which only began in 1981) which led to the competitiveness of Korean heavy industry. The liberalization of trade did go hand in hand with the expansion of heavy industries in the 1980s, but the *causal* factors were those market-unfriendly policies of state targeting and technical upgrading in the 1970s. Moreover, the Korean state has continued to protect high-technology sectors that would otherwise be undermined by foreign competition (Amsden 1993: 206–10).

Finally, the World Bank (1993: 266) argues that

In East Asia, more than elsewhere, governments resisted the temptation to intervene in the labor market to counter outcomes unpalatable in the short run to particular groups ... A relatively high level of efficiency in the allocation of labor was achieved by allowing wages and employment to be determined largely by the interaction of those supplying and those demanding labor services, rather than by government legislation, public sector leadership, or union pressure.

This view rests on the belief that there is a "natural" price for labour determined by a balance between labour demand and supply, which was criticized in Chapter Five. The East Asian scenario has been contrasted with Latin American labour markets, where "minimum wage legislation and union pressure raised wages above market-clearing levels" (Balassa et al. 1986: 134). In fact labour market distortions were low for a number of Latin American countries (Jenkins 1990: 45). Neo-liberals once again *assume* rather than *demonstrate* causality in their assertion that wages were determined by the laws of supply and demand. In Korea and Taiwan low wages were partly a product of state repression of labour (Deyo 1989). Moreover, the absence of minimum wage legislation or national collective bargaining agreements does not mean that state intervention in labour markets has been absent (Chang & You 1993). In the supposedly laissez-faire economies of Hong Kong and Singapore, the state has played a crucial role in regulating labour costs through access to cheap public housing, health-care and food (Schiffer 1991; Castells 1992; and Chapter Seven).

These examples show the inadequacies of the World Bank report, and its stubborn refusal to make a bold move beyond the neo-liberal paradigm. As Kwon (1994: 635) argues, the report

> is almost a textbook example of neoclassicists visibly confused but too proud to admit their failure – having been so quick to blame government for economic failures in the past, they are now reluctant to admit a positive role for government in a successful economy.

Such confusion leads to faulty logic in places and a number of contradictory claims. For example, the Bank (1993: 6) argues that

> It is very difficult to establish statistical links between growth and a specific intervention, and even more to establish causality. Because we cannot know what would have happened in the absence of a specific policy, it is difficult to test whether interventions increased growth rates.

However, this does not stop the Bank from using such a methodology in order to try to establish a causal link between growth and *non-intervention* (World Bank 1993: 325; Amsden 1994: 628). Thus, in arguing that industrial policy created a market-conforming industrial structure, the report concludes that industrial policy was ineffective. But as Amsden (1994: 629) states, "As this test is formulated, industrial policy cannot win: if it fulfills neo-classical expectations, it is 'ineffective'; if it violates them, it is inefficient."

One final, and most important, point must be made about the market-friendly approach. The basic argument is that interventions were largely irrelevant in East Asia because they were market-conforming, and therefore "relative price distortions were limited and indeed smaller than in most other developing countries" (World Bank 1993: 351). Of course this assertion can be subject to exactly the same criticisms as that of the price distortion index in the 1983 *World Development Report*, discussed above. But even leaving that aside, the evidence in the 1993 report can be used against the Bank's own arguments. This is because the Bank (1993: 301) recognizes that the degree of high outward orientation and low price distortion varies between the Asian NICs – Hong Kong, Malaysia, Singapore, Indonesia and Thailand have a low rate of price distortion, whereas Japan, Korea, Taiwan and China do not do so well. In fact, these latter countries actually rank *below* supposedly inefficient import-substituting industrializers such as Brazil, India, Mexico, Pakistan and Venezuela. Interestingly, the report only comments on the variations within the Asian NICs, rather than the fact that the Bank's evidence on prices implies that Brazil and India are more market-friendly than Korea and Taiwan – *even though the report is supposed to prove the opposite.*

An alternative approach is to completely break with the neo-liberal paradigm and its rigid "ISI bad, EOI good" dichotomy. One needs to recognize that the state played an active role in promoting industrialization, and in so doing deliberately "got prices wrong". In South Korea in the 1960s, many firms exported at a loss, including those in labour-intensive sectors such as textiles (Amsden 1989: ch. 6). As the previous chapter showed, losses were recovered through sales in the protected domestic market, but this reward was only granted to the most successful exporters – these sales were tied to performance standards set by the government. Hamilton (1986: 83) claims that in fact the average deviation of production prices from actual prices increased from 7.8 per cent in 1966 to 11.8 per cent in 1978. Such figures suggest that state manipulation of prices was far from market-friendly or irrelevant, and in fact was vital to Korea's export success. "Getting prices wrong" was therefore a major component of Korea's (and Taiwan's) transition to successful NIC status. The neo-liberal critique is narrowly concerned with the (static) "allocative efficiency" of getting prices right, and therefore lacks an account of the *dynamics* of the process of changing comparative advantage.[6]

A further result of such an approach is a failure to properly assess the results of import substitution strategies. As Schmitz (1984: 6) argues:

It is remarkable how little ... industrial performance has been investigated from a *dynamic* perspective. Most accounts remind us of the importance of learning-by-doing and external economies to industrial growth; but in the actual evaluation these considerations simply evaporate.

Individual sectors may thus be inefficient but "taken together, produce a macro-economically efficient result through developing linkages and extern-alities" (Colman & Nixson 1986: 296). This point applies not only to industrial policies in the East Asian NICs but to the "inefficient" industries in Brazil, India and elsewhere.[7] ISI can therefore be a useful strategy in preparing nations to later break into export markets (Singer & Alizadeh 1989: 323). Indeed, from the late 1960s/early 1970s, there were significant elements of *convergence* between East Asian EOI and Brazilian ISI, as the latter focused more on breaking into export markets and the former promoted a process of ISI based on heavy and chemical industries (Ellison & Gereffi 1990: 382).

This close connection between ISI and EOI can also be seen in the case of the most successful of the second-tier Asian NICs, Thailand. From the mid-1980s to the early 1990s, Thailand experienced an annual average rate of growth of exports of 30 per cent, and GDP grew by 9.2 per cent a year (Dixon 1995: 216). This manufacturing-led boom, undertaken at a time when the country was undergoing a number of structural adjustment policies, has led to claims that Thailand represents a new model of neo-liberal development (Handley 1991: 34–5). However, a careful consideration of the evidence shows that most of the structural adjustment policies were either limited in their implementation, or not carried out until well after the boom was under way (Sahasakul 1991; Dixon 1995). Whilst economic growth can partly be attributed to the relocation of labour-intensive manufacturing by first-tier Asian NICs, a vital role was also played by the utilization of excess capacity for export when regional and global conditions became more favourable for exporters. This excess capacity arose out of the expansion of heavily protected industries in a period of recession – thus, Thailand's improvement in its export position from 1986 arose partly out of the development of domestic industries that had been protected by import-substitution policies (Dixon 1995: 222). A similar case could also be made for Malaysian and Indonesian industrialization (Amsden 1992: 64–5; Jomo 1993: 297–300).

Neo-liberalism and the state

It is not surprising that neo-liberals argue that state intervention in East Asia was largely irrelevant, because the assumption that state intervention *must be inefficient* is built into their theoretical system. At the heart of the neo-liberal critique of the state is the contention that state officials *always* act in a self-interested way. These officials are said to expand the activity of the state for their own good, rather than the interest of society. Such self-interested activity is not necessarily harmful if the state adopts a role of limited government intervention in the economy, but problems arise as soon as it intervenes in the economic sphere. State intervention incurs costs when resources are diverted into unproductive activities by companies, and these are a product of monopoly "rents" created by state intervention. Such rents occur when an individual secures a payment above the value of the opportunity costs of the resources. So for instance an entrepreneur may innovate in order to capture a monopoly rent. The neo-liberal argument is that in this case, there is no problem because in the market economy there is competition and so the rent is secured through productive activity. Thus, as competitors enter this particular sector, competition will drive prices down, and so individual and social benefit coincides. However, in the state sector rents are created artificially, and so the resources spent on capturing them may be worthwhile from an individual point of view, but from a social point of view are wasted on unproductive economic activity. So, for example, import controls will lead to unproductive lobbying activity aimed at winning access to an import license, rather than the expansion of industrial (or other) output (Krueger 1974). Thus, rent-seeking in the "unrestricted" competitive market sector is healthy from both an individual and social point of view, while rent-seeking in the restricted monopolistic public sector is healthy from an individual point of view, but not for society as a whole (Buchanan 1980: 8).

Such a viewpoint represents a clear attempt by neo-liberals to explain politics, as well as economics, by sole reference to the self-interested, utility-maximizing individual. The best policy option is to secure the most effective context for such behaviour to operate efficiently, and this is one in which competitive market forces are allowed to flourish by a "nightwatchman state" (Buchanan 1986).

This perspective fails to come to terms with the experience of both the state and industrial development in East Asia (and Brazil and India). Clearly, there are many examples of unproductive rent-seeking activity throughout the world, but the neo-liberal argument is far stronger than this. It is that the state acts in its own interest *irrespective of time and place* (Toye 1991). Taken to its logical conclusion, such a view provides no justification for *any* state. As Evans (1995: 25) argues:

How does such a state arise out of individual maximizers? It is hard to explain why, if office-holders are primarily interested in individual rents, they do not all "free-lance" ... Neo-utilitarian logic provides little insight into what constrains individual incumbents to work together as a collectivity at all ... [S]trict adherence to a neo-utilitarian logic makes the existence of the state as a collective actor difficult to explain and the nightwatchman state a theoretical impossibility.

Given that the self-interested model of human behaviour cannot adequately explain the existence of the state, it logically follows that the motives for specific state interventions may not be simply self-interested.[8] In fact, it could be argued that the state has an active and productive role to play, as the East Asian examples above confirm. In terms of industrial policy, the case for state intervention rests on the related grounds that "free markets" are not cost-free, and that state promotion of industry may be productive.

First, as Lipton (1991: 27) points out, any policy based on promoting market forces "requires that states bear much of the cost of market development. Just as there is no free lunch, so there is no free market; markets are expensive." Neo-liberal analysis of the cost of rent-seeking in the public sector is misleading because it compares the costs of state activity with an implicit and purely hypothetical model of a costless market. As Chang (1994: 48) argues,

In the real world, *both state intervention and market transaction are costly*. Therefore the comparison must be between the costs of allocating resources through market transactions ... and the costs of allocating resources through state intervention.

Markets (and utility-maximizing behaviour) do not exist prior to particular social institutions and regulations, and the construction of these is not a costless exercise. For example, there is the expense of establishing and defining the rights of individuals, which involves costly processes of information collection, processing, bargaining, contract-writing and policing (Chang 1994: 47). Moreover, industrial production in capitalist economies is characterized by strategic uncertainty, as one firm attempts to second-guess the strategies of other firms operating in the same sector. This situation leads to the dangers of under-investment (as potential investors fear a price war and so fail to invest) or over-investment (as investors wrongly believe that competitors would not invest in this sector and secure economies of scale) in a particular sector. It is at this point that "the state can intervene in this industry to assure optimal entry by guaranteeing potential entrants that there will not be more than optimal entry" (Chang 1994: 66). For instance the state can restrict entry into a particular sector, or regulate capacity expansion (as in Japan's negotiated industry-wide investment plans in the 1960s – cf. Dore 1986).

Perhaps even more important is the relationship between industrial policy and long-term technological development, which ultimately determines the productivity and competitiveness of a particular economy. Given the nature of the technology involved in modern industrial production,[9] resources tend to be "locked up" and specific to current uses. For instance, the technology involved in steel production cannot quickly be shifted to the production of computers. Using less specific or "tied" assets may increase short-term flexibility but this may be at the cost of a commitment to long-term higher-productivity sectors, and therefore long-term economic growth. Similarly, there may be a conflict between individual and national flexibility – for example, the liberalization of capital flows makes capital flight much easier. As Chang (1995: 213) argues,

> there is an inherent conflict between short-run and long-run flexibilities, as short-run flexibilities may discourage productivity-enhancing investments, which are likely to increase long-run flexibility by providing a larger resource base and increased technological capabilities ... [I]n a world which has more than one national economy and assets with different mobilities, allowing individuals total flexibility may lead to a reduction in the flexibility of the national economy, because it may reduce the resource base and hamper the growth of productivity in the national economy.

There can be no clearer account of the rationale behind effective industrial policy in both South Korea and Taiwan, in which the state played a leading role in promoting the upgrading of technologies, and therefore productivity and economic growth (Amsden 1992). The World Bank's claim that industrial policy was largely ineffective is based on the assumption that a similarly efficient industrial structure would have emerged anyway. But this is just an assumption, which itself is based on the *a priori* belief that market forces allocate resources efficiently and promote economic growth. As Amsden (1994: 629) points out, "it is quite possible that if the Bank had determined East Asia's overall growth strategy, the outcome might have been a lot worse – rather than as good as or better than – what did happen". For instance, the absence of capital controls might have led to massive capital flight, and the absence of import controls might have led to domestic industry being swallowed up by foreign competition. In this situation Korea and Taiwan would still be exercising their "comparative advantages" in primary products, and thereby experiencing far lower rates of growth.

The experience of countries that have experimented with structural adjustment programmes[10] in the 1980s and 1990s clearly shows that the state cannot be by-passed. Assessing the impact of adjustment policies is a far from straightforward process, but the neo-liberal view that adjustment policies would promote long-term economic growth (and social development) has proved to be too optimistic.[11] Moreover, the theoretical basis of structural adjustment programmes is weak (Mosley 1994; Kiely 1995c: ch. 6), as it rests on the unfounded premiss that producers in the Third World can compete on a relatively equal basis with established producers in the First World. As Chang (1995: 215) argues,

this assumption ignores the fact that there are formidable entry barriers for developing countries attempting to move up the ladder of the international division of labour – because of cumulative causations in technical progress ... imperfect domestic and international financial markets ... and a lack of marketing skills and infrastructure, and so on.

Given these disadvantages, it is not surprising that industries were heavily protected in South Korea and Taiwan, and that exports initially made a loss that was only compensated for by the state.

Thus, it is not a question of the *quantity* of state intervention, but rather the *quality* – "[t]he appropriate question is not 'how much', but 'what kind' " (Evans 1995: 10). The 1993 World Bank Report appears to accept this point, but only insofar as interventions are deemed market friendly or unfriendly. As I have argued, this approach is not helpful – it is based on the *a priori* assumption that a state-guided industrial policy must either be inefficient or irrelevant. Instead, we need to address the question of why some state interventions have been more effective (in terms of promoting industrial growth) than others. As Seddon & Belton-Jones (1995: 333) put it:

It is one thing to emphasise the importance of state intervention, of strategic and selective planning or "guidance" as well as the capacity to shift policy when required ... It is quite another to explain the nature of "the state" and the conditions which enable it to act in such a fashion; and yet another to explain why some dirigiste states are successful both in encouraging policy adaptability and in promoting economic develop-ment, while others are not.

Such a task moves us on to the question of the role of the state, and its relationship to other social agents in the process of industrialization.

Industrialization and agency: social and political factors

This section is concerned with the role of agency in the process of late industrialization, and focuses on: (i) the state and its relationship with the dominant classes in civil society; (ii) land reform and agrarian–industry relations; and (iii) (exploited) classes and gender relations. Finally, I make some con-cluding remarks concerning the relationship between agency and contingency in industrialization processes.

The state and "civil society"

Some writers (Johnson 1982; White 1988; Wade 1990) have convincingly argued that some states are more inclined to promote industrial (and other) development than others. These developmental states are defined as states

whose politics have concentrated sufficient power, autonomy and capacity
at the centre to shape, pursue and encourage the achievement of explicit
developmental objectives, whether by establishing and promoting the
conditions and direction of economic growth, or by organising it directly,
or a varying combination of both. (Leftwich 1995: 401)

Leftwich has argued that such states are characterized by a developmentally-
oriented elite, relative autonomy from vested interests, a competent bureaucracy, a relatively weak civil society, the consolidation of state power prior to
the development of powerful economic interests, and the relative weakness of
civil rights (Leftwich 1994: 377–81; 1995: 405–19).

This approach has done a useful job in undermining neo-liberal approaches
that minimize the role of the state, but it is not without its weaknesses. Most
important, there is no guarantee that state autonomy and a weak civil society
will produce a developmental state. In fact such conditions are more likely to
produce a state which *impedes* economic transformation. Evans (1995: 44) has
referred to Zaire as a predator state, based on the "extract[ion of] . . . large
amounts of otherwise investible surplus while providing . . . little in the way of
'collective goods' ". In this case there is a strong state in the sense that it has
despotic power which it wields over civil society, but at the same time there is
little prospect for economic transformation without radical upheaval.

Instead of providing a rigid binary opposition of a strong state and weak civil
society, a more useful approach is to examine the way in which state autonomy
is "embedded" within particular social relations (Zhao & Hall 1994; Evans
1995; Weiss & Hobson 1995: ch. 6). Seddon & Belton-Jones (1995: 355) have
usefully summarized this approach:

the "relative autonomy of the state" and insulation from the immediate
pressures of the political arena do not necessarily mean a relatively low
level of interaction with different sections of civil society, or even with
specific pressure and interest groups. What they imply is a situation in
which the government and bureaucracy maintain effective control of the
commanding heights of decision-making and the policy-making process
and are able to manage the various competing special interests in such a
way that policy adaptability is maximized. The emphasis is less on
"relative autonomy" and more on the forms of control that enable "the
state" – the government and the bureaucracy – to intervene effectively.

For example, state–society relations in South Korea have been characterized by
a particular alliance between the bureaucracy, big business and to some extent
the rural sector (Moon & Kim 1996: 144). As Wade (1990: 320–21) has argued,

the Korean government has from time to time aggressively orchestrated the
activities of "private" firms. Sometimes it has directly ordered them to do
certain things and not do others. At the same time, its policies strengthened
some of those firms, helping the emergence of very large conglomerates
whose strength subsequently reduced both the government's leadership
potential as well as the economic advantages of government leadership.

On the other hand, big business played an active role in the formulation of plans for industrial development and it was the chaebols which were ultimately responsible for industrial transformation, which was the basis for the (never unquestioned) legitimacy of the Park regime (Evans 1995: 53).

In Taiwan the state played a more "hands-off" role in its relationship with the private sector, and representatives of the latter played only a limited role in policy formulation (Wade 1990: 295). Nevertheless, there were important network links between public and private sectors based on mutual interdependence. The case of textiles (supposedly a sector developed on the basis of static comparative advantage) provides a telling example of mutual interdependence. In the early 1950s, the state provided a set of incentives which made it difficult for the private sector to ignore, such as raw cotton supplies, working capital requirements and guaranteed purchase of products, as well as restricting both local entry and imports (Wade 1990: 79). At the same time the state never became the "prisoner" of a powerful industrial capitalist class content on maintaining oligopolistic rents (as in Latin America) as the new capitalists were progressively subject to selective regulations, such as making export quotas dependent on the quality of goods and diminishing protection (Evans 1995: 57).

Such cases of mutually reinforcing, economically dynamic, state–society relations arose out of the peculiar histories of the two countries, and the role of land reform and aid in boosting the potential for later industrial development were crucial (as discussed in Chapter Seven). In particular, the land reforms defeated powerful landowners, potential opponents of industrial development. They also created a particularly effective relationship between the state and agriculture, which had enormous implications for industrial development (see below). There was also strong ideological support for industrialization as powerful social actors in both Korea and Taiwan supported the militarization of society, as protection against the "Communist threat".

The comparative effectiveness[12] of state–society relations in Korea and Taiwan can be contrasted with mixed results elsewhere. In India the effectiveness of planning has been hindered by the continued domination of some propertied classes that lack an interest in structural transformation of the economy. Bardhan (1984: 61) has argued that the Indian state is dominated by three social classes – a weak industrial capitalist class, a class of rich farmers and a class of state bureaucrats. The relationship between these three groups is based on a mixture of compromise and conflict. Weak industrialists have relied on the state for permits and licenses while the state bureaucracy has a close relationship with rich farmers through administered prices, trade restrictions, and the distribution of credit and fertilizers (Bardhan 1984: 58–9). Industrial capital was in a weak position *vis-à-vis* the state because of the early development of the latter and late development of the former. However, it was precisely this relationship, with all its contradictions, that was necessary for the development of industry in India. As Evans (1995: 68) argues, "[w]hat private capital lost in autonomy they gained in security, but their gain was at the expense of the overall dynamism of the industrial sector". In particular, the development of infrastructure and the increase in domestic savings was successfully promoted through the state – even some neo-liberals concede this point (Lal 1988: 237).

Similarly in Brazil state–society relations have led to the promotion of elements of dynamism combined with the maintenance of uneven industrial growth. The early development of the state, along with the preservation of a powerful class of rural landowners, ensured that industrial classes remained largely dependent on the state. Brazil followed a pattern that is found in much of Latin America whereby

> enormous state apparatuses were, and are still, controlled by parties of a predominantly clientelistic or populistic character, or more generally by forces (civilian or military) whose interests of self-preservation and expansion systematically contradict requirements for the expanded reproduction of capitalism. . . . (Mouzelis 1994: 142)

At the same time, these institutions have not completely militated against the development of *some* close institutional–industrial ties, and some cases of (relative) industrial success, such as the domestically-owned computer industry (Hewitt 1992: 92; Evans 1995).

In South-East Asia the role of the state has varied. The Malaysian economy has had a high rate of state intervention. A period of import-substitution from 1957 laid the basis for rapid export-oriented industrial growth in the 1970s. The early 1980s saw a further period of import-substitution in heavy industry, albeit with mixed results (Edwards 1995: 240–43). At the same time, a major factor behind government intervention has been the question of ethnicity.[13] As Jomo (1993: 297) argues,

> It is widely believed that the ethnic Malay-dominated government has actually favoured industrialization under foreign transnational auspices in preference to the likely alternative of domestic ethnic Chinese dominance. Thus, ethnic obsessions may have undermined the most feasible and viable options for industrialization under domestic auspices.

In Indonesia ethnicity has also played a role in state–society relations, but more important has been the development of an alliance of senior state bureaucrats, a "client bourgeoisie", and the oil companies and manufacturing industries which lead the process of capital accumulation (Robison 1986).

These brief examples show the variety of state–society relations and how these are likely to lead to divergent industrial capitalisms.[14] This can be illustrated further by examining relations between agriculture and industry.

Land reform and agrarian–industrial relations

The relationship between industry and agriculture has been the subject of great controversy, as earlier chapters have shown. Many growth-based theorists of development in the 1950s (e.g. Lewis 1950) argued that it was essential to promote manufacturing growth because of its status as a productivity leader in the economy. The neo-classical resurgence has renewed the argument that there is no need for a sectoral distinction to be made, as capital can easily move between industry and agriculture. The market mechanism is therefore propagated as the institution which will lead to an efficient allocation of resources between the two sectors (Schiff & Valdes 1992).[15]

The problem with the latter view, as well as some versions of the growth-based argument, is that it neglects the issue of productivity (see also the discussion of industrial policy above). Manufacturing is important in its role as an "engine of growth" for the rest of the economy.[16] However, simply focusing on industry at the expense of agriculture is not necessarily the answer.[17] The resource flow from agriculture to industry will in part depend on the productivity of the former sector. A strategy which simply focuses on taxing agriculture may not be effective if the agricultural sector is stagnant. The most effective developing economies are therefore those in which there is a *dynamic complementarity* between the two sectors. As Karshenas (1995: 23) argues,

in a technologically progressive agricultural sector where new investment and increased input use is combined with fast rates of productivity, the complementary relationship between agricultural and industrial growth is most pronounced.

In the cases discussed, both Korea and especially Taiwan appear to fit the case of dynamic complementarity. A surplus outflow from agriculture was achieved through state regulation of terms of trade, fixed prices and higher taxation for agriculture (Wade 1983; Karshenas 1995). At the same time, the squeeze on agriculture did not hinder productivity growth, as it benefited from new technology, credit and a well developed infrastructure. Moreover, the land reforms in the 1940s and 1950s ensured that such benefits were distributed amongst most of the peasantry.

In the case of Brazil, the terms of trade have generally been fixed against food crops and domestic agriculture has provided some cheap food for industrial workers (Bernstein 1992a: 41–2). Although there have been some significant increases in sectors such as cotton, coffee and soybeans, productivity remains generally low and expansion has often been the result of an increase in the areas under cultivation rather than of technological innovation (Goodman & Redclift 1981: 137–8). Such low productivity, combined with the heavy concentration of land ownership, led to the generally sluggish growth of the agrarian sector and so a low-productivity, impoverished agriculture exists side-by-side with an unevenly developed industrial sector. These factors have paved the way for mass urbanization and the development of a massive informal sector.

In the case of India, agriculture has acted as an effective drain on potential resources available to industry.[18] In the 1950s low productivity in agriculture meant that surpluses were too small to act as a stimulus to industrial production, a situation that was exacerbated by rising food prices in the early 1960s (Bernstein 1992b: 56). As Chapter Six showed, the impact of the Green Revolution was uneven, but even where it led to productivity increases these were not sufficient to make up for the inflow of resources into agriculture. From 1964 to 1970, the terms of trade between the two sectors were more favourable to agriculture, a policy consciously designed by central and local government in order to make the new technological inputs of the Green Revolution affordable. The result was a rise in (some) farmers' incomes and a consequent rise in consumer spending goods far greater than the increase in output in agriculture. Thus Karshenas (1995: 202) explains that agriculture acted as a net drain on resources

> due to the extremely low tax burden on the agricultural incomes relative to the incomes generated in other sectors of the economy, and particularly the decline in the tax burden in the latter half of the 1960s, when agricultural incomes in real terms were rising due to the terms of trade effect.

These brief examples show that the relationship between agriculture and industry is more complex than a simple zero-sum game between the two sectors. Agriculture may be a burden but this does not necessarily prevent a process of sustained industrialization, as the examples of India and Brazil show.[19] However, a best-case scenario is one in which the two sectors complement each other, and efficiency is thereby raised in both sectors.

Class and gender

One of the stereotypical myths concerning the East Asian region is that the workforce is more passive than its Latin American or Indian counterparts. In fact, as Deyo (1989) has convincingly shown, all of the four tigers have witnessed major working-class mobilizations, and Taiwanese and particularly South Korean labour have demonstrated a strong capacity for militancy, despite state repression (Bello & Rosenfeld 1992). The related argument that the success of the East Asian NICs has rested on state repression of labour (Frank 1981) similarly fails to account for labour resistance, and in particular labour's successes in winning large wage increases and some political liberalization (Berry & Kiely 1993).

Whilst it is the case that labour may have had more influence over the state in Latin America than in East Asia (although one should not confuse populist appeals to the masses with genuinely pro-labour policies), this is largely a product of historical-structural factors. The greater concentration of larger industries and earlier organization of labour movements in urban centres is a far more convincing explanation for the relative subordination of East Asian labour than an appeal to a timeless cultural tradition. Moreover, new waves of unionization and militancy in Taiwan and especially South Korea undermine the myth of Asian docility (Deyo 1989).

Some suggestive contrasts can also be made concerning the relationship between industrialization and gender relations. The more capital-intensive industrialization processes in India and Brazil effectively marginalized most women from manufacturing employment in the formal sector. During the years of the Brazilian miracle women's industrial employment increased, but their share relative to men's declined. In 1970, at the height of the miracle, women constituted only 12 per cent of industrial workers (Pearson 1992: 228). In India women's share of industrial employment has remained fairly constant – the 1987 figure of 9.1 per cent was exactly the same as the figure in 1951 (Pearson 1992: 232). In the East Asian NICs, however, female employment in manufacturing has been much higher. The 1987 figures for South Korea, Hong Kong and the Philippines were all between 40 and 50 per cent (Pearson 1992: 232).

These figures to a large extent represent the fact that women are traditionally employed in more labour-intensive manufacturing operations, such as those more commonly utilized in the East Asian export industries – although of course this is now changing as some of the East Asian NICs have successfully upgraded their technology and Brazil and India have attempted to introduce labour-intensive export sectors as part of the process of structural adjustment. Such practices show that, at least in the initial stages of East Asian industrialization, the employment of women played a crucial role in securing a competitive export sector. Women in India and Brazil have also largely been restricted to labour-intensive sectors, although in these cases this has meant work in the urban informal sector and household (Young 1993: ch. 6). Women are often in the most vulnerable position in these cases, as they suffer from the dual burden of informal work in the cash economy combined with unpaid domestic labour, and the influence of sexist ideology (Hensman 1996).

The industrial employment of women has thus largely been contingent on the promotion of a particular industrial strategy. This does not mean, however, that women employed in the formal sector are necessarily in a better position than those working in other sectors. One needs to move beyond a simple cost–benefit analysis,[20] in which women are said to be better off because of the independence of a wage. As Pearson (1994: 349) argues:

in this situation women are not of course achieving equity alongside men. The construction of this labour force is – as ever – gendered – and women are the targeted group because social relations and socially constructed characteristics and skills make women the most profitable workers. . . .

What needs to be addressed, therefore, is how "actually existing industrializations" have (in some cases) led to a recomposition (Elson & Pearson 1981) of gender inequalities, both within and beyond the workplace. Thus, women in labour-intensive factories face a gendered hierarchy, in which women are largely concentrated in the lower-paid jobs, and face few prospects for promotion, and where women's skills (such as sewing) are generally taken for granted, when in fact they are the product of socially constructed gender roles (Phillips & Taylor 1980). Moreover, gender relations outside of the workplace may impact on women's industrial employment. In Taiwan and Hong Kong "young women are frequently pressured to seek and remain in factory employment in order to meet family goals such as the education of sons, rather than to follow their own choices in obtaining education or leaving the workforce to get married" (Pearson 1994: 355; cf. Cheng & Hsiung 1992). In some cases women may be the main wage earner within a family but this does not guarantee them control of the income generated from the employment (Elson & Pearson 1981: 99). Neither does it necessarily relieve women of the dual burden of paid industrial work and unpaid domestic labour.

These processes are not inevitable however, and the character of gender relations depends on a number of contingent factors. In South Korea technological upgrading has not benefited women workers, and they remain largely confined to the lower-paid, labour-intensive jobs. In Singapore on the other hand, the government has actively encouraged women to stay in the labour market through state subsidies for childcare and the conscious promotion of female training. As a result, women have become an established part of the labour market, in skilled, professional work as well as the traditional unskilled labour-intensive sectors. This more favourable outcome was not a result of a more enlightened policy by the government, but was instead a response to a tight labour market situation. The city-state faced a shortage of skilled labour in the context of a conscious attempt to upgrade the economy into high-technology industries and services (Pearson 1992: 239–43). In this respect, industrialization in Singapore has led to a (partial) *decomposition* of unequal gender relations.[21]

Social and political agency, and the rejection of models

What should be clear from my discussion in this section is that while the East Asian region may be more successful than India or Brazil, it can hardly constitute a model for others to follow. This is because the social and political agents that exist in East Asia do not necessarily exist elsewhere. Industrialization in Taiwan, South Korea and so on rested on contingent social factors particular to the history of those countries. Thus, recognizing the importance of a developmental state, a particular configuration of state–business and state–labour relations, and the success of land reform, is one thing. It is quite another for other regions or countries to repeat these processes – this will depend on the strengths and weaknesses of particular social forces within a country, and their ability to change existing power relations (Hamilton 1987; Byres 1991; Kiely 1994).

Late industrialization: the influence of the world market

Neo-liberalism contends that the world economy will tend towards equilibrium if market forces are allowed to operate unhindered by state regulations. Nation-states will exercise their comparative advantages and thereby concentrate production in those sectors in which they are cheap, efficient and competitive. Thus, as we have seen, successful East Asian industrialization is considered to be a product of the region's comparative advantage in cheap labour. This comparative advantage can only be exercised through a process of more or less open competition – as opposed to the protectionism of ISI (Balassa et al. 1986).

As an analysis of the reality of the world market, this perspective is clearly inadequate. As Chapter Five made clear, the global market does not tend towards equilibrium. It is based on unequal competition which itself is a product of unequal labour productivities, which themselves result from the concentration of mass production techniques, research and development, developed infrastructures and established markets in the First World. For these reasons Third World (and other) producers face unequal competition in terms of breaking into global markets (the "barriers to entry" discussed above), but also in terms of competing with overseas producers within their own domestic markets. It is for these reasons that states adopt industrial policies – to promote exporters attempting to break into the world market and to protect domestic producers from cheap imports produced by established overseas companies. In practice then, advanced technology (even in more labour-intensive sectors such as textiles) will more often than not out-compete cheap labour.[22] Late industrialization is more difficult "precisely because markets have been working, not failing" (Amsden 1992: 59).

In the cases discussed, *all* the countries concerned attempted to protect domestic producers from the constraints of unequal competition – in this sense, *none* of them adopted their (static) comparative advantage. Where they differed was in their attempts to take advantage of the opportunities generated by the world economy. Singapore and Hong Kong benefited from the peculiarities of their location, while South Korea and Taiwan benefited from large amounts of US aid and relatively open access to the lucrative US market. India was also a major beneficiary of aid. Brazil, on the other hand, attempted to draw on the opportunities generated by the attractions of foreign investment.

In the 1970s South Korea and Brazil both took advantage of the opportunity of cheap international credit and borrowed heavily. By the 1980s, economic performance diverged sharply. The neo-liberal argument that South Korea continued to grow (albeit after some slowdown) because of its adoption of neo-liberal policies while Brazil went into prolonged recession because it was locked into a policy of ISI is unconvincing.[23] Certainly, the loans acquired by South Korea were used more productively than Brazil's, but this was precisely *because of the state*, and its effective industrial policies, not in spite of it.

This brief discussion once again shows that the relationship between "local" nation-states and the "global" world economy is not as benign as neo-liberals suggest. Certainly the successes of Korean and Taiwanese exporters to Europe and the United States cannot easily be repeated by others in the context of an increase in some protectionist practices by First World nations (Cline 1982). Neither is it an inevitability that the later-industrializing Asian countries such as Thailand, Malaysia, Indonesia or indeed China will follow the lead of Japan,

Korea and Taiwan. If left to unregulated market forces, the likelihood is that the South-East Asian countries will at best continue to produce low-wage, labour-intensive goods, or at worst may face some de-industrialization as capital in these sectors relocates to lower-wage economies such as Vietnam, or such sectors technologically upgrade and therefore move back productive operations to the First World (Dixon & Drakakis-Smith 1993b: 220–21). Such a pessimistic scenario is not inevitable, and these economies may successfully upgrade to heavier and high-technology industries, but this occurrence depends on a coherent industrial policy put into effect by a developmental state. It is far from clear that such criteria exist in South-East Asia.[24]

Industrialization and development

This section returns to the question of the relationship between industrialization and social development. It shows how some of the industrializers have a better record than others in terms of issues such as income distribution, literacy rates, life expectancy, and so on. At the same time, however, I warn the reader of the negative consequences of all the processes of late industrialization – factors such as working conditions and environmental damage. Nevertheless, the differences between the case studies are significant, and I discuss these in the chapter's conclusion, which returns us to a discussion of the "Kitching thesis", and the question of the relationship between industrialization and development.

The figures in Tables 1–3 (from UNDP 1995: Tables 1, 2, 4 and 12) provide some suggestive indicators.[25] They indicate that, generally, the East Asian industrializers have a better developmental record in terms of life expectancy, literacy, and per capita income than either Brazil or India. The record of the South-East Asian countries is less clear – Thailand and Malaysia have a better record than Brazil, while the records of the Philippines and Indonesia are worse. Each of these countries fares better than India, which has a particularly poor record (UNDP 1995: 76–7). In terms of income inequalities and poverty,

Table 1 Comparative figures for life expectancy, literacy and per capita income

Country	Life expectancy (1992)	Literacy (1992)	Per capita income (1992)
South Korea	71	97%	$9,250
Singapore	75	n.d.	$18,330
Hong Kong	79	n.d.	$20,340
Malaysia	71	82%	$7,790
Philippines	66	94%	$2,550
Thailand	69	94%	$5,950
Indonesia	63	82%	$2,950
Brazil	66	82%	$5,240
India	53	46%	$1,356

Table 2 Income share
(ratio of highest 20% to lowest 20% – 1981–92)

South Korea	8.7
Singapore	9.6
Hong Kong	8.7
Malaysia	11.7
Philippines	7.4
Thailand	8.3
Indonesia	4.9
Brazil	32.1
India	4.7

Table 3 People in poverty (1990)

	Urban (%)	Rural (%)
South Korea	5	4
Singapore	n.d.	n.d.
Hong Kong	n.d.	n.d.
Malaysia	8	23
Philippines	40	54
Thailand	7	29
Indonesia	20	16
Brazil	38	66
India	38	49

the East Asian record is more impressive again, although the picture is more complicated. For the years 1981–92, India's levels of income equality were actually better than those of Hong Kong and South Korea, but the levels of poverty were far greater in India. In India in 1990, 38 per cent of urban dwellers and 49 per cent of those in the countryside were designated poor, compared to only 5 and 4 per cent respectively in South Korea – a reflection of the higher per capita income in the latter. Thus in Korea, 100 per cent of the population had access to decent sanitary facilities, while the figure for India was only 62 per cent in the towns and a derisory 12 per cent in the countryside (UNDP 1995: 178–9, 166–7). Brazil, on the other hand, had very high levels of inequality so that advantages over India in terms of per capita GNP were effectively cancelled out (UNDP 1995: 178). The South-East Asian countries have tended to do better than Brazil and India, but considerably worse than the first-tier Asian NICs. In the case of China, there were substantial increases in per capita consumption in the 1980s (Nolan 1995b: 253–5). Although per capita income was still low in the early 1990s (US$1,950), this partly reflects the fact that a large proportion of the population works in agricultural production (UNDP 1995: 158, 176). Nevertheless, the benefits of economic growth are distributed very unevenly. The coastal provinces and Beijing, favoured recipients of foreign investment, have grown far more rapidly than the west and the interior (Hirst & Thompson 1996: 107). The provinces of Guangdong and Fujian have far greater freedom to retain locally generated income, and there is a fear among other provinces that the (restricted) promotion of "market forces" will intensify, rather than alleviate, uneven development. Within the coastal provinces themselves, there is conflict over the perceived favouritism towards Guangdong over other areas (Breslin 1995: 69–70). The 1980s and 1990s also saw an increase in the number of people migrating to the towns without job contracts. The "floating population" of the bigger cities like Beijing, Shanghai and Guangzhou in each case was over 1 million by the late 1980s (Dwyer 1993: 160).

The (proportionate) annual growth rate of urban populations in the period from 1960 to 1992 was highest for South Korea, with an average increase of 3.2 per cent a year, compared to 1.7 per cent for Brazil and 1.2 per cent for India (UNDP 1995: 184). However, given Brazil and India's much larger populations (153 million and 884 million respectively, compared to 43 million in South Korea in 1992), the actual quantitative increase in the urban population was greater in the larger countries (UNDP 1995: 186–7). When combined with the fact that South Korea has lower rates of unemployment and higher per capita income than Brazil and India, it is not surprising that urban poverty is far higher (in both quantitative and proportional terms) in the latter countries (see above).

Nevertheless, although urban poverty and shanty-towns may be more common in Brazil and India, South Korea's record is far from perfect. The percentage of South Koreans living in urban areas increased from 28 per cent in 1960 to 71 per cent in 1990. Seoul, with a population of over 10 million accounts for 24 per cent of the population but only 0.6 per cent of the country's land-size. The Seoul metropolitan area of 18.6 million accounts for over 42 per cent of the national population (You 1995: 165–6). Between 1960 and 1988, the ratio of the number of housing units to the number of households declined from 82.5 per cent to 69.8 per cent (You 1995: 167). In Seoul, 28 per cent of households own no land. Around one-quarter of the Seoul population survives by either doubling or tripling up in rented accommodation, while another 20 per cent live as illegal squatters (Hart-Landsberg 1993: 260–61). Similarly in Hong Kong, housing conditions are extremely over-crowded. Most notoriously, there is the caged accommodation where people live in single-bed spaces and erect wire fencing to prevent theft of their belongings. In addition, there have been thousands of illegal (and largely unsafe) structures on private buildings used as dwellings. In the mid-1980s, these affected an estimated 200,000 people (Smart 1995: 100). On the whole, then, it seems fair to say that "the level of crowding and housing quality are still remarkably low for a territory as wealthy as Hong Kong, and even the middle class commonly live in extremely cramped quarters" (Smart 1995: 108–9).

The success stories also fare badly in terms of working conditions. South Korean workers had the longest working week in the world throughout the 1970s, and average hours increased from 50 to 54 between 1975 and 1983

(Hart-Landsberg 1993: 203). For much of the boom period Korea had the highest rate of industrial accidents in the world, with 130,000 workers affected by work-related accidents in 1979. Moreover, official figures underestimated the extent of the problem as they were based on reports by companies eager to avoid insurance payments for industrial accidents, and they did not include injuries in workplaces of less than ten people, which were often the most hazardous (Hart-Landsberg 1993: 204). Similarly, Taiwan in the late 1970s had the highest rate of workers killed in industrial accidents in factories in the world (Bello & Rosenfeld 1992: 217).

Those other Asian countries attempting to replicate the "Korean model" have also introduced harsh working conditions. The Chinese coastal miracle has been characterized as "a paradise built on remorseless exploitation of child labour, forced overtime, government strikebreaking, and worse" (Smith 1993: 95). In the Special Economic Zones a 96-hour working week is not uncommon and work conditions are often extremely hazardous. The Guangdong Provincial Fire Bureau reported that in 1990 there were 1,700 industrial fires in the Pearl River delta alone. In May 1991, 80 young female workers were burned to death in a fire at a factory at Shi Pai, Guangdong. Such conditions are not exclusive to China. In May 1993 a toy factory in Bangkok was burned down and 200 young women were killed (Smith 1993: 95).

These examples serve as reminders that official measures of development, based on expanding output and income, tell only one side of the story. To paraphrase Thompson on the British experience (see Chapter Three), "an upward curve" in statistical terms "might feel like immiseration" to (some of) the people concerned.

All of the cases discussed have also experienced a significant trade-off between rapid industrial development and environmental costs. Air pollution levels in the main cities of the late industrializers are extremely high. In the period from 1982 to 1985, the peak levels of airborne particulates and sulphur dioxide levels (measured in microgrammes per cubic metre) were measured as follows: particulates – Beijing 307, Brussels 97, London 77, New York 121, São Paulo 338, Bangkok 741, Manila 579, Calcutta 967 and Delhi 1,062; sulphur dioxide levels – Beijing 625, Frankfurt 230, London 171, New York 131, Manila 198 (Smith 1992: 289). These pollutants are closely linked to the inefficient burning of fossil fuels, and such figures, while not intended to blame the developing world for global environmental problems,[26] do show that environmental con-ditions in some Third World cities are poor. Furthermore, some governments, such as the Chinese, have actively promoted the country as a location for polluting industries and toxic dumps (Smith 1993: 96).

Although South Korea has experienced some environmental successes, most notably its reforestation programme initiated in 1973, it also has high levels of pollution (sulphur dioxide, carbon monoxide and nitrous oxide contents) associated with dirty industries and high rates of car use in over-crowded cities (You 1995: 171). In Taiwan the government's policy of promoting small-scale industry in rural areas has in some senses backfired as industries have been set up in rice fields, along waterways and by residential areas. Companies have ignored weak and badly enforced waste disposal regulations, and so many rivers are now polluted and an estimated 30 per cent of rice is contaminated with heavy metals, including mercury and arsenic (Bello & Rosenfeld 1992: 201).

In attempting to replicate the East Asian miracle, South-East Asian countries have cleared forests in search of foreign exchange and land for industry and agriculture. The proportion of the Philippines covered by forests declined from 50 per cent in 1950 to 25 per cent in 1990. Similarly high levels have been recorded in Thailand, Malaysia and Indonesia (Bello 1994: 50–51). One effect of this process has been an increase in "natural disasters" such as mudslides caused by flooding, which led to almost 400 deaths in Thailand in 1988, quickly followed by around 8,000 deaths in Ormoc in the Philippines (Bello 1994: 51–2). Deforestation in the Amazon region in Brazil has also left its legacy. The construction of steel plants, fuel terminals and agro-industry among others has left its legacy in terms of mass destruction of the rainforest, and the devastation of farming communities that have been dispossessed of their land. This has led to the growth of poor squatter camps and further fuelled urban growth (Hewitt 1992: 78).

Neo-liberals have made one final, valiant effort to explain the developmental success of the East Asian NICs compared to others in terms of technical policy making. They have argued that export oriented industrialization has contributed to increased employment, and in doing so, had a favourable effect on income distribution. So, as well as economic efficiency, market forces promote "development" (Balassa 1981). This technicist account of the relationship between growth and development is not convincing however, for as Colman & Nixson (1986: 308) argue,

> EOI may well be associated (indeed, may well depend upon) the employment of large numbers of workers at very low wages and it cannot be hypothesized a priori what the distributional implications of that particular strategy will be.

The greater rates of unevenness in the second-tier Asian NICs would appear to bear this out. More convincing as explanations are precisely the same reasons for the diversity in economic growth – that is, contingent social factors such as the role of the state, class and popular struggles, land reform, and so on. Thus, greater income disparities in Brazil compared to Taiwan[27] are not the product of a policy of ISI rather than EOI, but are in fact the product of more unequal class structures in the former, especially in land ownership.

Conclusion

Clearly then, all of the industrialization processes have had their "dark side". The question then becomes one of how much one would be prepared to sacrifice some economic growth in favour of better working conditions, shorter working hours, or stronger environmental regulations. In practice this is a hypothetical question – as I argued in Chapter Two, the motives of the agents of actually existing industrializations have rarely been to promote development; profitability, national security and economic strength have been far more powerful motives. Nevertheless, for all the developmental faults of each of the cases examined, it is still the case that *whatever the motives of the agents of industrialization, some cases have led to more favourable developmental effects than others.* This argument constitutes a revision of the Kitching thesis discussed in Chapter Two. I argued there that while there may be a theoretical case for industrialization, based on the limits to agrarian production, this told us nothing about actual cases of industrialization – not just the motives of the agents that promoted industrial development, but also how some processes were more conducive (even if only indirectly) to the promotion of social development than others. While anti-development theorists such as Sachs (1992a, b) and Escobar (1995) can point to the ill effects of any process of development, this does not take us very far. Certainly, South Korean and Taiwanese industrialization processes have occurred in the context of political repression, environmental destruction, working-class exploitation and female oppression, but these factors *alone* cannot explain their success. Other cases have experienced these processes too, but have not been as successful, either in terms of economic growth or social development. Of course this does not mean that the "successes" constitute a model for the "failures" – I have argued above that development is a far more contingent and social process than the simple advocacy of a technical neo-liberal model. But learning *specific lessons* from development processes is based on the realistic recognition "that development is about costs and benefits, and [we should be] ... more interested in the balance of these items than in the possibility of a painless development or non-development" (Corbridge 1995a: 10). Thus, to return again to Kitching, he is right to say that development is "an awful process" that "varies according to the degree of awfulness", but more attention needs to be paid to how such awfulness can be reduced, both in the short and long term. To do this we need to pay more attention to social actors and their struggles (class, gender, and so on) in and against the development process.

Notes

1. Confucianism is a philosophy which has its roots in the work of the Chinese scholar Confucius (551–479 BC). Its influence spread to most of East Asia as Chinese culture expanded (cf. Chapter Three). It emphasizes continuity, hierarchy, trust and loyalty.
2. Not all culturalist analyses are guilty of this problem. Berger & Tsaio 1988 and Lal 1988 attempt to integrate a cultural analysis with an economic one. However, both tend to regard free market economies as the norm and measure cultures simply by their (in)consistency with this ideology. We are left with one-dimensional views of both

culture and economics, neither of which necessarily fit the reality of the cases in question.

3. Cf. White 1988, Amsden 1989, Rodan 1989.

4. This view represents an important retreat from the neo-classical assumption that the costs of state intervention have typically been greater than the benefits, and that imperfect markets are superior to imperfect planning (Lal 1983: 106–7). As will become clear in the text however, the dogmatic and stubborn commitment to a variety of neo-liberal thinking has precluded the World Bank from going one step further, and accepting that state interventions can be not only neutral in their effects, but also *beneficial*.

5. South Korea (1.9 per cent of GNP in 1988) and Taiwan (1.2 per cent) have far greater levels of investment in research and development activities than most of the more industrialized developing countries – for example Argentina (0.5 per cent in 1988), India (0.9 per cent in 1986) and Brazil (0.4 per cent in 1985). This is lower than Japan (2.8 per cent in 1987) and Germany (2.8 per cent in 1987), but higher than Belgium (1.7 per cent in 1987) and Italy (1.2 per cent in 1987). See Singh 1994: 22.

6. This point relates to a major problem in neo-liberal thought, which asserts that getting prices right leads to static allocative efficiency. However, advocates of this theory often go on to make the far stronger claim that such efficiency unproblematically leads to development, without a convincing demonstration that one leads to the other.

7. A theoretical case for an industrial policy is outlined below.

8. The creation of welfare states, decent infrastructures and so on confirms the point that state intervention is not necessarily self-interested. Vulgar Marxists may respond that the creation of supposedly altruistic public bodies was simply a means of making the exploitation of the working class more efficient. The problem with this view is of course its circularity – the lack of welfare policies in capitalist societies shows the exploitative nature of capitalism, but so too does the creation of welfare. Such Marxists "know" this to be true because states must act in the interests of the capitalist class – but of course such "knowledge" is constructed in an *a priori* fashion (just as neo-liberals "know" that state officials act only for reasons of self-interest). Although he over-emphasizes the *influence* of vulgar Marxism on neo-liberal political economy, Toye (1987, 1991; cf. Mackintosh 1992) shows the dogmatic similarities of the two theories.

9. I leave aside for the moment computer-related high technology. This is discussed in Chapter Nine.

10. Structural adjustment can be defined as a set of policies designed to promote economic growth through the opening up of deregulated economies to competitive market forces. IMF stabilization policies designed to alleviate short-term balance of payments deficits involve currency devaluation and public spending cuts. World Bank adjustment policies, designed to promote longer-term development objectives, involve policies such as deregulation, privatization, the reduction of state protection and the removal of anti-export biases. In practice the extent of implementation of adjustment policies has varied, and has been dependent on the severity of economic recession within particular countries and the character of states and the politics of development (Mosley et al. 1991; Leftwich 1994).

11. The problems with assessing the impact of structural adjustment involve its uneven implementation, and the tendency of both critics and apologists to confuse correlations with causal factors. For instance, critical analysis has often focused on the "lost decade for development" (low growth rates, falling living standards, etc.) in the 1980s, and placed the blame largely on adjustment programmes. This perspective ignores the reasons why economies were forced to adjust in the first place, the impact of recession, shifts in the terms of trade which occur independently of adjustment programmes, and so on. Moreover, it wrongly assumes that a simple alternative exists. On the other hand, the World Bank is quick to claim credit for successful growth rates, and tends to ignore other factors (such as favourable shifts in the terms of trade, successful industrial policy, etc.) which may favour an increase in growth rates. Such a methodology is employed in

World Bank 1983, 1993, 1994 and in Handley 1991. Mosley & Weeks 1993 and Mosley et al. 1995 convincingly criticize the World Bank's claims that the most far-reaching adjusters in Africa have also seen the fastest growth rates. Lall (1995) provides a useful critique of the World Bank's position through an examination of adjustment and its effect on industry in Africa.

12. Such effectiveness should not be exaggerated, and there are prominent examples of industrial failures, such as automobiles in Taiwan. Moon & Prasad (1994: 381) have called for a change in the direction of research on Taiwan and South Korea towards state–society relations, focusing on tensions and failures as much as successes.

13. The argument here is that ethnicity *may* be a factor impinging on industrial development processes. I am not arguing – as do many stereotypical views of the Third World – that ethnicity automatically holds back development. Ethnicity and potential ethnic conflict should be analyzed *historically*. On Malaysia, see Lubeck 1992.

14. Excellent historical analyses of state–society relations leading to low rates of industrial and wider economic growth in parts of sub-Saharan Africa can be found in Sandbrook 1985, 1993.

15. This argument can be faulted on the same grounds as the neo-classical argument that the economy tends towards equilibrium. It assumes a perfectly mobile capital whereby investment in one sector/locality can easily move to another without cost. For a critique, see Chapter Five, and the second section of this chapter.

16. See Chapters One and Two for a fuller outline of this argument.

17. This has been made clear in the discussion on Soviet industrialization in Chapter Four.

18. This assertion is in marked contrast to the claims of Lipton, who has argued that poverty in the Third World is partly a product of an "urban bias" (Lipton 1977, 1982) – that is, a concentration of resources on a politically powerful urban class. This argument is based on a vague definition of class, and underestimates the fact that state elites often rely on political support from the countryside. Moreover, most importantly, the evidence for the thesis is very weak. For critiques, see Byres 1989, Corbridge 1989, and Toye 1987.

19. However, a relatively stagnant agriculture co-existing with industry is likely to intensify uneven development, via a process of massive rural–urban migration. This point applies to all the case studies, but is more marked in the cases of Brazil and India. It applies more to South Korea than it does to Taiwan – in the latter case rates of migration to towns have not been as great.

20. Such a methodology is employed by both neo-liberals and some fundamentalist Marxists, such as Lim 1990.

21. However, it remains the case that women remain subject to patriarchal ideologies within society more generally, and that the state has actively promoted such ideals.

22. Thus, given that neo-liberalism (wrongly) argues that a situation of perfect competition exists in a competitive market environment, it is not surprising that the World Bank's *East Asian Miracle* considers industrial policy to be irrelevant.

23. I remind the reader again that the World Bank's 1993 report accepts that South Korea has a higher rate of price distortion than Brazil.

24. This is not to say that successful industrial upgrading will not occur. My position is neither "inevitablist" (South-East Asia will continue to technologically upgrade) nor "impossiblist" (South-East Asia cannot technologically upgrade). The important point is that such upgrading depends on a variety of (contingent) factors, which make black and white predictions impossible. Specific lessons (as opposed to models) can be learnt, however, the most important of which is that global market forces have not on their own promoted industrialization.

25. Measures such as the Human Development Index and Gender Related Development Index, and some of the problems associated with quantifying development, are briefly discussed in Chapter One.

26. The advanced capitalist countries must take the bulk of the blame for global environmental problems. It is their earlier rounds of industrial development that have helped to create the global environmental problem, and these countries consume around half of the world's energy resources, compared to just one-sixth in the Third World. (This statement is not meant to imply that such resources are non-renewable. It does, however, show where the burden for greater environmental scrutiny lies.) The advanced capitalist countries pump out four-fifths of the world's greenhouse gases, and release almost 90 per cent of the CFC gases that destroy the ozone layer (*New Internationalist* 1992a: 18–19). Moreover, these countries are now in a position to afford tighter environmental controls. More meaningful environmental regulation could occur through a change in the distribution of wealth and income in the world, so that Third World societies could better afford stricter controls. Such a scenario, however, implies that there is a need for a radical redistribution of power relations in the global economy (Sutcliffe 1995). None of these comments are intended to let Third World governments "off the hook" in terms of environmental destruction, nor should they be read as downplaying the importance and progressiveness of some environmental movements operating in the Third World.

27. The prominence of small-scale (agricultural and industrial) enterprises in Taiwan challenges the idea that large-scale production is necessary for development to occur (cf. Kitching 1982; and Chapter Two). This debate is examined in Chapter Nine.

Chapter Nine

Flexible accumulation and the global economy: contemporary prospects for late industrializers

According to some writers, global capitalism has entered a new era of "disorganization", "flexible accumulation" or "post-Fordism" (Lash & Urry 1987; Harvey 1989; Lipietz 1992). This chapter examines these claims, and more importantly the implications for late industrializers in the developing world. My principal concern is therefore to examine the constraints and opportunities faced by late industrializers in the so-called "post-Fordist" world.

I undertake this task in three main sections. First, I examine the argument that capitalism has moved from a Fordist to a post-Fordist era based on flexible production. The claims made for a new era are treated with some scepticism, but I also acknowledge that significant changes have occurred. Second, I draw on this discussion – of the arguments both for and against a new period of capital accumulation – to draw out some of the implications for the Third World. Finally, in rejecting a blanket pessimism or optimism, I suggest a more nuanced approach, which examines different sectors, countries, and so on. This is then taken up through brief case studies of the clothing, automobile, and electronics sectors, and a brief re-examination of industrialization in Taiwan.

Post-Fordism/flexibility

The period from 1945 to 1973 has been called the era of "high Fordism" (Harvey 1989: 129–33). In the advanced capitalist world this was the era of mass production and consumption, in which the experiments and innovations introduced in 1909 by Henry Ford in the automobiles sector were extended to other sectors of the economy. Fordism was based on the mass production of standardized products, in which workers were allocated strictly demarcated tasks, and in which they utilized specialized machinery for each particular product – or part of a product (Dicken 1992: 116). This system of production was focused on the national market, which was usually protected from foreign competition, but there was considerable scope for competing in world markets, and for foreign investment in overseas markets. Within this system of production,

145

"[t]he economies came from the scale of production, for although mass production might be more costly to set up because of the purpose built machinery, once in place the cost of an extra unit was discontinuously cheap" (Murray 1989a: 39; cf. Chapter Two).

The implementation of Fordist practices was quite uneven. They were never uniformly introduced across all sectors of the economy, or all countries of the capitalist world. As we have seen, industrial development in the Third World was highly uneven. However, the strategy of import substitution industrialization was largely compatible with Fordist ideals in that it stressed the developmental potential of industrialization through large-scale, capital-intensive technology serving national markets (McMichael 1996: 40; cf. Chapter Six).

The Fordist era was never entirely stabilized, and there was widespread resistance to US dominance, cultural conformity and economic and social inequality in the capitalist world. However, it was in the period from the late 1960s onwards that the tensions in the system became more apparent. Social unrest and labour militancy took place in the context of growing international competition, declining US economic power, the rise of Japan, falling rates of profit and the effective collapse of post-war international economic agreements. The Bretton Woods system of fixed exchange rates was effectively abandoned from 1971 to 1973, when the US devalued the dollar against the price of gold, and in 1973–74 the world price of oil nearly quadrupled. The 1970s and 1980s therefore saw a marked slowdown in growth and periodic and widespread recession.

This was the context in which new experiments in industrial organization were implemented. The keyword that encapsulated these diverse experiments was *flexibility*.[1] Flexible production

> refers to forms of production characterized by a well-developed ability both to shift promptly from one process and/or product configuration to another (dynamic flexibility) and to adjust quantities of output rapidly up or down over the short run without any strongly deleterious effects on levels of efficiency (static flexibility). (Storper 1991: 107)

These forms of production may involve one or more of the following: flexible technologies; flexible relationships between core firms and suppliers; and flexible organization of the labour process.

Flexible technology will usually involve the use of computer-aided manufacturing which is directed towards diverse specifications. Thus, "what the machine actually *does* is programmed in via computer software rather than built into the machinery at the outset" (Schoenberger 1988: 252). Such practices can be seen in the case of retailing, where market leaders have developed a computerized system (the "bar code") to overcome the problems of underproduction (leading to loss of market share) and overproduction (leading to too much stock). Through computerized accounting of stocks in the shops, leading retailers can eliminate the problem of market uncertainty, thus allowing them to order (or produce) supplies which coincide with demand

(Murray 1989a: 42–3). Such technology also allows retailers to cater to the niche market, specializing in certain fragmented markets on the basis of age, income, occupation, and so on. Thus in this case, "the Fordist priority on mass production based on economies of scale has given way to economies of scope, cost savings based on producing a variety of products or services in small – even one of a kind – batches" (Malecki 1991: 236).

Thus flexible technology also presupposes a change in the relationship between core firms and suppliers. The Japanese automobile company Toyota has attempted to implement the "retail model" in its system of supplies, so that they are ordered on the basis of daily need, and components are produced on the day that they are assembled. This has enabled the company to speed up the passage of products through the factory system and eliminate waste in the process. This "just-in-time system" is based on producing according to actual demand, and thereby cutting down on time (Schoenberger 1994).

These changes in turn lead to the need for a more flexible labour force. Flexible labour can refer both to the skills utilized by a small proportion of the workforce and to the extended division of the labour market into core and periphery. As regards the former, the Toyota system developed a core of multi-skilled workers able to undertake a number of tasks and whose shopfloor knowledge is utilized by management to promote continuous improvement in the production process. These core workers are therefore granted a job for life, are continuously trained, and are paid according to seniority (Kenney & Florida 1988). There is a marked shift away from the rigid division of labour of Fordism

> since it is characteristic of the flexible labour process that the same labourers who are involved in operating the machines will also be responsible for changing the settings of machines and for routine functions of maintenance and repair. (Kaplinsky 1989b: 15)

On the other hand, the maintenance of a core of privileged workers co-exists with an increase (compared to Fordism) in the size of the secondary labour market. As Murray (1989a: 46) states,

> The cost of employing lifetime workers means an incentive to subcontract all jobs not essential to the core. The other side of the Japanese jobs-for-life is a majority of low-paid, fragmented peripheral workers, facing an underfunded and inadequate welfare state.

Under the Toyota system, most manufactured inputs are not produced by the end producer but by formally independent supplier firms. Toyota developed a hierarchical system of supply networks, with (in 1988) around 230 first-tier suppliers, which subcontracted work to around 5,000 second-tier suppliers, which in turn were supplied by around 20,000 third- and fourth-tier suppliers (Ruigrok & van Tulder 1995: 53). Profits tend to decline the lower one's place in the hierarchy.

This scenario stresses how smaller firms in Japan have been marginalized by core firms. Other writers (Piore & Sabel 1984) have argued that the new era of flexibility presents new opportunities for such firms. Over the past twenty years, small firms in the Emilia Romagna region of Italy have established a competitive position in world markets in shoes, leather goods, furniture, musical instruments and in the machinery which makes these products (Humphrey 1995a: 1). The Italian experience of *flexible specialization* is based on the development of a cluster of small firms, spatially concentrated and sectorally specialized, developing forward and backward linkages such as exchange of goods, information and people, and supported by local government institutions (Humphrey 1995a: 1; Rasmussen et al. 1992). The basic idea is that "clusters of predominantly small firms can gain economies of scale and scope by increased flexibility through specialization and interfirm cooperation" (Humphrey 1995a: 1).

The Toyota system and flexible specialization are regarded by some writers as potentially viable strategies for industrial producers in the post-Fordist world. Toyotaism (Wood 1991) thus becomes *Japanization*, a strategy of generalizing the Toyota system to all sectors of the economy (including services and agriculture) in all countries (Womack et al. 1990). Similarly the Italian industrial district becomes a model for other countries to follow (Piore & Sabel 1984).

In terms of "flexible futures", at least three perspectives can be identified: the neo-Schumpeterian, the flexible specialization, and the regulation approach (Amin 1994b). The first of these is influenced by the technological approach to development taken by Joseph Schumpeter, and it argues that we have entered a new period (or long wave) of development based on new, knowledge-intensive technology. Summarizing this approach, Amin (1994a: 17) states that the new information technology involves "a shifting emphasis in production from scale economies, rigid technologies and compartmentalization, towards scope economies, flexible manufacturing systems and integration of design, production and marketing", and a post-industrial utopia of teleshopping, flexible work, and so on – a "cybernetic economy". The flexible specialization approach is also optimistic in that it believes that non-hierarchical relations can be developed between small companies producing high-quality goods for niche markets. The regulation school on the other hand is far more pessimistic concerning (post-) industrial futures, as labour market differentiation intensifies, trade unions are disempowered and new rates of intensification of work are imposed by capital – as in the case of Japanese production (cf. Amin 1994a: 22–3).

Clearly then, there are important differences between different schools of thought over the desirability (or otherwise) of the post-Fordist future. Having said that, they are united in the belief that we have entered a new period of capitalism based on flexible accumulation. Before examining the implications of such flexible systems for the Third World, and indeed whether these strategies represent new ways forward for late industrializers, some cautionary observations are necessary.

First, there is some question concerning the viability of a Japanese model of industrial production. Humphrey (1995b: 151–2) warns us that models can easily abstract from specific social contexts, and thus lack clarity over what is, and is not, vital to the content of a posited model. In the case of the Toyota system, the innovations in the labour process were introduced in the specific context of the defeat of radical unions in post-war Japan, a resultant systematic drive by the company to intensify work and dominate the local labour and supplies market and a limited market in the post-war period (Elger & Smith 1993b: 40; Dohse 1985; Chalmers 1989). Moreover, the production system in automobiles is not necessarily in place in other sectors, either in Japan or in other advanced capitalist countries which receive Japanese foreign investment. For instance, Taylor et al. (1993) have found little evidence for the existence of Just-in-Time practices in Japanese electronics plants operating in Britain. Dedoussis & Littler (1993) have similarly shown that a stereotypical Japanese model has at best been unevenly implemented in Australian plants. There is some question over the degree to which Japanese TNCs set up new production sites overseas which rely on locally sourced inputs, rather than imports from Japan[2] (Williams et al. 1992).

Questions concerning flexible specialization also focus on the universal applicability of Italian industrial districts, and other new regions, to the rest of the world, and indeed on whether the source of the model has itself been properly understood. Much of the new technology which facilitates flexible production is simply too expensive for small firms, and it is no surprise that in the high-technology sectors themselves, design and manufacturing is dominated by a few large firms (Harrison 1994: 5–6, 22). The new technology is generally not so flexible that one simply presses a few buttons which lead to new models, and so the costs of programming can often only be met by large companies which require a large scale of production (Williams et al. 1987; Tomaney 1994: 161). Moreover, recent mergers, takeovers and strategic alliances within the advanced capitalist world confirm a tendency towards the concentration of capital – and not the growth of dynamic small industries (Rainnie 1993: 58).

True, there has been a growth in the number of small industries, but this is partly a product of the vertical disintegration of large firms, rather than a product of the alleged inherent inefficiency of large firms. Large firms are in many cases maintaining control by contracting out lower-value-added work to small industrial enterprises, rather than being out-competed by supposedly more efficient small-scale production (Murray 1987: 92–3). Moreover, there is some evidence that hierarchies are now emerging *within* as well as beyond the industrial districts themselves, as single firms in a cluster gain a competitive advantage (Ruigrok & van Tulder 1995: 31). Thus, rather than the autonomous localisms of the flexible specialization school, we appear to be witnessing a situation where large capital/transnational companies are sometimes prepared to draw on or even contract out work to specific localities, but in a relationship in which the former dominates the latter (Amin & Robbins 1990; Amin 1994b: 25).

These qualifications to the Japanization and flexible specialization theses lead one to question the foundation for the argument that we now live in a world of flexible accumulation. Too often, arguments are couched in a covertly reductionist framework in which the demands of the new technology lead to an inevitable flexible future. Such technological determinism in turn leads to a dualist analysis in which the outmoded Fordist regime will be replaced by a (post)modern flexible regime, irrespective of the actions of human beings or the social context in which they live (Rustin 1989: 308). Such a dualism

is only anomalous to a vision of capitalism as a mass production paradigm, and not as an economic system committed to profitability and capital accumulation, where the existence of diversity, whether in a mass and batch production or large and small capital, is normal. (Smith 1989: 216)

The argument that mass markets have been replaced by more volatile niche markets repeats this dualism, in that what is seen is one inevitably replacing the other, rather than the reality of the two existing together (Williams et al. 1987). Moreover, insofar as mass markets have been undermined, this should be seen as a *consequence* of the slowdown in economic growth over the last twenty years, and growing social inequalities, and not as the sign of a move towards a dynamic, flexible future (Gough 1986: 63).

Clearly then,

The argument that there is an acute danger of exaggerating the significance of any trend towards increased flexibility and geographical mobility, blinding us to how strongly implanted Fordist production systems still are, deserves careful consideration. (Harvey 1989: 191)

On the other hand, this does not mean that nothing has changed, as capital attempts to relocate, and to introduce new flexible labour contracts, flexible work practices, and new technologies. As Rustin (1989: 305) argues,

What seems to be emerging is not one "progressive" mode of information-based production, but a plethora of co-existing and competing systems, whose ultimate relative weight in the system is impossible to predict.

Thus, in terms of the implications for the less developed countries, we need to examine the impact of flexible accumulation on potential industrializers, but at the same time bear in mind the unevenness of this flexibility in both First and Third Worlds.

Implications for LDCs

In Chapter Five I argued that the world economy did not conform to the free market utopia of perfect competition, but was instead an unequal playing field in which late industrializers suffered certain competitive disadvantages. This was not to deny that the world economy also offered certain opportunities, such as foreign investment, large export markets, cheap labour in some sectors, and so on. Nevertheless, if left solely to unregulated "market forces", the dominant tendency was for capital to concentrate in particular areas of accumulation. It was in this context that the strategies of ISI and EOI were located. What then of the movement towards flexible accumulation? Does this mean an increase or a decrease in the constraints and opportunities faced by late industrializers?

The most important tendency acting as a constraint is the movement towards regional agglomeration. Although the Fordist era still saw the concentration of industrial capital in the First World, there was a gradual tendency for some labour-intensive tasks to be relocated to the periphery, where costs were lower.[3] One impact of flexible accumulation is the possibility that industrial production – including the lower-value end – will relocate back to the established regions of accumulation. This is because with flexible accumulation, *time* becomes an important dimension of a firm's competitive strategy. As Schoenberger (1994: 58) argues,

> The firm that can bring new products to market faster or turn around an order more quickly and reliably gains a significant advantage – in effect, it is selling speed (and reliable service) as well as the physical product itself.

Thus in the case of flexible markets, clothing manufacturers are limited by a highly competitive and volatile market, so that some of the brand leaders only have product runs of six weeks. Similarly Just-in-Time practices operate on the principle of close proximity to the core firm – thus in the case of Toyota, many of its suppliers are located within a range of 100 kilometres of what is actually called Toyota City (Ruigrok & van Tulder 1995: 53). Furthermore, automated technologies may increase productivity to such an extent that the competitive advantage of cheap labour in the periphery is undermined. This may be reinforced by the existence of non-tariff barriers in the First World which sometimes force the assembly stage of a product to the same location as the product's final market (Kaplinsky 1989b: 15). Clothing production utilizing new technology has partly relocated to the advanced capitalist countries as a result (Kaplinsky 1982c: 3; cf. below).

These tendencies conform to the data on global capital flows presented in Chapter Five. Briefly, the last twenty-five years have seen an intensification of capital concentration in the First World and the NICs. This has coincided with a recent move towards increased foreign investment in certain parts of the developing world, as strategic countries "act as nodes in the trade and investment circuits reaching out from the key First World states" (McMichael 1996: 107). Thus countries like China, Mexico, South Korea and Indonesia are favoured recipients of investment, due to the size of their domestic markets, and their proximity to other large affluent markets.

Clearly then, insofar as flexible accumulation has been introduced, it has not altered global capitalism's tendency towards uneven development (Storper 1991: 116). Given that this has coincided with a partial move towards a global free market,[4] it is not surprising that it has if anything intensified it. However, at the same time flexible production has facilitated the growth of new regions of accumulation such as the Third Italy and Silicon Valley, and it is for this reason that some writers point to the opportunities that flexibility can offer to the Third World.

For those writers influenced by Schumpeter (Perez 1985; Freeman 1987), the new flexible technology offers new opportunities for the Third World because it has the potential to enable them not only to close the technological gap, but actually to leapfrog over earlier industrializers (Perez 1985: 457). This opportunity can be fulfilled if appropriate institutional arrangements are adapted to the new techno-economic paradigm. The problem with this approach is its technological determinism – institutional change, the role of the state, and so on, is measured purely in relation to its adaptation to the new paradigm. Ruigrok & van Tulder (1995: 16) reject such technological determinism:

> In reality, technological change is far from a socially neutral process. Some groups or interests will be better able to grab the opportunity offered by technical change than others. Technological change is therefore always subject to political bargaining and power struggles. This means that one has to analyse the position of the societal groups affected by technological change, and their industrial, social or political embeddedness.

Of particular relevance here is the continued concentration of research and development facilities in the advanced capitalist world. On the other hand, Soete (1985: 416–18) argues that this is less important a concern than the market situation faced by potential high-technology importers. Rather than the expensive capital-intensive technology of the ISI period, late industrializers now face a buyer's market due to intense competition in the new technology spheres combined with a rapid rate of innovation. Thus, the potential may exist for at least some late industrializers (Soete confines his analysis to the most successful NICs) to acquire new technology on competitive terms.

Such optimism may also apply to flexible forms of work organization. The possibility exists that flexible specialization and Japanization techniques will allow new industries to leapfrog the First World's entrenched Fordist values and so develop competitive advantage in flexible and dynamic new industries (Kaplinsky 1989a: 4). The adoption of these work-practices has the advantage of being relatively cheap, at least compared to the expensive imports of capital-intensive technology under ISI (ibid.). The most optimistic proponent of flexible specialization, Charles Sabel (1986: 43), has argued that the informal sector may be a way forward for the periphery as it has the potential to form clusters of small-scale independent producers, adapting to flexible markets and even new technology.

The evidence on these issues is far from conclusive, which probably reflects the fact that such strategies have been implemented in a very uneven way throughout the periphery.[5] This point refers us back to the problem of transferability of models discussed above. In particular, to fully adopt the practices of flexible accumulation, the periphery faces the problem of the diffusion of new technology, and the development of an appropriate infrastructural base, including skilled labour (Hoffman & Kaplinsky 1988: 334–5; Kaplinsky 1994). Neither of these requirements is an impossibility, but nor are they an inevitability. Even if the technology can be acquired on competitive terms from abroad, many local capitalists are likely to attempt to remain competitive through the maintenance of low wages rather than introduce the new technology. A local infrastructure may also be developed, but this is an expensive and time-consuming process which may be costly to the Third World, especially given the agglomeration tendencies associated with flexible accumulation outlined above. In the case of investment and infrastructure, the role played by a developmental state is crucial, but as the previous chapter showed, the emergence of such states is largely a product of contingent, historical circumstances which are not easily introduced into an economy. Moreover, the growing liberalization of many Third World economies undergoing structural adjustment programmes militates against the emergence of such states.

These problems are particularly acute for strategies of flexible specialization. In both so-called "Fordist" and "flexible" firms, economies of scale remain significant. Flexible specialization theorists underestimate both the expense of the new technology and the ease with which it can be transferred to new product lines, which further enforces high costs (Tomaney 1994: 161). The strategy also exaggerates the degree of co-operation between firms in clusters and the means by which large firms can control smaller subcontractors.[6]

On the whole then, we can see that flexible accumulation presents new opportunities and constraints for late industrializers. Just as the opportunities and constraints discussed in Chapter Five worked in different ways in different countries, as global and local factors interacted, so too will they operate differently in the current period. Moreover, we must again be sensitive to the uneven implementation of flexible accumulation in different industrial sectors. I expand on these points below.

Transcending the debate: tendencies and counter-tendencies

The general points made in the previous section need to be made more concrete. This section briefly examines the clothing and textiles, automobile and semiconductor/electronics industries, and looks again at Taiwan, a country that has enjoyed considerable success in small-scale industrial production. Some conclusions are then made regarding the opportunities and constraints for Third World nations, as well as a critical reassessment of the notion of flexible accumulation.

Textiles and clothing

In the twenty-five years to 1990, the Third World's share of global output in both the textiles and clothing industries increased. In textiles, it increased from 18.6 per cent in 1975 to 26.1 per cent in 1990; in clothing, it increased from 11.7 per cent in 1970 to 20.4 per cent in 1990 (Elson 1994: 190–91). Although the Third World's share has increased, the First World's share of textile exports remains higher – in 1989, Western Europe accounted for 46 per cent of global textile exports, while Japan and the United States combined accounted for a further 10 per cent. Moreover, the so-called Third World's share is dominated by four East Asian NICs – China, South Korea, Taiwan and Hong Kong (Dicken 1992: 238). In clothing, the so-called Third World's share is greater, but it is similarly dominated by the East Asian NICs, with Hong Kong, South Korea, China and Taiwan all among the top six exporters in the world. Others have made considerable headway however, including Thailand, Venezuela, Turkey and the Dominican Republic, and to some extent, albeit from a more established base, India (Dicken 1992: 241–2). The increase in exports from the Third World has occurred despite the implementation of the Multi-Fibre Agreement from 1974, which restricted the amount of clothing imports from particular Third World countries.[7]

These figures are also reflected in the changes in employment in the industries. Between 1963 and 1987, there were massive job losses in many parts of the First World, while in the Far East there were sharp rises. From 1971 to 1978, South Korean employment in textiles rose by 111 per cent and in clothing by 224 per cent, while in Hong Kong employment in clothing rose by 138 per cent between 1970 and 1980 (Elson 1989: 81).

Such figures have sometimes been taken as evidence for a relocation of manufacturing from high-cost First World to low-cost Third (cf. Frobel et al. 1980). However, we should be careful to avoid simple zero sum games by which employment gains in one region lead to losses elsewhere (and vice versa). Many of the job losses in the First World can be attributed to changes in domestic demand and increases in productivity, rather than simple relocation.[8] In fact, foreign investment is not particularly high, and the (often indirect) employment of cheap labour is just one of the strategies used by TNCs in the clothing and textiles sectors.

The restructuring of clothing and textiles must be seen in the context of changes in retailing, global sourcing, intensified competition, market fragmentation and the development of new technologies (Gereffi 1994b). For instance, with the increase in the proportion of single people and double income couples in the West, retailers have been forced to adapt to the reality of changes in the market place. These changes, reinforced by periodic recession and increasing inequalities, have led retailers to go either upscale into niche marketing, or into the low price sectors. With the increase in niche markets, there has been an increase in the turnover time of particular products, which partly undermines the advantages of using long-distance but cheap labour. In addition new technologies in both (parts of) manufacturing and retailing have increased labour productivity, and control over manufacturers. These points are best illustrated through a few brief examples.

Tootal was a British TNC which ran down its operations in Britain in the 1970s. Instead, it used subcontractors in East Asia and re-established itself as a service industry, concentrating on design, marketing, distribution, and so on. Its motive for using subcontractors was not only cheaper labour costs in the Far East, but market access to industrial sewing thread in the region. Interestingly, its restructuring attempts were not successful and it was taken over by a rival in 1990 (Elson 1994: 197–8).

Levi Strauss, the largest jeans company in the world, had 104 manufacturing plants in 1983. Of these 66 were in the United States. These were mainly concentrated in the southern states, where labour costs were cheaper, but not as cheap as in the Caribbean or Mexico. Plants abroad tended to be concentrated in cheap labour areas, such as Glasgow, Dundee and North Shields in Britain, but still not in countries where labour costs were far lower (Elson 1989: 91).

Nike is the market leader in the athletic footwear industry. It draws on manufacturing subcontractors, mainly in East Asia. In recent years, it has increasingly used subcontractors in China, where labour costs are particularly low. However, this is not without its problems, and "[t]he advantages of lower labor costs in the developing manufacturing areas had to be weighed against disadvantages in production flexibility, quality, raw material sourcing, and transportation" (Korzeniewicz 1994: 259). The development of new model specifications took four months in South Korea, compared to eight months in China; the ratio of A-grade (perfect quality) shoes to B-grade (aesthetically flawed but structurally sound) shoes was 99:1 in Korea compared to 80:20 in China; South Korea sourced 100 per cent of its raw materials needed for production, while China managed only 30 per cent; and shipping time from Korea was 20–25 days compared to 35–40 days from Shanghai (Korzeniewicz 1994: 259).

Finally, there is the case of Benetton, often cited as the classic example in using flexible specialization techniques (Murray 1989b). This Italian company started as a small family business and has now emerged as Europe's largest producer of clothes. In fact, it directly owns very few factories and instead relies on manufacturing by relatively small workshops in Italy. In the early 1980s the company employed only 1,600 people, but through subcontracting it indirectly employed over 10,000. Benetton owns over 3,000 shops and sells its products through franchise agreements. A computer at the company's headquarters links every shop, and detailed information of sales is transmitted on a daily basis. Production is then planned according to daily sales figures. Thus, Benetton "can control *without* owning because of its possession of the information vital for both successful production and successful retailing" (Elson 1989: 103). Although there was some considerable optimism concerning the work conditions and wages of employees in the small workshops employed by Benetton (Piore & Sabel 1984), recent evidence points to a sharp divsion between a minority of core workers and a majority of peripheral workers, the latter suffering low pay and long working hours (Curry 1993: 104).

These brief examples then show a variety of strategies used by companies in the clothing and textiles sectors. While the industries (especially clothing) remain relatively labour-intensive, and so opportunities exist for competitive production in the Third World, cheap labour is clearly not the only criterion by which investment decisions are made. New technologies used by retailers and changes in market structures have in some cases encouraged production near to the final market. Furthermore, some (limited) technological advances in manufacture, such as automation of cutting, have also encouraged location in the First World (Dicken 1992: 250; Malecki 1991: 242). As far as generalizations can be made, the higher-value, fashion-oriented products tend to be dominated by First World countries, while lower-cost products are more likely to rely on sources from the Third World (Gereffi 1994b: 110–11). There are, however, important exceptions to this rule, especially as many designer labels are "basically a device to *differentiate* what are often relatively similar products" (Dicken 1992: 246). Similarly, companies utilizing labour in the Third World may not rely on the very cheapest labour but instead draw on labour which is both relatively cheap *and skilled* – hence the use of South Korea and Taiwan as favoured locations by companies like Nike.

There is some disagreement among analysts as to whether such practices represent an intensification or a break with Fordist production methods. Korzeniewicz (1994: 261) characterizes Nike's strategy as post-Fordist and Gereffi (1994b) is happy to generalize this description to the American clothing industry. Taplin (1994: 220) takes a different view:

At the respective production sites, standardized mass market firms rely upon technological innovation (introduction of design, production and processing technology) and labor intensification, whereas fashion-oriented firms are more likely to use decentralized production techniques (subcontractors and related wage–depressing tactics). Both procedures imply forms of flexible accumulation that remain decidedly Fordist in character.

I return to this question below.

Automobiles

The automobiles sector is far more concentrated globally. Ownership, investment and trade are dominated by a handful of companies, most of which have their home base in the First World. In the late 1980s the ten leading producers accounted for 76 per cent of production and the top twenty accounted for 96 per cent (Dicken 1992: 268). Around 80 per cent of production was concentrated in the United States, Japan and the European Community (Dicken 1992: 272). Around 96 per cent of world trade in automobiles was between these core areas (Dicken 1992: 272). These figures are not likely to have changed much since the late 1980s.

Over the last twenty years the most significant development has been the rise of Japan. In 1960, the United States produced more than 50 per cent of the world's automobile output. By 1980, Japan had emerged as the world's leading producer of passenger cars (Dicken 1992: 272). Before 1960, no Japanese company was in the top fifteen car producers in the world; by 1989, Toyota was challenging Ford for second place, Nissan was sixth, Honda ninth and Mazda tenth (Dicken 1992: 289). In the United States, employment fell by 24 per cent from 470,000 in 1978 to 355,000 in 1989, while Ford in Europe cut its blue-collar labour force from 104,000 to 77,500 in the same period (Dicken 1992: 306). Britain produced 10.4 per cent of the world's cars in 1960, but by 1989 this had declined to just 3.7 per cent (Dicken 1992: 272). Its output fell by half between 1972 and 1982, and by 1989 the industry had a deficit of £6.5 billion (Law 1991: 17–18).

The initial response of Ford and General Motors to Japanese competition was an extension of Fordist principles and the creation of the "world car" strategy. Cars would be produced for a world market, and production transnationally integrated so that manufacturing would locate in least-cost locations on a global scale (Gwynne 1991: 65). In this strategy, large economies of scale would occur through specialization in particular plants and the use of low-cost labour. As early as 1967 Ford Europe was established. The Fiesta model was designed in Europe, engines produced in Valencia (Spain), transaxles in Bordeaux (France), and assembly took place in Valencia, Dagenham (England) and Saarlouis (Germany). The low-cost Fiera model was made in the Philippines, Taiwan and Thailand, with components supplied from England, Argentina, Australia and Japan. General Motors adopted a similar strategy, and its Chevette model was produced in the United States, Germany, Britain, Japan, Australia, Brazil and Argentina (Hill 1987: 27). The world car strategy thus relied heavily on foreign investment – in 1989, almost 60 per cent of Ford's passenger car production was located outside of its US base, while for General Motors the figure was 42 per cent (Dicken 1992: 290).

The Japanese strategy on the other hand conformed more closely to the Just-in-Time system outlined above. Thus a closely integrated system of supplier networks was established at Toyota City which relies on inventory-saving techniques and faster turnover time. Rather than competing through massive economies of scale and low-cost labour, Japanese companies have relied on flexible, automated plants with close relations between suppliers and manufacturers.[9] This strategy lacks the advantage of lower labour costs, but it avoids the problem of co-ordinating a massive flow of goods from around the world and the need for large stockpiles for security against easily disrupted production lines. It has been estimated that Toyota's production per worker was until recently three times greater than that of Ford, and that a Toyota engine plant takes up only 300,000 square feet compared to 900,000 at comparable Ford facilities (Hill 1987: 30).

Given the agglomeration of economic activity implied by Japanese techniques, it is not surprising that Japanese direct foreign investment has been low. Before 1982, Toyota had no production plants outside of Japan. Even by 1989, only 8 per cent of its operations were outside of its home base. This figure compared to 18 per cent for Mazda, 14 per cent for Nissan and 30 per cent for Honda (Dicken 1992: 290).

The increase in foreign investment in the 1980s was primarily in response to protectionist threats from mainly First World competitors, and the advantage of locating near final markets to facilitate response to variety in demand. By the early 1990s, there were twelve Japanese automobile plants in North America and Japanese cars produced in the US had captured 21 per cent of the US domestic market (Dicken 1992: 295). Nevertheless, direct foreign investment is limited in amount and is primarily concerned with continued access to lucrative markets. Competitors have responded to the rise of Japan through the establishment of joint ventures with Japanese companies and attempts at implementing Japanese practices within the workplace.[10]

These developments have important implications for the Third World. During the 1980s, the share of the NICs in world automobile production grew from 6.4 per cent in 1980 to 7.7 per cent in 1990 (Kim & Lee 1994: 282). South Korea increased its exports of cars from 20,000 in 1983 to 390,000 in 1991. By the year 2000, it is expected that Korea will produce 4.2 million cars and export 2.5 million of them (Kim & Lee 1994: 283–4). Hyundai, the most successful of the Korean manufacturers, has established links with the Japanese company Mitsubishi, which owns 15 per cent of Hyundai. The Hyundai model Pony Excel successfully entered the US market from 1986, taking advantage of protectionism against Japanese products, and the upgrading of Japanese companies into more expensive models. Hyundai was able to take advantage of Mitsubishi's technology in order to do this. More recently the formerly state-run Malaysian company Proton[11] has taken advantage of Mitsubishi technology and made some leeway in foreign markets (Perspectives 1996: 1). Other Korean companies have taken advantage of the world car strategy and entered joint ventures with General Motors (Daewoo) and Ford (Kia) (Gwynne 1991: 73; Hill & Lee 1994: 304).

Brazil and Mexico have also increased their exports. In the case of the former, this has occurred because of export incentives introduced by Brazilian governments, and the necessity of TNCs in Brazil finding new markets because of the collapse of the Brazilian domestic market in the recessionary 1980s. Mexico has experienced some direct foreign investment in the late 1980s as companies take advantage of proximity to the US market, but it has so far been limited to just two assembly plants and a few engine plants (Gwynne 1991: 84).

Automobile production in the so-called Third World is thus largely limited to a few NICs in Latin America and East Asia. Potential automobile industrializers face the disadvantages of limited markets (in an industry where proximity to final market as a location decision appears to be increasing in importance), lack of technology and skills, and limited experience in advanced methods of industrial organization.[12] Hill (1987: 34) describes the tendencies accurately:

Direct foreign investment in the poorer countries is still a small percentage of total outlays by transnational auto corporations. The auto giants are unlikely to locate major export platforms in very poor countries. The commitment of capital is great, and without a relatively assured home market, too heavy dependence on exports harbours many economic and political risks. Because the car companies depend upon a spectrum of suppliers, they are unlikely to develop big export-oriented production complexes without a pre-existing manufacturing base of sufficient magnitude to produce some of the required materials and components at competitive prices. So, auto production will increase in the Third World but mainly in larger countries with growing markets which require domestic manufacture in return for market access.

Semiconductors and electronics

The electronics industry can now be described as the key industry in the world today. It offers the possibility of higher productivity and value added, and favourable spin-offs such as links with suppliers and buyers in other industries, and the need for an educated workforce (Henderson 1994: 258–9). Key technological developments in the industry include the development of the transistor in 1948, which made possible the development of a microelectronics industry; the development of the integrated circuit in the late 1950s, which connected a number of transistors on a single silicon chip; and in the early 1970s, when a number of circuits (effectively a computer) were put on a single chip (Dicken 1992: 309).

The growth in the production of semiconductors has been enormous. Output virtually doubled every year in the 1970s (Dicken 1992: 311). Until the 1980s, the United States dominated production, but it has since been overtaken by Japan. By 1989, Japan accounted for 42 per cent of global production, the United States 26 per cent and Europe 12 per cent (Dicken 1992: 311). The trade in semiconductors has been dominated by US–Japanese rivalry, with Europe attempting to hold its own (Ernst 1987). The location of production and trading patterns correlates closely with demand for semiconductors, which are used in a wide variety of industries. Initial demand was greatest in defence, but this has spread as demand for electronic goods has increased, and as other industries such as automobiles have drawn on computer technology in parts of the production process.

The barriers to entry in the industry are high. The rapid pace of tech-nological change has meant that the cost of establishing a semiconductor plant has grown enormously. In the 1960s, the cost was around $2 million, by the early 1970s it was $15 million, and by the late 1980s it was $150 million. In 1990, Japanese companies spent $7 billion on production facilities for 4-megabyte chips. Thus, even allowing for inflation, cost barriers to entry have soared (Dicken 1992: 320). Ownership in the industry has therefore become more concentrated. In the case of the United States, the cluster of small firms at Silicon Valley has gradually given way to dominance by larger firms, while in Europe and Japan larger firms were dominant from the outset (Castells & Hall 1993: ch. 2). In 1989 ten companies accounted for almost 60 per cent of world output[13] (Dicken 1992: 328–9). This concentration increased in the 1980s with the growth of strategic alliances and mergers between companies (Henderson 1989: 142–3).

Having said that, small firms are still common in the assembly stage of production. Unlike the design and wafer fabrication stage, assembly of semiconductors does not require skilled personnel or a developed infrastructure. Moreover, the low weight and high value of semiconductors means that there are few restrictions on their movement across long distances. This break in the production process has enabled companies to draw on low-cost, unorganized labour. From the early 1960s, US companies set up offshore assembly facilities in the Far East, and similar facilities were established in Mexico and parts of the Caribbean in the 1970s. Japanese companies have similarly invested in offshore assembly operations in East Asia.

The four first-tier NICs used this opportunity to develop and upgrade their industries. For instance, in the 1980s the state in Singapore increased labour costs as part of a deliberate strategy to encourage TNCs to invest in more technology and skill-intensive processes, such as computer-controlled operations, circuit design and wafer fabrication (Henderson 1994: 263). South Korea has developed through the promotion of domestic firms relying on foreign technology. As early as 1959, Goldstar produced radios. By the early 1980s, the four main chaebols (Hyundai, Goldstar, Samsung and Daewoo) were producers of VCRs, TVs, microwaves and semiconductors. Samsung had successfully moved into the fabrication of 4- and 16-megabyte DRAM (dynamic random access memories) production. By 1988 Taiwan was responsible for around 10 per cent of world Personal Computer production, and electronics was the country's largest export sector[14] (Henderson 1994: 266).

Despite these advances, there is still considerable dependence on foreign companies. In the case of Taiwanese computers for instance, Original Equipment Manufacturing[15] (OEM) agreements with foreign companies accounted for 43 per cent of production in 1989. In Korea in 1988, OEM arrangements accounted for 60–70 per cent of local firm output, and 30 per cent of all manufactured exports (Henderson 1994: 268). This dependency is all the greater in the second-tier Asian NICs which, with the possible exception of Malaysia, concentrate on the low-value, unskilled assembly end of production (Henderson 1989: 150).

A number of tendencies can be identified in the semiconductor and electronics industries. Companies have located labour-intensive assembly operations in the Third World, but this is only one tendency in the industry. Most of the global investment in semiconductor production is either domestically based or foreign investment in other First World countries. This may actually *increase* in the future. The rise of automated assembly operations and the rise in demand for customized semiconductors and higher product quality is likely to increase the advantages of locating all stages of production close to the final market. This is because automated assembly (such as Motorola's automated plant in Scotland) leads to higher productivity and therefore undermines the advantages of low labour costs, and global monitoring of product quality is both cumbersome and expensive. Furthermore, the rise of

Japanese companies and US companies attempting to copy perceived Just-in-Time practices reinforces the tendency towards re-agglomeration in the First World.[16] The supply of large pools of cheap, unorganized labour in the First World acts as a further incentive to invest there.[17]

The first-tier NICs (except for Hong Kong), on the other hand, have upgraded and have made considerable advances in technology, skills and infrastructure. However, even these successes face the problem of competing in the world market, where strategic technological and financial alliances between established market leaders and producers are being made (Henderson 1989: 150). For most of the Third World, the prospects are far worse, as most countries lack the skills and infrastructure required for assembly, or the potential to become a market in the near future.

Taiwan

Chapter Seven provided some data concerning the dynamism of small companies in Taiwan. This experience "casts doubt on the taken-for-granted advantages of scale, and ... demonstrate[s] the competitiveness of flexibly networked small firms" (Cheng & Gereffi 1994: 214). Such firms rest on the development of a particular institutional framework, such as state support, market access, family ties and supportive networks of similar firms. This has led to favourable comparison with the Italian industrial district model (Orru 1991).

However, one needs to exercise caution in putting forward the view that Taiwan represents a model of small-firm flexible specialization.[18] From the 1950s to the 1970s, Taiwan's economy was dominated by big business. The manufacturing value added share of firms employing more than 500 workers at the beginning of the 1970s was 56.4 per cent, higher than Brazil (36 per cent) and even South Korea (52.7 per cent), and possibly the highest in the world. The move towards smaller businesses was partly a product of the state encouraging a move by industry to the suburbs (Amsden 1991: 1123–6). This move was linked to high land prices in the urban centres, and urban congestion. Moreover, as Taiwan moved into newer sectors such as electronics, so it became incorporated into "global commodity chains[19] which provide[d] resources based on distinctive patterns of forward and backward linkages" (Cheng & Gereffi 1994: 214). This can be seen with the commonality of OEM arrangements in Taiwan, discussed in the case of electronics above (Hobday 1995: 132–3).[20] If Taiwan wishes to further upgrade its electronics industry, and move beyond OEM arrangments, then it will have to confront the problem of cost barriers to entry and therefore scale (see above).

Conclusion: flexible accumulation, comparative advantage, commodity chains and late industrialization

The idea of flexible accumulation clearly points to some important changes that have occurred in the world economy in recent years. There is a need for caution however, in that much of the literature exaggerates the shift from Fordism to post-Fordism, often with contradictory results. For instance, in the clothing and electronics sectors, the (limited) relocation of labour-intensive manufacturing to parts of the Third World is often cited as evidence of the flexible practices of TNCs (Gereffi 1994b). At the same time, in the automobiles sector the world car strategy, based on relocation of labour-intensive segments to lower-cost areas, tends to be regarded as an extension of Fordism. In this sector, it is the extension of Japanese practices, which involve the re-agglomeration of productive activity within the First World, which is seen as an extension of the principles of flexibility (Hill & Lee 1994). Thus, both a hyper-mobile capital which operates on a global scale, and a more entrenched capital which operates within established regions, are taken as evidence of a post-Fordist era (cf. Murray 1989a: 45–8; Urry 1989: 97–8).

Clearly there is a need to avoid such over-generalizations and contradictions. At the same time there is a need to recognize the reality of flexible accumulation, while being sensitive to its uneven implementation. First it needs to be stressed that flexible accumulation offers new opportunities to the Third World, as competitiveness in some sectors may be achieved through the promotion of small businesses and the adoption of Japanese organizational methods. The unprecedented rise of the NICs suggest that a completely pessimistic analysis is misguided.

On the other hand, optimistic scenarios deserve a more vehement rejection. First, the opportunities presented by flexible accumulation are limited in that their success rests on particular institutional structures such as a developmental state, skilled labour and particular patterns of work organization. Some of these institutions – and especially the developmental state – have been undermined by the implementation of structural adjustment policies in the 1980s and 1990s.[21] But even more important is the fact that flexibility does not promote a level playing field in the global economy. In other words, while post-Fordism may lead to the establishment of new areas of capital accumulation and agglomeration, and the decline of others, it does not alter the facts that (i) capital will accumulate in some areas and therefore marginalize others; and (ii) given the advantages enjoyed by First World countries (skills, infrastructure, research and development in new technology, etc.), the new areas are still more likely to be in the established regions or countries.

A commodity chains approach is one fruitful way of understanding the hierarchical location of production (and other economic activity) in the world economy. Such a chain can be defined as "a network of labor and production processes whose end result is a finished commodity" (Hopkins & Wallerstein 1986: 159). A global commodity chain links such processes at a global level. Gereffi (1994a: 219) distinguishes between two kinds of commodity chains. The first type, producer-driven, is where the site of production is relatively immobile and tends to agglomerate within established areas of accumulation. In these cases, manufacturers making advanced products like aircraft, automobiles and computer systems are the key economic agents in these producer-driven chains not only in terms of their earnings, but also in their ability to exert control over backward linkages with raw material and component suppliers, as with forward linkages into retailing.

Buyer-driven commodity chains, the second type, are characterized by more mobility as production is more labour-intensive and therefore more likely to take place in the Third World. However,

> these same industries are also design- and marketing-intensive, which means that there are high barriers to entry at the brand-name merchandising and retail levels where companies invest considerable sums in product development, advertising and computerized store networks to create and sell these items. Therefore, whereas producer-driven commodity chains are controlled by core firms at the point of production, control over buyer-driven commodity chains is exercised at the point of consumption. (ibid.)

Two final points need to be made which take us back to Kitching's arguments, and the relationship between industrialization and development. The first point, which in some ways supports Kitching's contentions, is that a commodity chains framework undermines the flexible specialization thesis because it shows how small industries are often subordinated to large capital. Small is often not so much beautiful or efficient, but subordinate.[22] The second point, which partly undermines Kitching's thesis, is that the relationship between industrialization and development is not as direct as he implies. For as Gereffi (1994a: 226) points out,

> while industrialization may be a necessary condition for core status in the world economy, it no longer is sufficient. Mobility within the world economy should not be defined simply in terms of a country's degree of industrialization, but rather by a nation's success in upgrading its mix of economic activities toward technology- and skill-intensive products and techniques with higher levels of local value added.

Notes

1. Following Harvey (1989: ch. 9), I use the term flexible accumulation (or flexible production). Although this term is more vague than some phrases used to describe the new era, it has the advantage of being a "catch-all" category, which in turn can recognize the changes that have occurred in capital accumulation, but at the same time can problematize some of the more sweeping arguments made concerning post-Fordism.

2. The issue of import of technology has been discussed in Chapter Five. It is also examined later in this chapter when I present some sectoral case studies of flexible accumulation.

3. This is the basis for the theory of the new international division of labour, critically discussed in Chapter Five (cf. Jenkins 1984b; Kiely 1994). As should be clear by now, the push factor of cheap labour was strictly limited and combined with local pull factors such as the role of the state.

4. This can be seen in the movement towards tariff reductions, the creation of a World Trade Organisation and the implementation of structural adjustment programmes. This does not mean that the free market globalization thesis is correct however. Capital is not completely footloose or stateless, as Chapter Five makes clear. On the limits of globalization theses of both left and right, see Kiely 1997b.

5. On Japanization, see Humphrey 1993, Harriss 1995b. On flexible specialization, see the articles in *IDS Bulletin* 1992, Schmitz & Musyck 1994, Rabellotti 1995, Schmitz 1995.

6. See further the case studies below, particularly clothing.

7. Under the Uruguay round of the GATT (1986–93), the Multi-Fibre Agreement will be gradually phased out over a ten-year period.

8. In practice of course, these factors may have been partly caused by import penetration by the NICs. Nevertheless, the fact remains that a correlation between First World job losses and "Third World" (or East Asian) job gains is not the same as a causal process.

9. These comments do not imply that economies of scale are unimportant in Japanese automobile companies. On the contrary, assembly plants still have an optimum run of 250,000 units a year, although the specific model optimum may be lower (Dicken 1992: 282).

10. For example, General Motors have a joint venture with Toyota in North America, while Honda established a deal with what was British Leyland (now Rover) as early as 1979. The European and American companies hope to gain managerial know-how from such deals, while for the Japanese companies it guarantees them access to markets.

11. Proton is the brand name. The company is actually called Perusahaan Otomobil Nasional Berhad.

12. Humphrey (1993) documents cases of the adoption of Japanese production techniques in Brazil, and even argues that established patterns of work flexibility and the absence of clear job specifications may act as an advantage for late industrializers hoping to adopt advanced management techniques. Nevertheless, Humphrey's relatively upbeat argument is undermined by his acceptance that such practices are the exception rather than the norm, and that the recession of the early 1990s undermined management promises of increased job security.

13. This figure needs some qualification, however, as it does not take into account those companies (such as IBM) that produce semiconductors solely for use within the company. Nevertheless, these in-house consumers are also large companies and so the basic point that semiconductor production is dominated by large companies remains valid.

14. Brazil is another example of the successful development of a domestic computer industry, actively fostered by state intervention. The industry is still, however, confined to the lower quality end of the market (cf. Schmitz & Hewitt 1992; Evans 1995).

15. This is where factories make finished goods where the specifications are supplied by the buyers, who are usually the companies that design the goods.

16. I do not mean that JIT practices are uniformly practised by Japanese or US electronics companies. I refer the reader to my comments concerning the limitations of the Japanese model in the first section of this chapter. What is important is the *perception* that Japanese practices – including locational proximity to suppliers – are the most effective way forward for companies.

17. Employment conditions for assembly workers are often appalling in the industry, including in Silicon Valley (cf. Fuentes & Ehrenreich 1983).

18. Not only is this the case for the reasons cited here, it also applies to the problems associated with the flexible specialization model applied to Italy, discussed earlier in this chapter.

19. Global commodity chains are discussed in more detail below.

20. These arrangements are not unlike those between small clothing companies/workshops

and Benetton in Italy. They do not however constitute independent regional development as flexible specialization theorists contend.

21. This is not to deny that many states are inefficient, but it is to deny that they are *necessarily* inefficient and that late industrializers can do without sustained intervention in the economy. See the discussion in Chapter Eight.

22. This point needs qualification. The "small is beautiful" and "small is efficient" schools are obviously very different and I have put them together here only because they implicitly challenge an over-emphasis on scale economies. More important, I do not reject the obvious point that small industry can be viable or that Third World producers may carve out specific niches for themselves in certain markets, which may later be used for the upgrading of industrial activity. What I do reject, however, is the argument that such industries are inherently more efficient or that they enjoy considerable autonomy from large capital.

Part IV
Conclusion

Chapter Ten

Capitalism, industrialization and alternatives

This book has focused on the questions of agency, lateness and development in various industrialization processes. In this final chapter, I briefly review the issues. Also, in returning to the question of socialism, I examine the questions raised by alternative industrialization strategies.

Agency and industrialization

The technological determinist case associated with, for example, the convergence thesis, should be rejected. Whilst technology is undoubtedly one factor in any case of industrialization, it clearly is not the only one. Social and political factors have been crucial in the taking of decisions on whether or not to adopt a particular technology, and the effect of this technology has had different effects on social groups such as classes and genders. Current debates around the potential of information technology must be seen in this light, just as historical decisions to invest in new technology should be situated in the context of specific social relations of production.

Questions around the agency for industrialization are historically specific. There is, then, a need for care in making generalizations. Insofar as these can be made, the most important question appears to revolve around the role of the state. All industrializations have relied on a strong state, but *the later the industrialization, the greater the need for strong state intervention in the economy*.[1] States can of course be inefficient and oppressive, in both socialist and capitalist contexts. However, states are not *necessarily* inefficient. Markets, on the other hand, are unequal, hierarchical and incapable of working without the existence of states.

Actually existing industrializations rest on the development of a particular *social structure of accumulation* (SSA). This refers to

the complex of institutions which support the process of capital accumulation. The central idea of the SSA approach is that a long period of relatively rapid and stable economic expansion requires an effective SSA.[2] (Kotz et al. 1994: 1)

Thus, our case studies have shown the importance of class formation, state organization, gender and sectoral relationships (between industry and agriculture for instance) in any pattern of capital accumulation. These factors have impacted both on the rate of capital accumulation and on wider questions of social development.

Late industrialization and the global economy

The global economy comprises hierarchies of production which in turn mean that the world market is not the level playing field that neo-liberals imagine. Late industrializers face enormous constraints, both in developing effective producers that can compete with foreign capital in their domestic economy, and in breaking into export markets and thereby competing in the world economy. These barriers are not completely insurmountable however, and the East Asian NICs have enjoyed some considerable success on both fronts. Having said that, their success rested on favourable world market factors and the existence of a strong, effective state that disciplined capital as well as labour. Neo-liberal dominance of international trade, financial and development institutions hinders the prospects for successful late industrialization in the current period. On the other hand, a scenario of completely unregulated global market forces is unlikely to be implemented and the world economy does offer opportunities for late developers as well as constraints. These opportunities include the prospects (with all the contradictions these entail) of foreign investment, established overseas markets, and advanced technology. The prospect for successful late industrialization then appears to rest on a policy of being "in and against the (world) market".[3] Successful late industrializers will be *in* the world market in that they attempt to draw on its opportunities, but are *against* it in that the state plays a crucial role in removing its constraints. Any delinking from the world economy (in a capitalist or socialist framework – see below) must be selective.

Industrialization and development

The link between industrialization and development is not as direct as some advocates (like Kitching) make out. The case studies have shown considerable diversity in the relationship, which suggests that the character of the agents that promote industrialization also affects the nature of the wider development process. Thus, the relatively egalitarian nature of Korean and Taiwanese industrialization has its roots in the land reforms that were implemented in those countries, which in turn were a product of pressures from below (although, in the latter case, the pressure came from the Chinese mainland, which influenced KMT action on reaching Taiwan).

Contrary to the claims of some writers (Sachs 1992a, b), capitalist industrialization *can* be progressive and empowering, even if it is at the same time exploitative. The degree to which it is progressive may depend partly on the fact that capitalism promotes the expansion of output and new technologies. Some of these developments will (even if indirectly) have a beneficial effect in terms of health and education, as Kitching reminds us. However, that is only part of the story. Development also depends on the actions of lower classes and other oppressed groups in alleviating the worst effects of capitalism, for current as well as future generations.

Kitching's position of being *in* development therefore underestimates the social costs of industrialization, while Sachs' position of being *against* development underestimates the potential benefits. A position of being "in and against" development recognizes both the costs and benefits of new technologies, and promotes the minimization of the former and maximization of the latter (even if this has "negative" trade-offs in terms of lower economic growth).

Alternative industrializations? Capitalism, socialism and appropriate technology

So far this concluding chapter has focused on the relationship between industrialization and development. But what of the alternatives, and particularly the question of socialism and industrial development? Chapter Four made clear that the record of socialist industrializers was not a good one, and so, to finish this work, I want to briefly address three questions that relate to alternative development strategies. First, are rural utopias based on delinking from the world economy viable? Second, what is the best way of industrializing – by capitalist or socialist methods? Third, are we doomed to make a trade-off between technological development and better living standards on the one hand, and hierarchy, alienation and exploitation on the other?

The argument that nations are better off if they avoid industrialization is a romantic fallacy. As I showed in Chapter Two, the great strength of Kitching's work is his theoretical case for industrialization. Although this may not tell us much about "actually existing industrializations", it tells us a great deal about would-be agrarian societies totally cut off from the world economy. Such utopias would involve the relatively equal distribution of scarcity – people would share poverty. These societies would be authoritarian so that the activities of potential entrepreneurs, who could drive ahead of competitors, would have to be controlled. Finally, delinking would lead to economic collapse as imports ended, including those required for domestic production. Such wishful thinking then, is not only patronizing and romantic, it is positively dangerous.

What, then, is the best route available for late industrializers? For some "new realist" Marxists, including Kitching (1983), the best way is through the development of capitalist relations of production (cf. Sender & Smith 1986; Warren 1980). These would later be replaced by socialism, presumably at the "appropriate time". The mixed developmental record of socialist countries is often cited to back up these claims (Kitching 1983; Sender & Smith 1990). However, these writers only put forward a model of capitalism in the abstract, and fail to properly distinguish between different capitalisms in the world (cf. Chapter Two). Moreover, while they may be right to point to the terrible costs of socialist industrializations, they fail to see how the leaders of these societies operate within a similar framework. Both Stalinism and "new realist" Marxism assume that the key issue is the development of the productive forces, at the cost of human development. The latter therefore ignore how capitalist technology may be inappropriate for a socialist future (Leys 1984; Sutcliffe 1992: 343–4). One thinks of the massive production of motor cars, armaments, hierarchies in the labour process, and so on. Thus, writers such as Kitching are certainly too optimistic about advanced capitalism – both in terms of its attainability for late developers, and its desirability for the whole world.

Are we left, then, with a Faustian bargain, a trade-off between advanced technology and alienation (cf. Berman 1984: ch. 1)? Does industrialization offer the possibility of social development, but at the cost of hierarchy and lack of democracy? It is at this point that debates around the issue of "appropriate technology" become important? A genuinely alternative approach to technology would cease to consider workers (and others) as the objects of "progress", as they have been in capitalist and state socialist societies. "Externalities" such as environmental hazards and job dissatisfaction would cease to be treated as such, and would be treated as a central consideration in the development and introduction of new technologies. However, *contra* the arguments of many populists, such appropriate technology could only exist in a particular social context, which presupposes a radical change in power relations, both globally and locally. Such a genuinely radical approach to technology is well summarized by Andrew Feenberg (1991: 19):

> [T]he technical enterprise itself is immanently disposed to address the demands we formulate as potentialities, but ... it is artificially truncated in modern industrial societies. Opening technical development to the influence of a wider range of values is a technical project requiring broad democratic participation. Radical democratization can thus be rooted in the very nature of technology, with profound substantive consequences for the organization of industrial society.

Notes

1. I am purposely using the language of neo-liberalism here. The idea of a separate state "intervening" in a separate economic sphere actually fetishizes both economics and politics, and in reality the two are inextricably linked (Kiely 1995c: ch. 6). My use of language is therefore deliberately polemical, designed to undermine the fallacies of neo-liberalism.
2. The approach in this work is not completely compatible with the SSA approach

however. First, SSA approaches have largely focused on the appropriate micro-institutional framework for capital accumulation, such as work organization. Apart from my discussion in Chapter Nine, my focus has been on the macro-institutional framework. More important is the danger that SSA approaches can lead to functionalism. In focusing on appropriate foundations for capital accumulation, the SSA school can exaggerate the degree of integration of any SSA, and thereby downplay the reality of conflict within all capitalist societies. In this way, an appropriate SSA can be regarded as an appropriate structure which functions for the hegemony of capitalism, thereby ignoring the contradictions of *any* social structure of accumulation and the role of exploited classes as makers of their own history. My approach has attempted to utilize the strength of the SSA school – the reality of different capitalist industrializations based on the emergence of particular social relations. However, I continue to recognize the contradictions of all capitalist industrializations, and the *contingent* nature of the emergence of social structures of accumulation (on theorizing contingency see McLennan 1996).

3. The idea of being "in and against" capitalism is derived from the work of the Conference of Socialist Economists on the state (CSE 1979; London to Edinburgh Weekend Return Group 1980). It is based on the recognition that important reforms (opportunities) can be gained from being *in* the capitalist state, but that these are always compromised (constrained) by the dominance of capitalist social relations and the role of the state in securing this dominance, and so there is a need to be simultaneously *against* the state.

References

Adorno, T. 1991. *The culture industry*. London: Routledge.

Afshar, H. (ed.) 1996. *Women and politics in the third world*. London: Routledge.

Alavi, H. 1989. Formation of the social structure of South Asia under the impact of colonialism. In *South Asia*, H. Alavi & J. Harriss (eds), 5–19. London: Macmillan.

Alavi, H. & T. Shanin (eds) 1982. *An introduction to the sociology of developing societies*. London: Macmillan.

Alexander, J. 1995. *Fin de siècle social theory: relativism, reduction, and the problem of reason*. London: Verso.

Allen, T. 1992. Prospects and dilemmas for industrializing nations. In Allen & Thomas (1992), 379-90.

Allen, T. & A. Thomas (eds) 1992. *Poverty and development in the 1990s*. Oxford: Oxford University Press.

Amin, A. 1994a. Post-Fordism: models, fantasies and phantoms of transition. See Amin (1994b), 1–39.

Amin, A. 1994b. *Post-Fordism: a reader*. Oxford: Blackwell.

Amin, A. & K. Robbins 1990. The re-emergence of regional economies? The mythical geography of flexible accumulation. *Environment and Planning D: Society and Space* 8, 7–34.

Amsden, A. 1985. The state and Taiwan's economic development. In *Bringing the state back in*, P. Evans, D. Rueschmeyer & T. Skocpol (eds), 78–106. Cambridge: Cambridge University Press.

Amsden, A. 1989. *Asia's next giant*. Oxford: Oxford University Press.

Amsden, A. 1991. Big business and urban congestion in Taiwan: the origins of small enterprise and regionally decentralized industry (respectively). *World Development* 19, 1121–35.

Amsden, A. 1992. A theory of government in late industrialization. In *The state and market in development*, L. Putterman & D. Rueschmeyer (eds), 53–84. Boulder: Lynne Rienner.

Amsden, A. 1993. Trade policy and economic performance in South Korea. In *Trade and growth*, M. Agosin & D. Tussie (eds), 187–214. London: Macmillan.

Amsden, A. 1994. Why isn't the whole world experimenting with the East Asian model to develop? Review of 'The East Asian miracle'. *World Development* 22, 627–33.

Amsden, A. & Y-D. Euh 1990. Republic of Korea's financial reform: what are the lessons? *UNCTAD Discussion Paper* no. 30. Geneva: UNCTAD.

Anderson, P. 1974. *Lineages of the absolutist state*. London: Verso.

Andors, S. 1977. *China's industrial revolution*. London: Martin Robertson.

Appelbaum, R. & J. Henderson (eds) 1992. *States and development in the Asian Pacific Rim*. London: Sage.

Arnot, B. 1988. *Controlling Soviet labour*. London: Macmillan.

Ashton, T. 1948. *The industrial revolution*. London: Routledge.

Aston, T. & C. Philpin (eds) 1985. *The Brenner debate*. Cambridge: Cambridge University Press.

Atkinson, D., A. Dallin & G. Lapidus 1978. *Women in Russia*. London: Harvester.

Bahro, R. 1978. *The alternative in Eastern Europe*. London: New Left Books.

Balassa, B. 1981. *The newly industrializing countries and the world economy*. New York: Pergamon.

174

Balassa, B., G. Bueno, P. Kuczynski & M. Simonsen 1986. *Adjusting to success: balance of payments policy in the East Asian NICs*. Washington: Institute of International Economics.

Balsubramanyam, V. 1980. *Multinational enterprises and the third world*. London: Trade Policy Research Centre.

Banuri, T. and F. Appfel Marglin (eds) 1993. *Who will save the forests?* London: Zed.

Baran, P. & P. Sweezy 1966. *Monopoly capital*. New York: Monthly Review Press.

Bardhan, P. 1984. *The political economy of development in India*. Oxford: Blackwell.

Barnet, R. & R. Muller 1974. *Global Reach*. New York: Simon & Schuster.

Barone, C. 1984. Reply to Hart-Landsberg. *Review of Radical Political Economics* 16, 194–7.

Bayat, A. 1991. *Work, politics and power*. London: Zed.

Becker, D. & R. Sklar 1987. Why postimperialism? See Becker et al., 1–18.

Becker, D., J. Frieden, S. Schatz & R. Sklar 1987. *Postimperialism*. Boulder: Lynne Rienner.

Bello, W. 1994. *People and power in the Pacific*. London: Pluto.

Bello, W. & S. Rosenfeld 1992. *Dragons in distress*. London: Penguin.

Benewick, R. & P. Wingrove (eds) 1995. *China in the 1990s*. London: Macmillan.

Bensel, R. 1990. *Yankee leviathan*. Cambridge: Cambridge University Press.

Berger, F. 1979. Korea's experience with export-led development. In *Export promotion policies*, B. de Vries (ed.), 60–82. Washington: World Bank.

Berger, P. & H-H. Tsaio 1988. *In search of an East Asian model of development*. New Brunswick: Transaction Books.

Berman, M. 1984. *All that is solid melts into air*. London: Verso.

Bernstein, H. 1979. Sociology of development versus sociology of underdevelopment? In *Development theory: four critical essays*, D. Lehmann (ed.), 77–106. London: Frank Cass.

Bernstein, H. 1982. Industrialization, development and dependence. See Alavi & Shanin (1982), 218–35.

Bernstein, H. 1992a. Agrarian structures and change: Latin America. See Bernstein et al. (1992b), 27–50.

Bernstein, H. 1992b. Agrarian structures and change: India. See Bernstein et al. (1992b), 51–64.

Bernstein, H. 1994. Agrarian classes in capitalist development. See Sklair (1994), 40–71

Bernstein, H. & B. Crow 1988. The expansion of Europe. See Crow & Thorpe (1988), 9–29

Bernstein, H., T. Hewitt & A. Thomas 1992a. Capitalism and the expansion of Europe. See Allen & Thomas (1992), 168–84

Bernstein, H., B. Crow & H. Johnson (eds) 1992b. *Rural livelihoods*. Oxford: Oxford University Press.

Berry, S. & R. Kiely 1993. Is there a future for Korean democracy? *Parliamentary Affairs* 46, 594–604.

Bettelheim, C. 1974. *Cultural revolution and industrial organisation in China*. New York: Monthly Review Press.

Bhagwati, J. & T. Srinivasan 1975. *Foreign trade regimes and economic development: India*. New York: Columbia University Press.

Bhaskar, V. & A. Glyn (eds) 1995. *The north, the south and the environment*. London: Earthscan.

Bideleux, R. 1985. *Communism and development*. London: Methuen.

Bienefeld, M. 1994. Capitalism and the nation-state in the dog days of the twentieth century. *The Socialist Register*, 94–129. London: Merlin.

Blackburn, R. (ed.) 1991. *After the fall*. London: Verso.

Blecher, M. 1986. *China: politics, economics and society*. London: Macmillan.

Booth, D. (ed.) 1994. *Rethinking social development*. London: Longman.

Bradford, C. 1990. Policy interventions and markets: development strategy typologies and policy options. See Gereffi & Wyman (1990), 32–51.

Bradshaw, Y. & M. Wallace 1996. *Global inequalities*. London: Pine Forge.

Brenner, R. 1977. The origins of capitalist development: a critique of "neo-Smithian" Marxism. *New Left Review* 104, 25–92.

Brenner, R. 1986. The social basis of economic development. In *Analytical Marxism*, J. Roemer (ed.), 23–53. Cambridge: Cambridge University Press.

Breslin, S. 1995. Centre and province in China. See Benewick & Wingrove (1995), 63–72.

Brett, E. A. 1983. *International money and capitalist crisis*. London: Macmillan.

Brewer, A. 1990. *Marxist theories of imperialism*. London: Routledge.

Bronfenbrenner, M. 1982. The Japanese development model re-examined: why concern ourselves with Japan? In *The struggle for development*, M. Bienefeld & M. Godfrey (eds), 93–109. Toronto: Wiley.

Buchanan, J. 1980. Rent-seeking and profit seeking. In *Towards a theory of the rent seeking society*, J. Buchanan, R. Tollison & G. Tullo (eds), 1–21. Texas: A & M University Press.

Buchanan, J. 1986. *Liberty, market and the state*. Brighton: Wheatsheaf.

Byres, T. 1974. Land reform, industrialisation and the marketed surplus in India: an essay on the power of rural bias. In *Agrarian reform and agrarian reformism*, D. Lehmann (ed.), 73–117. London: Faber.

Byres, T. 1989. Agrarian transition and the agrarian question. See Harriss (1989), 82–93.

Byres, T. 1991. The agrarian question and differing forms of capitalist agrarian transition: an essay with reference to Asia. In *Rural transformation in Asia*, J. Breman & S. Mundle (eds), 5–72. Oxford: Oxford University Press.

Byres, T. & B. Crow 1988. New technology and new masters for the Indian countryside. See Crow & Thorpe (1988), 163–81.

Cammack, P. 1991. Brazil: the long march to the New Republic. *New Left Review* 190, 21–58.

Carr, E. H. 1952. *The Bolshevik revolution*. London: Macmillan.

Castells, M. 1992. Four Asian tigers with a dragon head: a comparative analysis of the state, economy and society in the Asian Pacific rim. See Appelbaum & Henderson (1992), 33–70.

Castells, M. & P. Hall 1993. *Technopoles of the world*. London: Routledge.

Chalmers, N. 1989. *Industrial relations in Japan: the peripheral workforce*. London: Routledge.

Chandra, N. 1992. Bukharin's alternative to Stalin: industrialisation without forced collectivisation. *Journal of Peasant Studies* 20, 97–159.

Chandra, R. 1992. *Industrialization and development in the third world*. London: Routledge.

Chang, H-J. 1994. *The political economy of industrial policy*. London: Macmillan.

Chang, H-J. 1995. Explaining "flexible rigidities" in East Asia. See Killick (1995), 197–221.

Chang, H-J. & J. You 1993. The myth of free labour market in Korea. *Contributions to Political Economy* 12, 29–46.

Chenery, H., M. Ahluwalia, C. Bell, J. Duloy & R. Jolly 1974. *Redistribution with growth*. Oxford: Oxford University Press.

Cheng, L. & G. Gereffi 1994. The informal economy in East Asian development. *International Journal of Urban and Regional Research* 18, 194–219.

Cheng, L. & P. Hsiung 1992. Women, export-oriented growth and the role of the state: the case of Taiwan. See Appelbaum & Henderson (1992), 233–66.

Cheng, T. 1990. Political regimes and development strategies: South Korea and Taiwan. See Gereffi & Wyman (1990), 139–78.

Clairmonte, F. and J. Cavanagh 1988. *Merchants of drink: transnational control of world beverages*. Penang: Third World Network.

Clark, A. 1919. *Working life of women in the seventeenth century*. London: Routledge.

Clarke, S. 1992. Privatisation and the development of capitalism in Russia. *New Left Review* 196, 3–28.

Clarke, S. 1993. The contradictions of "state socialism". In *What about the workers?*, S. Clarke, P. Fairbrother, M. Burawoy & P. Krotov (eds), 1–29. London: Verso.

Clarke, S. 1995. Formal and informal relations in Soviet industrial production. In *Management and industry in Russia*, S. Clarke (ed.), 1–27. Aldershot: Edward Elgar.

Cliff, T. 1974. *State capitalism in Russia*. London: Pluto.

Cline, W. 1982. Can the East Asian model of development be generalized? *World Development* 10, 41–50.

Cohen, S. 1973. *Bukharin and the Bolshevik Revolution*. New York: Knopf.

Colclough, C. & J. Manor (eds) 1991. *States or markets?* Oxford: Clarendon.

Colman, D. and F. Nixson 1986. *Economics of change in less developed countries*. Hemel Hempstead: Philip Allan.

Corbridge, S. 1986. *Capitalist world development*. London: Macmillan.

Corbridge, S. 1989. Urban bias, rural bias and industrialization: an appraisal of the work of Michael Lipton and Terry Byres. See Harriss (1989), 94–116.

Corbridge, S. 1994. Post-Marxism and post-colonialism: the needs and rights of distant strangers. See Booth (1994), 90–117.

Corbridge, S. 1995a. Thinking about development. See Corbridge (1995b), 1–17.

Corbridge, S. (ed.) 1995b. *Development studies: a reader*. London: Edward Arnold.

Corrigan, P., H. Ramsey & D. Sayer 1978. *Socialist construction and Marxist theory*. London: Macmillan.

Cowen, M. & R. Shenton 1996. *Doctrines of development*. London: Routledge.

Crow, B. and A. Thomas 1983. *Third world atlas*. Milton Keynes: Open University Press.

Crow, B. & M. Thorpe (eds) 1988. *Survival and change in the third world*. Cambridge: Polity.

Crush, J. (ed.) 1995. *Power of development*. London: Routledge.

CSE 1979. *Struggles against the state*. London: CSE Books.

Cumings, B. 1987. The origins and development of the north-east Asian political economy: industrial sectors, product cycles and political consequences. See Deyo 1987, 44–83.

Curry, J. 1993. The flexibility fetish: a review essay on flexible specialisation. *Capital and Class* 50, 99–126.

Davidoff, L. & C. Hall 1987. *Family fortunes: men and women of the English middle class 1780–1850*. London: Hutchinson.

Davies, R. 1995. Forced labour under Stalin. *New Left Review* 214, 62–80.

Day, R. 1973. *Leon Trotsky and the politics of economic isolation*. London: Macmillan.

Day, R. 1977. The troubled unity of the Left Opposition. *Studies in Comparative Communism* 10, 77–91.

Dedoussis, V. & C. Littler 1993. Understanding the transfer of Japanese management practices: the Australian case. See Elger & Smith (1993b), 175–95.

Deutscher, I. 1970. *The prophet unarmed*. London: Penguin.

Deyo, F. (ed.) 1987. *The political economy of the new Asian industrialism*. Ithaca: Cornell University Press.

Deyo, F. 1989. *Beneath the miracle: labour subordination in the new Asian industrialism*. Berkeley: University of California Press.

Dicken, P. 1992. *Global shift*. London: Paul Chapman.

Dixon, C. 1991. *South-east Asia in the world economy*. Cambridge: Cambridge University Press.

Dixon, C. 1995. Structural adjustment in comparative perspective: lessons from Pacific Asia. In *Structurally adjusted Africa*, D. Simon, W. van Spengen, C. Dixon & A. Narman (eds), 202–28. London: Pluto.

Dixon, C. & D. Drakakis-Smith (eds) 1993a. *Economic and social development in Pacific Asia*. London: Routledge.

Dixon, C. & D. Drakakis-Smith 1993b. Conclusion: towards the Pacific century? See Dixon & Drakakis-Smith (1993a), 219–22.

Dohse, K. 1985. From "Fordism" to "Toyotism"? The social organisation of the labour process in the Japanese automobile industry. *Politics and Society* 14, 115–46.

Donaghu, M. & R. Barff 1990. Nike just did it: international subcontracting and flexibility in athletic footwear production. *Regional Studies* 24, 537–52.

Dore, R. 1986. *Flexible rigidities: industrial policy and structural adjustment in the Japanese economy, 1970–80*. London: Athlone Press.

Drakakis-Smith, D. 1992. *Pacific Asia*. London: Routledge.

Dreze, J. & A. Sen 1989. *Hunger and public action*. Oxford: Clarendon.

Dunning, E. 1993. *Multinational enterprises in a global economy*. Wokingham: Addison-Wesley.

Dutt, A. K. & K. Kim 1994. Market miracle and state stagnation? The development experience of South Korea and India compared. In *The state, markets, and development*, A. K. Dutt, K. Kim & A. Singh (eds), 169–216. Aldershot: Edward Elgar.

Dwyer, D. 1993. China: the consequences of liberalization. See Dixon & Drakakis-Smith (1993a), 152–68.

Edwards, C. 1985. *The fragmented world*. London: Methuen.

Edwards, C. 1992. Industrialization in South Korea. See Hewitt et al. (1992b), 97–127.

Edwards, C. 1995. East Asia and industrial policy in Malaysia: lessons for Africa. In *Asian industrialisation and Africa*, H. Stein (ed.), 239–56. London: Macmillan.

Eisenstadt, S. 1966. *Modernization, protest and change*. New York: Prentice-Hall.

Elger, T. & C. Smith 1993a. Introduction. See Elger & Smith (1994b), 1–24.

Elger, T. & C. Smith 1994 Global Japanization? Convergence and competition in the organization of the Labour process, in Elger & Smith 1994b, pp. 31–59.

Elger, T. & C. Smith (eds) 1994b. *Global Japanization?* London: Routledge.

Ellison, C. & G. Gereffi 1990. Explaining strategies and patterns of industrial development. See Gereffi & Wyman (1990), 368–403.

Ellman, M. 1975. Did the agricultural surplus provide the resources for the increase in investment in the USSR during the first Five Year Plan? *Economic Journal* 85, 844–63.

Elson, D. 1988. Dominance and dependency. See Crow & Thorpe (1988), 264–87.

Elson, D. 1989. The cutting edge: multinationals in textiles and clothing. In *Women's employment and multinationals in Europe*, D. Elson & R. Pearson (eds), 80–110. London: Macmillan.

Elson, D. 1994. Uneven development and the textiles and clothing industry. See Sklair (1994), 189–210.

Elson, D. & R. Pearson 1981. Nimble fingers make cheap workers: an analysis of women's employment in third world manufacturing. *Feminist Review* 7, 87–107.

Emmanuel, A. 1974. Myths of development versus myths of underdevelopment. *New Left Review* 85, 61–82.

Emmanuel, A. 1982. *Appropriate or underdeveloped technology?* Chichester: Wiley.

Ernst, D. 1987. US–Japanese competition and worldwide restructuring of the electronics industry: a European view. See Henderson & Castells (1987), 38–59.

Escobar, A. 1995. *Encountering development*. Princeton: Princeton University Press.

Esteva, G. 1992. Development. See Sachs (1992a), 6–25.

Evans, P. 1979. *Dependent development*. Princeton: Princeton University Press.

Evans, P. 1991. The state as problem and solution: predation, embedded autonomy and adjustment. In *The politics of economic adjustment*, S. Haggard & R. Kaufman (eds), 60–88. Princeton: Princeton University Press.

Evans, P. 1995. *Embedded autonomy*. Princeton: Princeton University Press.

Feenberg, A. 1991. *Critical theory of technology*. Oxford: Oxford University Press.

Filtzer, D. 1986. *Soviet workers and Stalinist industrialisation*. London: Pluto.

Fishlow, A. 1989. Latin American failure against the backdrop of Asian success. *Annals of the American Academy of Political and Social Science* 505, 117–28.

Frank, A. G. 1969. *Capitalism and underdevelopment in Latin America*. New York: Monthly Review Press.

Frank, A. G. 1981. *Crisis in the third world*. London: Heinemann.

Frank, A. G. 1982. Asia's exclusive models. *Far Eastern Economic Review*, 25 June, 22–3.

Frank, A. G. 1983. Global crisis and transformation. *Development and Change* 14, 323–46.

Frederickson, G. 1981. *White supremacy*. Oxford: Oxford University Press.

Freeman, C. 1987. *Technology policy and economic performance*. London: Pinter.

Friedman, M. & R. Friedman 1981. *Free to choose*. London: Penguin.

Frith, S. 1983. *Sound effects*. London: Constable.

Frith, S. 1988. *Music for pleasure*. Cambridge: Polity.

Frobel, F., J. Heinrichs & O. Kreye 1980. *The new international division of labour*. Cambridge: Cambridge University Press.

Fuentes, A. & B. Ehrenreich 1983. *Women in the global factory*. Boston: South End Press.

Fukui, H. 1992. The Japanese state and economic development: a profile of a nationalist-paternalist capitalist state. See Appelbaum & Henderson (1992), 199–225.

Furtado, C. 1970. *Economic development of Latin America*. Cambridge: Cambridge University Press.

Gamble, A. 1985. *Britain in decline*. London: Macmillan.

George, S. 1976. *How the other half dies*. Harmondsworth: Penguin.

Geras, N. 1995. *Solidarity in the conversation of humankind*. London: Verso.

Gereffi, G. 1983. *The pharmaceutical industry and dependency in the third world*. Princeton, NJ: Princeton University Press.

Gereffi, G. 1990. Paths of industrialization: an overview. See Gereffi & Wyman (1990), 3–31.

Gereffi, G. 1992. New realities of industrial development in East Asia and Latin America: global, regional and national trends. See Appelbaum & Henderson (1992), 85–112.

Gereffi, G. 1994a. Capitalism, development and global commodity chains. See Sklair (1994), 211–31.

Gereffi, G. 1994b. The organization of buyer-driven global commodity chains: how US retailers shape overseas production networks. See Gereffi & Korzeniewicz (1994), 95–122.

Gereffi, G. and L. Hempel 1996. Latin America in the global economy: running faster to stay in place. NACLA 39 (4), 18–27.

Gereffi, G. and M. Korzeniewicz (eds) 1994. *Commodity chains and global capitalism*. Westport, CT: Greenwood Press.

Gereffi, G. and D. Wyman (eds) 1990. *Manufacturing Miracles*. Princeton: Princeton University Press.

Gerschenkron, A. 1962. *Economic backwardness in historical perspective*. Cambridge, MA: Belknap Press.

Ghosh, J. & K. Bharadwaj 1992. Poverty and employment in India. See Bernstein et al. (1992b), 139–64.

Gilpin, R. 1987. *The political economy of international relations*. Princeton: Princeton University Press.

Girvan, N. 1971. *Foreign capital and economic underdevelopment in Jamaica*. Mona: UWI-ISER.

Goodman, D. & M. Redclift 1981. *From peasant to proletarian*. Oxford: Blackwell.

Gordon, D. 1988. The global economy: new edifice or crumbling foundations? *New Left Review* 168, 24–64.

Gough, J. 1986. Industrial policy and socialist strategy. *Capital and Class* 29, 58–79.

Griffin, K. 1978. *International inequality and national poverty*. London: Macmillan.

Gulalp, H. 1986. Debate on capitalism and development: the theories of Samir Amin and Bill Warren. *Capital and Class* 28, 135–59.

Gunnarsson, C. 1985. Development theory and third world industrialisation. *Journal of Contemporary Asia* 15, 183–206.

Gwynne, R. 1991. New horizons? The third world motor vehicle industry in an international framework. In *Restructuring the global automobile industry*, C. Law (ed.), 61–87. London: Routledge.

Habermas, J. 1987. *The philosophical discourse of modernity*. Cambridge: Polity.

Haggard, S. & Cheng 1987. State and foreign capital in the East Asian NICs. See Deyo (1987), 84–135.

Hall, C. 1982. The home turned upside down? The working class family in cotton textiles, 1780–1850. In *The changing experience of women*, E. Whitelegg (ed.), 17–29. Oxford: Martin Robertson.

Hall, S. & M. Jacques (eds) 1989. *New Times*. London: Lawrence & Wishart.

Halliday, F. 1991. The ends of Cold War. See Blackburn (1991), 78–99.

Halliday, J. & B. Cumings 1988. *Korea: the unknown war*. New York: Pantheon.

Hamelink, C. 1983. *Cultural autonomy in global communications*. New York: Longman.

Hamilton, C. 1984. Class, state and industrialisation in South Korea. *IDS Bulletin* 15, 38–43.

Hamilton, C. 1986. *Capitalist industrialization in Korea*. London: Westview.

Hamilton, C. 1987. Can the rest of Asia emulate the NICs? *Third World Quarterly* 87, 1225–56.

Hamilton, G. & C. Kao 1987. Max Weber and the analysis of East Asian industrialisation. *International Sociology* 2, 289–300.

Handley, P. 1991. Growth without tears. *Far Eastern Economic Review*, 18 July, pp. 34–5.

Harris, N. 1986. *The End of the Third World*. London: Penguin.

Harris, N. 1991. A Comment on National Liberation. *International Socialism* 53, 79–91.

Harrison, B. 1994. *Lean is mean: the changing landscape of corporate power in an age of flexibility*. New York: Basic Books.

Harriss, J. (ed.) 1989. *Rural development*. London: Routledge.

Harriss, J. 1995a. Does the "depressor" still work? Agrarian structure and development in India. See Corbridge (1995b), 121–46.

Harriss, J. 1995b. "Japanization": context and culture in the Indonesian automotive industry. *World development* 23, 117–28.

Hart-Landsberg, M. 1984. Capitalism and third world economic development: a critical look at the South Korean miracle. *Review of Radical Political Economics* 16, 181–93.

Hart-Landsberg, M. 1993. *The rush to development*. New York: Monthly Review Press.

Harvey, D. 1989. *The condition of postmodernity*. Oxford: Blackwell.

Healey, J. & M. Robinson 1992. *Democracy, governance and economic policy*. London: Overseas Development Institute.

Henderson, J. 1989. *The globalisation of semi-conductor production*. London: Routledge.

Henderson, J. 1991. Urbanisation in the Hong Kong–South China region: an introduction to dynamics and dilemmas. *International Journal of Urban and Regional Research* 15, 169–79.

Henderson, J. 1994. Electronics industries and the developing world. See Sklair (1994), 258–88.

Henderson, J. & M. Castells (eds) 1987. *Global restructuring and territorial development*. London: Sage.

Hensman, R. 1996. The role of women in the resistance to political authoritarianism in Latin America and South Asia. See Afshar (1996), 48–72.

Hewitt, T. 1992. Brazilian industrialization. See Hewitt et al. (1992b), 66–96.

Hewitt, T. & D. Wield 1992. Technology and industrialization. See Hewitt et al. (1992b), 201–21.

Hewitt, T., H. Johnson & D. Wield 1992a. Introduction. See Hewitt et al. (1992b), 1–9.

Hewitt, T., H. Johnson & D. Wield (eds) 1992b. *Industrialization and development*. Oxford: Oxford University Press.

Hill, R. C. 1987. Global factory and company town: the changing division of labour in the international automobile industry. See Henderson & Castells (1987), 18–37.

Hill, R. C. & Y. J. Lee 1994. Japanese multinationals and East Asian development: the case of the automobile industry. See Sklair (1994), 289–315.

Hilton, R. (ed.) 1976. *The transition from feudalism to capitalism*. London: Verso.

Hirst, P. & G. Thompson 1996. *Globalization in question*. Cambridge: Polity.

Hobday, M. 1995. *Innovation in East Asia*. Aldershot: Edward Elgar.

Hobsbawm, E. 1962. *Age of revolution*. London: Weidenfeld & Nicolson.

Hobsbawm, E. 1968. *Industry and empire*. London: Penguin.

Hobsbawm, E. 1969. *Labouring men*. London: Weidenfeld & Nicolson.

Hofheinz, R. & K. Calder 1982. *The East Asia edge*. New York: Basic.

Hoffman, J. & R. Kaplinsky 1988. *Driving force*. Boulder: Westview.

Hopkins, T. & I. Wallerstein 1986. Commodity chains in the world economy prior to 1800. *Review* 10, 157–70.

Hosking, G. 1990. *A history of the Soviet Union*. London: Fontana.

Howell, J. 1992. The myth of autonomy: the foreign enterprise in China. In *Labour in transition*, C. Smith & P. Thompson (eds), 205–26. London: Routledge.

Huang, C. 1989. The state and foreign investment: the cases of Taiwan and Singapore. *Comparative Political Studies* 22, 93–121.

Humphrey, J. 1988. Industrialization in Brazil. See Crow & Thorpe (1988), 216–41.

Humphrey, J. 1993. "Japanese" methods and the changing position of direct production workers: evidence from Brazil. See Elger & Smith (1993b), 327–47.

Humphrey, J. 1995a. Introduction. *World Development* 23, 1–7.

Humphrey, J. 1995b. Industrial reorganization in developing countries: from models to trajectories. *World Development* 23, 149–62.

Hyden, G. 1980. *Beyond ujamaa in Tanzania*. London: Heinemann.

Hymer, S. 1982. The multinational corporation and the law of uneven development. See Alavi & Shanin (1982), 128–52.

IDS Bulletin 1992. Flexible specialisation: a new view on small industry. 23, 2–57.

Inkster, I. 1991. *Science and technology in history*. London: Macmillan.

Ip, O. 1995. Changing employment systems in China: some evidence from the Shenzhen special economic zone. *Work, Employment and Society* 9, 269–85.

Jackson, C. 1995. Radical environmental myths: a gender perspective. *New Left Review* 210, 124–40.

Jenkins, R. 1984a. *Transnational corporations and the industrial transformation of Latin America*. London: Macmillan.

Jenkins, R. 1984b. Divisions over the international division of labour. *Capital and Class* 22, 28–57.

Jenkins, R. 1987. *Transnational corporations and uneven development*. London: Methuen.

Jenkins, R. 1988. Transnational corporations and third world consumption: implications of competitive strategies. *World Development* 16, 1363–70.

Jenkins, R. 1990. Learning from the gang: are there lessons for Latin America from East Asia. *Bulletin of Latin American Research* 10, 37–54.

Jenkins, R. 1991. The political economy of industrialization: a comparison of Latin American and East Asian newly industrializing countries. *Development and Change* 22, 197–231.

Jenkins, R. 1992a. Industrialization and the global economy. See Hewitt et al. (1992b), 13–40.

Jenkins, R. 1992b. Theoretical perspectives. See Hewitt et al. (1992b), 128–66.

Jenkins, R. 1992c. (Re-)interpreting Brazil and South Korea. See Hewitt et al. (1992b), 167–98.

Johnson, C. 1982. *MITI and the Japanese miracle*. Stanford: Stanford University Press.

Johnson, C. 1995. *Japan: who governs?* New York: W. W. Norton.

Johnson, H. 1988. Survival and Change on the Land. See Crow & Thorpe (1988), 147–62.

Jomo, K. S. 1993. Prospects for Malaysian industrialisation in light of East Asian experience. In *Industrialising Malaysia*, K. S. Jomo (ed.), 286–301. London: Routledge.

Kane, P. 1995. Population and family policies. See Benewick & Wingrove (1995), 193–203.

Kaplinsky, R. (ed.) 1982a. *Third world industrialisation in the 1980s*. London: Frank Cass.

Kaplinsky, R. 1982b. The international context for industrialisation in the coming decade. See Kaplinsky (1982a), 75–96.

Kaplinsky, R. 1982c. Editorial. *IDS Bulletin* 13, 1–4.

Kaplinsky, R. 1989a. Editorial introduction: industrial restructuring and the global economy. *IDS Bulletin* 20, 1–6.

Kaplinsky, R. 1989b. "Technological revolution" and the international division of labour in manufacturing: a place for the third world? In *Technology and development in the third industrial revolution*, R. Kaplinsky & C. Cooper (eds), 5–37. London: Frank Cass.

Kaplinsky, R. 1990. *The economies of small*. London: Intermediate Technology.

Kaplinsky, R. 1994. *Easternisation: the spread of Japanese management techniques to developing countries*. London: Frank Cass.

Kaplinsky, R. 1995. Technique and system: the spread of Japanese management techniques to devloping countries. *World Development* 23, 57–71.

Karshenas, M. 1995. *Industrialisation and agricultural surplus*. Cambridge: Cambridge University Press.

Kay, G. 1975. *Development and underdevelopment*. London: Macmillan.

Kemp, T. 1978. *Historical patterns of industrialization*. London: Longman.

Kemp, T. 1983. *Industrialisation in the non-western world*. London: Longman.

Kemp, T. 1990. *The climax of capitalism*. London: Longman.

Kennedy, P. 1988. *African Capitalism*. Cambridge: Cambridge University Press.

Kenney, M. & R. Florida 1988. Beyond mass production: production and the labour process in Japan. *Politics and Society* 16, 121–58.

Kerr, C., J. Dunlop, F. Harbison & C. Myers 1962. *Industrialism and industrial man*. London: Heinemann.

Kiely, R. 1994. Development theory and industrialisation: beyond the impasse. *Journal of Contemporary Asia* 24, 133–60.

Kiely, R. 1995a. Marxism, post-marxism and development fetishism. *Capital and Class* 55, 73–101.

Kiely, R. 1995b. Third worldist relativism: a new form of imperialism. *Journal of Contemporary Asia* 25, 159–78.

Kiely, R. 1995c. *Sociology and development: the impasse and beyond*, London: UCL Press.

Kiely, R. 1995d. Review Article: "Rethinking social development" and "Capitalism and development". *Journal of Contemporary Asia* 25, 307–16.

Kiely, R. 1996. *The politics of labour and development in Trinidad*. Kingston: The Press – University of West Indies.

Kiely, R. 1997a. The crisis of global development. See Kiely & Marfleet (1997).

Kiely, R. 1997b. Global capital flows, TNCs and the third world. See Kiely & Marfleet (1997).

Kiely, R. & P. Marfleet (eds) 1997. *Globalization and the third world*. London: Routledge (forthcoming).

Kiernan, V. 1981. *America: the new imperialism*. London: Zed.

Killick, T. (ed.) 1995. *The flexible economy*. London: Routledge.

Kilmister, A. 1992. Socialist models of development. In Allen & Thomas 1992, 238–52.

Kim, H-K. & S-H. Lee 1994. Commodity chains and the Korean automobile industry. See Gereffi & Korzeniewicz (1994), 281–96.

Kirkpatrick, C., N. Lee & F. Nixson 1984. *Industrial structure and policy in less developed countries*. London: Allen & Unwin.

Kitching, G. 1980. *Class and economic change in Kenya: the making of an African petite-bourgeoisie 1905–70*. New Haven and London: Yale University Press.

Kitching, G. 1982. *Development and underdevelopment in historical perspective*. London: Methuen.

Kitching, G. 1983. *Rethinking socialism*. London: Methuen.

Kitching, G. 1987. The role of a national bourgeoisie in the current phase of capitalist development: some reflections. In *The African bourgeoisie: capitalist development in the Ivory Coast, Kenya and Nigeria*, P. Lubeck (ed.), 27–55. Boulder: Lynne Rienner.

Kitching, G. 1989. Postscript. In *Development and underdevelopment in historical perspective* (see Kitching 1982), 2nd edn, 185–95. London: Methuen.

Koo, H. & E. M. Kim 1992. The developmental state and capital accumulation in South Korea. See Appelbaum & Henderson (1992), 121–49.

Kotz, D., T. McDonough & M. Reich (eds) 1994. *Social structures of accumulation*. Cambridge: Cambridge University Press.

Korzeniewicz, M. 1994. Commodity chains and marketing strategies: Nike and the global athletic footwear industry. See Gereffi & Korzeniewicz (1994), 247–66.

Krueger, A. 1974. The political economy of the rent-seeking society. *American Economic Review* 64, 291–303.

Krueger, A. 1978. *Foreign trade regimes and economic development*. Cambridge: Ballinger.

Kucinski, B. 1982. *Brazil: state and struggle*. London: Latin America Bureau.

Kwon, J. 1994. The East Asia challenge to neo-classical orthodoxy. *World Development* 22, 635–44.

Kyong-Dong, K. 1994. Confucianism and capitalist development in East Asia. See Sklair (1994), 87–106.

Lal, D. 1983. *The poverty of development economics*. London: Institute of Economic Affairs.

Lal, D. 1988. Ideology and industrialization in India and East Asia. In *Achieving industrialization in East Asia*, H. Hughes (ed.), 195–240. Cambridge: Cambridge University Press.

Lall, S. 1978. *The growth of the pharmaceutical industry in developing countries.* New York: UNIDO.

Lall, S. 1980. *The multinational corporation.* London: Macmillan.

Lall, S. 1984. Transnationals and the third world: changing perceptions. *National Westminster Bank Quarterly Review* (May), 2–16.

Lall, S. 1994. "The East Asian miracle" study: does the bell toll for industrial strategy? *World Development* 22, 645–54.

Lall, S. 1995. Structural adjustment and African industry. *World Development* 23, 2019–31.

Larrain, J. 1989. *Theories of development.* Cambridge: Polity.

Lash, S. & J. Urry 1987. *The end of organized capitalism.* Cambridge: Polity.

Latouche, S. 1993. *In the wake of the affluent society: an exploration of post-development.* London: Zed.

Law, C. 1991. Introduction. In *Restructuring the global automobile industry*, C. Law, 1–21. London: Routledge.

Leftwich, A. 1994. Governance, the state and the politics of development. *Development and Change* 25, 363–86.

Leftwich, A. 1995. Bringing politics back in: towards a model of the developmental state. *Journal of Development Studies* 31, 400–27.

Lenin, V. I. 1977a. Two tactics of social democracy in the democratic revolution. In *Selected Works.* 50–147. Moscow: Progress.

Lenin, V. I. 1977b. Imperialism: the highest stage of Capitalism. In *Selected Works*, 169–262. Moscow: Progress.

Lewin, M. 1974. *Lenin's last struggle.* London: Pluto.

Lewis, W. A. 1950. *The industrialisation of the British West Indies.* West Indies: W. A. Lewis.

Leys, C. 1984. Relations of production and technology. In *Technological capability and the third world*, M. Fransman & K. King (eds), 3–30. London: Macmillan.

Lim, L. 1990. Women's work in export factories. In *Persistent inequalities: women and world development*, I. Tinker (ed.), 63–90. Oxford: Oxford University Press.

Lipietz, A. 1987. *Miracles and mirages.* London: Verso.

Lipietz, A. 1992. *Towards a new economic order.* London: Macmillan.

Lipton, M. 1977. *Why poor people stay poor.* London: Temple Smith.

Lipton, M. 1982. Why poor people stay poor. See Harriss 1989, 66–81.

Lipton, M. 1991. Market relaxation and agricultural development. See Colclough & Manor (1991), 26–47.

Little, I. 1979. The experience and causes of rapid labour-intensive development in Korea, Taiwan province, Hong Kong and Singapore and the possibilities of emulation. In *Export-led industrialization and development*, E. Lee (ed.), 23–45. Geneva: ILO.

Littler, C. 1985. Soviet type societies and the labour process. In *Work, employment and unemployment*, K. Thompson (ed.), 85–95. London: Macmillan.

Lockett, M. 1980. Bridging the division of labour? *Economic and Industrial Democracy* 1, 447–86.

London to Edinburgh Weekend Return Group 1980. *In and against the state.* London: Pluto.

Long, N. and M. Villareal 1993. Exploring development interfaces: from the transfer of knowledge to the transfer of meaning. In *Beyond the impasse*, F. Schuurman (ed.), 187–206. London: Zed.

Lubeck, P. 1992. Malaysian industrialization, ethnic divisions, and the NIC model: limits of replication. See Appelbaum & Henderson (1992), 176–98.

Luedde-Neurath, R. 1988. State intervention and export oriented development in South Korea. In *Developmental states in East Asia*, G. White (ed.), 68–112. London: Macmillan.

MacFarquhar, R. 1980. The post-Confucian challenge. *The Economist* 9, 67–72.

Mackintosh, M. 1990. Abstract markets and real needs. In *The food question*, H. Bernstein, B. Crow, M. Mackintosh & C. Martin (eds), 43–53. London: Earthscan.

Mackintosh, M. 1992. Questioning the state. In *Development policy and public action*, M. Wuyts, M. Mackintosh & T. Hewitt (eds), 61–90. Oxford: Oxford University Press.

Maitan, L. 1976. *Party, army and masses in China*. London: New Left Books.

Malecki, E. 1991. *Technology and economic development*. London: Longman.

Mandel, E. 1983. Uneven Development. In *A dictionary of Marxist thought*, T. Bottomore, L. Harris, V. Kiernan & R. Miliband (eds), 502–3. Oxford: Blackwell.

Marx, K. 1976. *Capital*, vol. 1. London: Penguin.

Marx, K. & F. Engels 1964. *The German ideology*. Moscow: Progress.

Marx, K. & F. Engels 1965. *Selected correspondence*. Moscow: Progress.

Maynard, M. 1985. Housework. In *Work and Society*, Open University, Block 1, 75–90. Milton Keynes: Open University.

McClelland, D. 1961. *The achieving society*. New York: Free Press.

McLennan, G. 1992. The Enlightenment project revisited. In *Modernity and its futures*, S. Hall, D. Held and T. McGrew (eds), 327–77. Cambridge: Polity.

McLennan, G. 1996. Post-Marxism and the "four sins" of modernist theorizing. *New Left Review* 218, 53–74.

McMichael, P. 1996. *Development and social change*. London: Pine Forge.

Mies, M. and V. Shiva 1993. *Ecofeminism*. London: Zed.

Mitchell, B. 1988. *British historical statistics*. Cambridge: Cambridge University Press.

Mitchell, T. 1992. The Gap: can the nation's hottest retailer really stay on top? *Business Week*, 9 March, 58–64.

Mitter, S. 1986. *Common fate, common bond*. London: Pluto.

Molyneux, M. 1991. The "woman question" in the age of perestroika. See Blackburn (1991), 47–77.

Moon, C. & R. Prasad 1994. Beyond the developmental state: networks, politics and institutions. *Governance* 7, 360–86.

Moon, C. & Y-C. Kim 1996. A circle of paradox: development, politics and democracy in South Korea. In *Democracy and development*, A. Leftwich (ed.), 139–67. Cambridge: Polity.

Moore, B. 1966. *The social origins of dictatorship and democracy*. Harmondsworth: Penguin.

Morris, M. 1967. Values as an obstacle to economic growth in South Asia: an historical survey. *Journal of Economic History* 27, 588–607.

Morris-Suzuki, T. 1994. *The technological transformation of Japan*. Cambridge: Cambridge University Press.

Mosley, P. 1994. Decomposing the effects of structural adjustment: the case of sub-Saharan Africa. In *Structural adjustment and beyond in sub-Saharan Africa*, R. van der Hoeven & F. van der Kraaj (eds), 70–98. London: James Currey.

Mosley, P. & J. Weeks 1993. Has recovery begun? "Africa's adjustment in the 1980s" revisited. *World Development* 21, 1583–99.

Mosley, P., J. Harrigan & J. Toye 1991. *Aid and power* (2 volumes) London: Routledge.

Mosley, P., T. Subasat & J. Weeks 1995. Assessing Adjustment in Africa. *World Development* 23, 1459–73.

Mouzelis, N. 1980. Modernization, underdevelopment, uneven development: prospects for a theory of third world formations. *Journal of Peasant Studies* 7, 353–74.

Mouzelis, N. 1986. *Politics in the semi-periphery*. London: Macmillan.

Mouzelis, N. 1988. Sociology of development: reflections on the present crisis. *Sociology* 22, 23–44.

Mouzelis, N. 1994. The state in late development: historical and comparative perspectives. See Booth (1994), 126–51.

Mu, A. 1996. Social policies and rural women's fertility behaviour in the People's Republic of China, 1979–90. See Afshar (1996), 106–20.

Mukherjee, R. 1974. *The rise and fall of the East India Company*. New York: Monthly Review Press.

Muller, M. 1974. *The baby killer*. London: War on Want.

Muller, M. 1982. *The health of nations*. London: Faber.

Munck, R. 1984. *Politics and dependency in the third world*. London: Zed.

Munck, R. 1987. The labour movement in Argentina and Brazil: a comparative perspective. In *International labour and the third world*, R. Boyd, R. Cohen & P. Gutkind (eds), 108–36. Aldershot: Avebury.

Murray, F. 1987. Flexible specialization in the "Third Italy". *Capital and Class* 33, 84–95.

Murray, R. 1972. Underdevelopment, international firms and the international division of labour. In *Towards a new world economy*, papers and proceedings of the fifth European conference of the Society for International Development, 159–247. Rotterdam: Rotterdam University Press.

Murray, R. (ed.) 1981. *Multinationals beyond the market*. Brighton: Harvester.

Murray, R. 1989a. Fordism and post-Fordism. See Hall & Jacques (1989), 38–52.

Murray, R. 1989b. Bennetton Britain. See Hall & Jacques (1989), 54–64.

Myrdal, G. 1957. *Asian drama*, vol. 1. New York: Pantheon.

New Internationalist 1992a. Green justice, 230.

New Internationalist 1992b. The rise of Japan, 231.

New Internationalist 1992c. Development: a guide to the ruins, 232.

New Internationalist 1993. The new globalism, 246.

New Internationalist 1995. Unmasked: the East Asian economic miracle, 263.

Nicholas, S. & D. Oxley 1994. The industrial revolution and the genesis of the male breadwinner. See Snooks (1994), 96–111.

Nolan, P. 1988. *The political economy of collective farms*. Cambridge: Cambridge University Press.

Nolan, P. 1995a. Political economy and the reform of Stalinism: the Chinese puzzle. In *The transformation of the communist economies*, H-J. Chang & P. Nolan (eds), 400–17. London: Macmillan.

Nolan, P. 1995b. Politics, planning, and the transition from Stalinism: the case of China. In *The role of the state in economic change*, H-J. Chang & B. Rowthorne (eds), 237–61. Oxford: Clarendon.

Nove, A. 1969. *An economic history of the U.S.S.R.* London: Allen Lane.

Nuti, D. 1979. The contradictions of socialist economies: a Marxian interpretation. In *The Socialist Register 1979*, R. Miliband & J. Savile (eds), 228–73. London: Merlin.

Nzula, A. 1979. *Forced labour in colonial Africa*. London: Zed.

O'Brien, P. 1982. European economic development: the contribution of the periphery. *Economic History Review* 35, 1–18.

O'Donnell, K. & P. Nolan 1989. Flexible specialization and the Cyprus industrial strategy. *Cyprus Journal of Economics* 2, 1–20.

Ogle, G. 1990. *South Korea: dissent within the economic miracle*. London: Zed.

Olle, W. and W. Schoeller 1982. Direct investment and monopoly theories of imperialism. *Capital and Class* 16, 41–61.

Ong, A. 1987. *Spirits of resistance and capitalist discipline*. Albany: SUNY Press.

Open University 1985. *Work and Society*, Block 2. Milton Keynes: Open University.

Orru, M. 1991. The institutional logic of small-firm economies in Italy and Taiwan. *Studies in Comparative International Development* 26, 3–28.

Oxfam 1991. *Brazil: a mask called progress*. Oxford: Oxfam.

Palma, G. 1978. Dependency and development: a formal theory of underdevelopment or a methodology for the analysis of concrete situations of underdevelopment? *World Development* 6, 881–924.

Pearce, D. 1989. *Blueprint for a green economy*. London: Earthscan.

Pearce, J. 1982. *Under the Eagle*. London: Latin America Bureau.

Pearson, R. 1992. Gender issues and industrialization. See Hewitt et al. (1992b), 222–47.

Pearson, R. 1994. Gender relations, capitalism, and third world industrialization. See Sklair (1994), 339–58.

Peet, R. 1986. Industrial devolution and the crisis of international capitalism. *Antipode* 21, 35–50.

Perez, C. 1985. Microelectronics, long waves and world structural change: new perspectives for developing countries. *World development* 13, 441–63.

Perspectives 1996. *Second special report on Malaysia*. 21 July. London.

Petras, J. and M. Morley 1974. *How Allende fell*. Nottingham: Spokesman.

Phillips, A. 1977. The concept of development. *Review of African Political Economy* 8, 7–20.

Phillips, A. 1989. *The enigma of colonialism*. London: James Currey.

Phillips, A. & B. Taylor. 1980. Sex and skill: notes towards a feminist economics. *Feminist Review* 6, 79–88.

Pinchbeck, I. 1930. *Women workers and the industrial revolution, 1750–1850*. London: Routledge.

Piore, M. and C. Sabel 1984. *The second industrial divide*. London: Basic.

Plekhanov, G. 1976. *The materialist conception of history*. London: Lawrence & Wishart.

Pollert, A. (ed.) 1991. *Farewell to flexibility*. London: Macmillan.

Portes, A. 1976. On the sociology of national development. Rep. in *Development and underdevelopment*, M. Seligson & J. Passe-Smith (eds), 183–90. Boulder: Lynne Rienner.

Poulantzas, N. 1973. *Political power and social classes*. London: Verso.

Prebisch, R. 1959. Commercial policy in the underdeveloped countries. *American Economic Review* 44, 251–73.

Preobrazhensky, E. 1965. *The new economics*. Oxford: Clarendon.

Rabellotti, R. 1995. Is there an "industrial district model"? Footwear districts in Italy and Mexico compared. *World development* 23, 29–41.

Rabushka, A. 1979. *Hong Kong: a study in economic freedom*. Chicago: University of Chicago Press.

Rai, S. 1992. Watering another man's garden. In *Women in the face of change*, S. Rai, H. Pilkington & A. Phizacklea (eds), 20–40. London: Routledge.

Rai, S. 1995. Gender in China. See Benewick & Wingrove (1995), 181–92.

Rainnie, A. 1993. The reorganisation of large firm subcontracting. *Capital and Class* 49, 53–76.

Raj, K. & A. Sen 1961. Alternative patterns of growth under conditions of stagnant export earnings. *Oxford Economic Papers* 13, 1–21.

Rasmussen, J., H. Schmitz & P. van Dijk 1992. Introduction: exploring a new approach to small scale industry. *IDS Bulletin* 23, 2–7.

Redclift, M. 1987. *Sustainable development: exploring the contradictions*. London: Methuen.

Reed, M. 1986. Nineteenth-century rural England: a case for "peasant studies"? *Journal of Peasant Studies* 14 (1), 78–99.

Richards, E. 1974. Women in the British economy since about 1700. *History* 58, 137–57.

Riskin, C. 1987. *China's political economy*. Oxford: Oxford University Press.

Robison, T. 1986. *Indonesia: the rise of capital*. Canberra: Asian studies association of Australia.

Rodan, G. 1989. *The political economy of Singapore's industrialisation*. London: Macmillan.

Rostow, W. 1985. *The Stages of Economic Growth*. Oxford: Oxford University Press.

Rothermund, D. 1993. *An economic history of India*. London: Routledge.

Roxborough, I. 1987. Populism and class conflict. In *Latin America*, E. Archetti, P. Cammack & B. Roberts (eds), 119–24. London: Macmillan.

Ruigrok, W. & R. van Tulder 1995. *The logic of international restructuring*. London: Routledge.

Rustin, M. 1989. The trouble with New Times. See Hall & Jacques (1989), 303–20.

Sabel, C. 1982. *Work and politics*. Cambridge: Cambridge University Press.

Sabel, C. 1986. Changing models of economic efficiency and their implications for industrialisation in the third world. In *Development, democracy and the art of trespassing*, A. Foxley, M. McPherson & G. O'Donnell (eds), 35–80. Notre Dame: University of Notre Dame Press.

Sachs, W. (ed.) 1992a. *The development dictionary*. London: Zed.

Sachs, W. 1992b. Development: a guide to the ruins. *New Internationalist*, July.

Sader, E. & K. Silverstein 1991. *Without fear of being happy*. London: Verso.

Sahasakul, C. 1991. *Lessons from the World Bank experience of structural adjustment loans: the case of Thailand*. Bangkok: Thailand Development Research Institute.

Sakwa, R. 1990. *Gorbachev's politics*. London: Philip Allan.

Sampson, A. 1974. *Sovereign state: the secret history of ITT.* London: Hodder & Stoughton.

Sandbrook, R. 1985. *The politics of Africa's economic stagnation.* Cambridge: Cambridge University Press.

Sandbrook, R. 1993. *The politics of Africa's economic recovery.* Cambridge: Cambridge University Press.

Schelling, V. 1992. Culture and industrialization in Brazil. See Hewitt et al. (1992b), 248–76.

Schiff, M. & A. Valdes 1992. *The plundering of agriculture in developing countries.* Washington: World Bank.

Schiffer, J. 1981. The changing pattern of post-war development. *World Development* 9, 515–37.

Schiffer, J. 1991. State policy and economic growth: a note on the Hong Kong model. *International Journal of Urban and Regional Research* 15, 180–96.

Schmitz, H. 1984. Industrialisation strategies in less developed countries: some lessons of historical experience. See Kaplinsky (1982a), 1–21.

Schmitz, H. 1995. Small shoemakers and Fordist giants: tale of a supercluster. *World Development* 23, 9–28.

Schmitz, H. & T. Hewitt 1992. An assessment of the market reserve for the Brazilian computer industry. In *Hi-tech for industrial development: lessons from the Brazilian experience in electronics and automation*, H. Schmitz & J. Cassolato (eds), 21–52. London: Routledge.

Schmitz, H. & B. Musyck 1994. Industrial districts in Europe: policy lessons for developing countries? *World Development* 22, 889–910.

Schoenberger, E. 1988. From Fordism to flexible accumulation: technology, competitive strategies and international location. *Environment and Planning D: Society and Space* 6, 245–62.

Schoenberger, E. 1994. Competition, time and space in industrial change. See Gereffi & Korzeniewicz (1994), 51–66.

Schumacher, E. 1973. *Small is Beautiful.* London: Blond & Briggs.

Schuurman, F. 1968. *Ideology and organisation in Communist China.* Berkeley: University of California Press.

Scott, A. 1988. *New industrial spaces.* London: Pion.

Seddon, D. & R. Belton-Jones 1995. The political determinants of economic flexibility, with special reference to East Asia. See Killick (1995), 325–64.

Seers, D. 1979. The meaning of development. In *Development theory: four critical essays*, D. Lehmann (ed.), 1–15. London: Frank Cass.

Selden, M. 1988. *The political economy of Chinese socialism.* London: M. E. Sharpe.

Sen, Amartya 1981. *Poverty and famines.* Oxford: Oxford University Press.

Sen, Amartya 1990. How is India doing? In *The Indian economy and its performance since independence*, R. Choudhury, S. Gamkhar & A. Ghose (eds), 7–22. Delhi: Oxford University Press.

Sen, Amartya 1992. Development: which way now? See Wilber & Jameson (1992), 5–26.

Sen, Anupam 1984. *The state, industrialization and class formation in India.* London: Routledge & Kegan Paul.

Sender, J. & S. Smith 1986. *The development of capitalism in Africa.* London: Methuen.

Sender, J. & S. Smith 1990. *Poverty, class and gender in rural Africa.* London: Routledge.

Shaikh, A. 1978. Foreign trade and the law of value: part two. *Science & Society* 44, 27–57.

Shanin, T. (ed.) 1984. *Late Marx and the Russian road.* London: Routledge.

Shapiro, H. & L. Taylor 1992. The state and industrial strategy. See Wilber & Jameson (1992), 432–64.

Singer, H. 1988. The World development report 1987 on the blessings of outward orientation: a necessary correction. *Journal of Development Studies* 24, 232–36.

Singer, H. & P. Alizadeh 1989. Import substitution revisited in a darkening external environment. Reprinted in *Development studies*, R. Ayres (ed.), (1995), 321–41. Dartford: Greenwich University Press.

Singh, A. 1994. How did East Asia grow so fast? *UNCTAD Discussion Paper* no. 97. Geneva: UNCTAD.

Skidmore, T. & P. Smith. 1992. *Modern Latin America*. Oxford: Oxford University Press.

Sklair, L. 1991a. *Sociology of the global system*. London: Harvester Wheatsheaf.

Sklair, L. 1991b. Problems of socialist development: the significance of Shenzhen special economic zone for China's open door development strategy. *International Journal of Urban and Regional Research* 15, 197–215.

Sklair, L. 1993. *Assembling for development*. San Diego: University of California Press.

Sklair, L. (ed.) (1994) *Capitalism and development*, London: Routledge.

Smart, A. 1995. Hong Kong's slums and squatter areas. In *Housing the urban poor*, B. Aldrich & R. Sandhu (eds), 96–111. London: Zed.

Smith, C. 1989. Flexible specialisation, automation and mass production. *Work, Employment and Society* 3, 203–20.

Smith, P. 1992. Industrialization and environment. See Hewitt et al. (1992b), 277–302.

Smith, R. 1993. The Chinese road to capitalism. *New Left Review* 199, 55–99.

Smith, S. 1981. Class analysis versus world system: critique of Samir Amin's typology of underdevelopment. *Journal of Contemporary Asia* 11, 86–99.

Snooks, G. (ed.) 1994. *Was the industrial revolution necessary?* London: Routledge.

Soete, L. 1985. International diffusion of technology, industrial development and technological leapfrogging. *World Development* 13, 409–22.

Solow, B. and S. Engerman (eds) 1987. *British capitalism and Caribbean slavery*. Cambridge: Cambridge University Press.

Spalding, H. 1977. *Organized labour in Latin America*. New York: Harper & Row.

Spraos, J. 1983. *Inequalising trade?* Oxford: Clarendon.

Stallings, B. 1990. The role of foreign capital in economic development. See Gereffi & Wyman (1990), 55–89.

Stavrianos, L. 1981. *Global rift*. New York: William Morrow.

Stopford, J. and E. Dunning 1983. *Multinationals: company performance and global trends*. London: Macmillan.

Stopford, J. and S. Strange 1991. *Rival states, rival firms: competition for world market shares*. Cambridge: Cambridge University Press.

Storper, M. 1991. *Industrialisation, economic development and the regional question in the third world*. London: Pion.

Strinati, D. 1995. *An introduction to theories of popular culture*. London: Routledge.

Sutcliffe, B. 1971. *Industry and underdevelopment*. London: Addison-Wesley.

Sutcliffe, B. 1972. Imperialism and industrialisation in the third world. In *Studies in the theory of imperialism*, R. Own & B. Sutcliffe (eds), 171–92. London: Longman.

Sutcliffe, B. 1992. Industry and underdevelopment re-examined. See Wilber & Jameson (1992), 331–45.

Sutcliffe, B. 1995. Development after ecology. See Bhaskar & Glyn (1995), 232–58.

Taplin, I. 1994. Strategic reorientations of US apparel firms. See Gereffi & Korzeniewicz (1994), 205–22.

Taylor, B., P. Fairbrother & T. Elger 1993. Transplants and emulators: the fate of the Japanese model in British electronics. See Elger & Smith (1993b), 196–225.

Tellmann, S. 1995. Happy face fascism. *New Internationalist* 263, 10–12.

Thomas, C. 1974. *Dependence and transformation*. New York: Monthly Review Press.

Thomas, M. 1985. The development of capitalism in the Third World. *Workers Liberty* 1.

Thompson, E. P. 1963. *The making of the English working class*. London: Penguin.

Thompson, E. P. 1991. *Customs in common*. London: Merlin.

Ticktin, H. 1973. Towards a political economy of the USSR. *Critique* 1, 20–41.

Tomaney, J. 1994. A new paradigm of work organization and technology? See Amin (1994b), 157–94.

Tomlinson, J. 1991. *Cultural imperialism*. London: Pinter.

Toye, J. 1987. *Dilemmas of development*. Oxford: Blackwell.

Toye, J. 1991. Is there a new political economy of development? See Colclough & Manor (1991), 321–38.

Trotsky, L. 1975. Towards socialism or capitalism? *The challenge of the Left Opposition, 1923–5.* New York: Pathfinder.

Trotsky, L. 1976. *The permanent revolution and results and prospects.* New York: Pathfinder.

Tsiang, S. & R. Wu 1985. Foreign trade and investment as boosters of take off: the experience of the four Asian NICs. In *Foreign trade and investment*, W. Galenson (ed.), 320–43. Madison: University of Wisconsin Press.

Tsuru, S. 1993. *Japan's capitalism.* Cambridge: Cambridge University Press.

Ullrich, O. 1992. Technology. See Sachs (1992a), 275–87.

UNCTAD 1994a. *World investment report 1994.* Geneva: UNCTAD.

UNCTAD 1994b. World investment report 1994: transnational corporations, employment and the workplace. An executive summary. *Transnational Corporations* 3, 73–113.

UNDP 1995. *Human development report 1995.* Oxford: Oxford University Press.

Urry, J. 1989. The end of organised capitalism. See Jacques & Hall (1989), 94–102.

Vaitsos, C. 1976. *Employment problems and transnational enterprises in developing countries.* Geneva: ILO.

Vanaik, A. 1990. *The painful transition.* London: Verso.

Vernon, R. 1977. *Storm over the multinationals: the real issues.* London: Macmillan.

Wade, R. 1983. South Korea's agricultural development: the myth of the passive state. *Pacific Viewpoint* 24, 11–29.

Wade, R. 1990. *Governing the market.* Princeton: Princeton University Press.

Walder, A. 1983. Organised authority and cultures of dependency in Chinese industry. *Journal of Asian Studies* 43, 51–76.

Walder, A. 1986. *Communist neo-traditionalism.* Berkeley: University of California Press.

Warren, B. 1973. Imperialism and capitalist industrialisation. *New Left Review* 81, 9–44.

Warren, B. 1980. *Imperialism: pioneer of capitalism.* London: Verso.

Webster, A. 1991. *An introduction to the sociology of development.* London: Macmillan.

Weeks, J. 1982. Equilibrium, uneven development and the tendency of the rate of profit to fall. *Capital and Class* 16, 62–77.

Weiss, J. 1990. *Industry in developing countries.* London: Routledge.

Weiss, L. & J. Hobson 1995. *States and economic development.* Cambridge: Polity.

Wheatcroft, S., R. Davies & J. Cooper 1986. Soviet industrialization reconsidered: some preliminary conclusions about economic development between 1926 and 1941. *Economic History Review* 39, 12–42.

White, G. 1982. Revolutionary socialist development in the third world: an overview. In *Revolutionary socialist development in the third world*, G. White, R. Murray & C. White (eds), 1–34. Brighton: Hassocks.

White, G. (ed.) 1988. *Developmental states in East Asia.* London: Macmillan.

White, G. 1993. *Riding the tiger.* London: Macmillan.

Whitley, R. 1991. The social construction of business systems in East Asia. *Organisation Studies* 12, 1–28.

Wield, D. 1988. Industry and Industrialization. See Crow & Thorpe (1988), 187–215.

Wilber, C. and K. Jameson (eds) 1992. *The political economy of development and underdevelopment.* New York: McGraw-Hill.

Williams, E. (1987) *Capitalism and slavery.* London: André Deutsch.

Williams, K., T. Cutler, J. Williams & C. Haslam 1987. Review article: the end of mass production. *Economy and Society* 16, 405–38.

Williams, K., C. Haslam, J. Williams & T. Cutler 1992. Against lean production. *Economy and Society* 21, 321–54.

Williamson, J. 1988. *Consuming passions.* London: Marion Boyars.

Wolfe, J. 1978. *Women under communism.* Baltimore: Johns Hopkins University Press.

Womack, J., D. Jones & H. Roos 1990. *The machine that changed the world.* New York: Rawson Associates.

Wood, S. 1991. Japanization and/or Toyataism? Work Employment and Society 5 (4), 567–600.

World Bank 1983. *World development report*. Oxford: Oxford University Press.

World Bank 1989. *World development report*. Oxford: Oxford University Press.

World Bank 1991. *World development report*. Oxford: Oxford University Press.

World Bank 1993. *The East Asian miracle*. Oxford: Oxford University Press.

World Bank 1994. *Adjustment in Africa*. Oxford: Oxford University Press.

Worsley, P. 1984. *The three worlds*. London: Weidenfeld & Nicolson.

You, J-I. 1995. The Korean model of development and its environmental implications. See Bhaskar & Glyn (1995), 158–83.

Young, K. 1993. *Planning development with women*. London: Macmillan.

Zhao, D-X. & J. Hall 1994. State power and patterns of late development: resolving the crisis of the sociology of development. *Sociology* 28, 211–30.

Index

For Product Safety Concerns and Information please contact our EU
representative GPSR@taylorandfrancis.com
Taylor & Francis Verlag GmbH, Kaufingerstraße 24, 80331 München, Germany

www.ingramcontent.com/pod-product-compliance
Lightning Source LLC
Chambersburg PA
CBHW070422270326
41926CB00014B/2900

9 781857 285451